Monaco

INSIDE F1'S GREATEST RACE

Malcolm Folley

CENTURY

1 3 5 7 9 10 8 6 4 2

Century
20 Vauxhall Bridge Road
London SW1V 2SA

Century is part of the Penguin Random House group of companies
whose addresses can be found at global.penguinrandomhouse.com.

Penguin
Random House
UK

First published by Century in 2017

www.penguin.co.uk

A CIP catalogue record for this book is available from the British Library.

ISBN 9781780896168

Typset in 11/15.5 pt ITC Stone Serif by Jouve (UK), Milton Keynes
Printed and bound in Great Britain by Clays Ltd, St Ives plc

Penguin Random House is committed to a sustainable future for
our business, our readers and our planet. This book is made from
Forest Stewardship Council® certified paper.

To all my old sports editors who paid for me to travel the world for four decades – send more money! Importantly, thank you all for your unwavering faith.

Contents

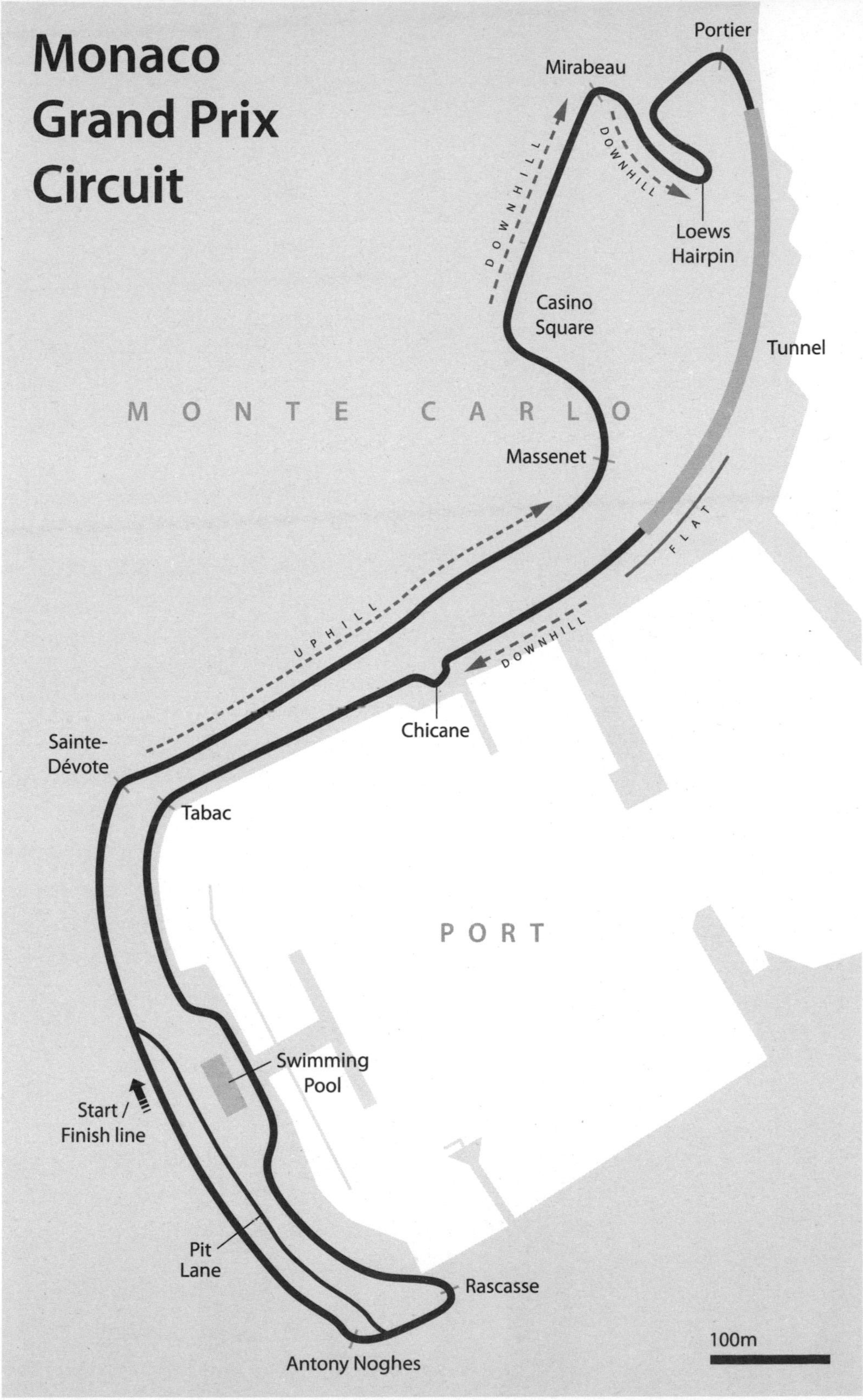

Monaco
Grand Prix
Circuit

MONTE CARLO

Mirabeau

Portier

DOWNHILL

DOWNHILL

Loews
Hairpin

Casino
Square

Tunnel

Massenet

FLAT

UPHILL

DOWNHILL

Chicane

Sainte-
Dévote

Tabac

PORT

Swimming
Pool

Start /
Finish line

Pit
Lane

Rascasse

Antony Noghes

100m

Prologue

Rhythm of the Streets, 13 April 2016

He is dressed behind the wheel in an unbranded polo shirt and a pair of chinos, but he is still trim enough to fit into the racing suit he discarded eight years ago, after leaving the paddock in São Paolo as a Formula One driver for ever.

His right foot instinctively entices maximum torque from the Mercedes engine at his command on the piece of tarmac that is the start–finish line for the Monaco Grand Prix, which has been staged each year since 1955. To trace the winners, from Fangio and Moss, to Hill and Stewart, is to follow a lineage of motor-racing aristocracy which runs through the labyrinth of these streets to the barons of the sport these past forty years: Lauda, Prost, Senna, Schumacher, Alonso, Hamilton, Vettel and Nico Rosberg.

Having made his home in Monaco since 1994, David Coulthard is the perfect guide to these streets. His authenticity to act as our chaperone is reinforced by the fact that Coulthard has won the Monaco Grand Prix twice, an accomplishment that will not be diminished by time. While the

Mercedes power unit under his control may not be delivering the 825 horsepower that was in the back of his McLaren MP4-15 when he won here for a second time in 2002, he manages to tease his Smart Brabus into effortlessly shadowing the racing line as buses, trucks, cars, even a motorised tourist train, jostle for position around us.

It is beyond dispute that the Monaco Grand Prix is unique, a race that would never be sanctioned today; yet it is also a race that Formula One relies on to be the centrepiece of the world championship because of its history, because of a harbour that sparkles diamond-bright in the sun, because of its glamour, and because of the privilege of witnessing the spectacle – and the spectacular – provided by the greatest drivers in the world racing on narrow, unforgiving streets normally governed by a 50kph speed limit, or less.

Coulthard was instantly addicted to the challenge of Monaco, a place where pain and pleasure can be experienced within the confines of one qualifying session; a place where a driver's aggression has to be tempered by a tenderness of feel and touch. 'I know a lot of tracks very well in my mind, but this one I know particularly well because it is such an intimate driving experience,' says Coulthard, as we gently slipstream a white van on Boulevard Albert 1er, which still shows the faint outline of the grid markings from the last Grand Prix. 'If you don't feel at home on the streets of Monaco you will never perform,' says Coulthard. 'You become incredibly tuned into your environment, your senses are heightened. You have to feel you own the road. You have to take ownership of this space, know every inch in the same way as you know, if the power goes out in your house, how many steps it is to the door handle, and where every cupboard is located, so you can successfully find your way around instinctively.'

Coulthard is giving us a close-up and personal tour. 'My

head will be down where your belly button is – below the top of the Armco barriers,' he says, looking across at me in the passenger seat of the Smart car. 'You don't need to see the scenery. All you need to see are your braking points and your apex points. It is a matter of having total focus. What you can't do on this circuit is look away and look back up again. At Silverstone, for example, you can switch off at 200mph on the Hangar Straight. Here you cannot switch off for a second.

'It is a very short run to the first corner, Sainte-Dévote. What you don't see on television is the way the road rises to the first corner. That rise helps you under braking. One of the things I tell all young drivers, including Sebastian Vettel in his first year racing here with Toro Rosso in 2008, is a simple message: "Don't get greedy braking into Turn One." Instead get on the brakes early; because otherwise if you make a mistake you will be in the barrier or be going down the escape road. In my opinion, you never drive at 100 per cent at Monaco. I understand that purists will look at laps by Ayrton Senna, especially his astonishing pole-winning lap here in 1988, when he was 1.4 seconds faster than the second-placed driver, Alain Prost, his McLaren team-mate, and go: "Well, there's a lap at 100 per cent." I am not going to have an argument with anyone by disputing that. But I had a very reasonable level of success here, and it's about knowing where you can push, and it's about trying to maximise braking, hitting the apex and making a good exit from the corners. You do have to compromise into Sainte-Dévote. Out of that right-hand corner, you are heading up the hill in the middle of the road, more or less, to a blind crest at Massenet at 275kph. The point where you brake for the entry to Casino Square is where you just come over the rise in the road before the pedestrian crossing. You use engine braking, shifting down in the middle of the circuit, just rolling the car left, rolling the car.'

Awaiting the drivers is Casino Square. On the left is the five-star hotel called the Hotel de Paris, with its liveried door-men and American Bar. Classic upmarket brands such as Chanel, Gucci, Piaget and Dior are all opening boutiques next door in a complex named La Promenade. On the right is the Casino de Monte-Carlo, a gorgeous belle époque building housing the most fabled gambling establishment in the world, in business since 1863. Both are owned and operated by SBM (Société des Bains de Mer), a company in which the government and the ruling family have a majority stake. Stunning cars seem not to be parked, but put on display. Casino Square is a showroom to flaunt your wealth.

It is also a test of a racing driver's nerve, skill and powers of concentration. 'See the kerb not far from the front door of the Hotel de Paris – that's the point where the barrier will stick out,' says Coulthard, who raced a Formula One car fourteen times at Monaco. 'So, the apex from Massenet is a long way round the corner and that's the point you are aiming for. If you get that right, you carry the speed through there. After cornering right out of Casino Square, we all tend to come over to the right side of the road after passing the small police station on the left because of a bump in the road. As you drop down to Mirabeau, this is another corner where you have to compromise. If you carry too much speed into the entry of this right-hand corner you scare yourself. By that I mean you frighten yourself, as you have increased your chances of crashing – and round here that's game over. I guess it can be likened to gambling in the casino, where the next card wins you a lot, or loses you a lot; it's that kind of nervous excitement. You must get right on to the red-and-white kerb at Mirabeau. Then it's downhill fast, before braking for the 65kph hairpin which used to be called Loews, after the hotel situated there, but is now known as Fairmont after the hotel changed hands.'

Another red-and-white kerb outside the hotel, on the out-side of the hairpin, is scarred with tyre marks, reflecting the frenetic scramble of men who have wrestled with their cars here down the years. 'It is such a long hairpin, you basically throw the car in on the front axle and let it slow down on the front tyre,' explains Coulthard. 'The risk is that you can create graining on your front right, but the upside is that you carry a lot more speed. Now it's downhill towards Portier. You aim to just miss the barrier jutting out on the right. A lot of young drivers leave too much space, because they are scared of the barriers. You have to see the barriers as your friend. If you feel like you are kissing the barriers in places like this, that's where the lap times come at Monaco.'

Ross Brawn remembers the absolute commitment Michael Schumacher exhibited every time he belted himself into his car at Monaco. 'Michael would scuff every wheel on the car on a qualifying lap,' said Brawn in conversation with me for this book. 'He brushed the Armco where he knew you could brush it without causing damage to the suspension, because it was the fastest racing line. He just kissed the barriers with his car . . . at 140mph.' Brawn smiled at the memory of the style and courage of his great friend, whose life was so catastrophic-ally affected by a ski accident in December 2013. Schumacher won the Monaco Grand Prix five times, having started on the front row of the grid on eleven occasions. He actually won a fourth pole position, aged forty-three, with a memorable lap in 2012, but it was erased from the records by a five-place grid penalty that Schumacher was served for an infringement at the previous race in Spain. Schumacher and controversy were not strangers, in spite of his brilliance – or perhaps because of it, we will hear. One of his more bizarre rushes of blood took place here. 'I can tell you Michael loved Monaco from the beginning,' said Brawn.

After Portier, drivers then upshift to top gear as they flash through the tunnel with its flat-out right-hand corner. It took me three minutes and thirty-five seconds to walk the length of the tunnel; in a Formula One car it is a journey lasting a matter of seconds. At full throttle, drivers go from sunlight into artificial light and back into sunlight at around 295kph. They pass in a blur the service bays for the Fairmont Hotel and Monte Carlo Star in the tunnel on their right. 'They paint the ceiling and the wall white and always double up the lights,' says Coulthard. Yet the charge back into daylight is still obviously disconcerting for drivers at such high speed. 'You really get attacked by the sunlight as you come out,' he says. 'You learn to look at the side of the road – just as you wouldn't stare into the lights of an oncoming car at night.'

Immediately on the left of the exit is the new Yacht Club de Monaco, sheltered behind Armco, yet unable to hide its status as a symbol of the wealth and privilege of those permitted access. Marker boards on the opposite side of the track count down the metres to the chicane: 200, 150, 100. Drivers brake hard to make the left–right transition on to the quayside. 'The only place you can really hope to catch someone out at Monaco, to overtake them, is down into that chicane,' says Coulthard. It is a manoeuvre fraught with peril, as drivers have been known to have accidents on their own here, without the additional strain of trying to out-brake a rival. 'I ended up in the barriers here during my last race weekend,' he says. It shook up Coulthard, but, mercifully, the strength of his Red Bull car and the trajectory of his journey, bouncing from one barrier to another, ushering him down an escape road, kept him from greater harm. 'After the first impact I wished I was anywhere but strapped in a racing car,' said Coulthard when he had returned to the paddock after that accident in 2008. 'When you lose a corner of the car, you lose the brakes. At that point, it's in the lap of the gods if you hit one barrier or another; today, I was obviously very lucky.' There was a sobering truth at the core of this experience. 'No matter how much experience you have at the track, it can still bite you,' explains Coulthard, feathering our Smart car beyond the chicane.

In a Formula One car, it is an invitation to get hard on the power and move up through the gearbox in a rush of speed towards Tabac, a left-handed corner. 'The barrier on the right comes just a little bit closer as you approach Tabac because it juts out,' says Coulthard. It is not perceptible at the speed we are travelling, but Coulthard waves his hands towards his chest to show how the barrier deviates from a straight line as you hog the racing line. 'That throws a few drivers at first. But once you are comfortable with this sensation you can focus on Tabac. The entry speed is so fast, around 225kph, and you aim for the barrier as you turn in early. It looks like you will collide with it, but the momentum of your car will take you away. If you get that right, it sets you up for the swimming-pool section. There is a huge amount of time to be made here. It is the fastest collection of corners on the circuit and the car is dancing around. It is a fantastic feeling and you are so exhilarated because the most difficult part of the lap, the first half, is behind you. We used to have great images of us just kissing the barriers as we passed the swimming pool, but, sadly, this is now an open chicane.'

It is a sun-splashed morning as we cruise through crowded and noisy streets. Grandstands are being erected around the harbour as though a giant Meccano set has been gifted to teams of construction workers as a belated Easter present. Men hammer out a day-long soundtrack as a reminder that Monaco is once more getting dressed, in Armco and wire netting, and laying out thousands of seats in temporary grandstands, to welcome the world to the most glamorous motor race on the planet. The hard graft is being carried out with practised efficiency, an art form re-enacted annually that attracts the attention only of visitors. Monégasques – as well as those who commute from France to work in the principality – understand the inconvenience and disturbance is a small tariff to pay for the fiscal benefits of playing host to a Grand Prix that is on the bucket list of the rich and famous, as well as Formula One cognoscenti.

In all, it takes seven weeks for the grandstands to be constructed and the streets to be protected to the satisfaction of the Automobile Club de Monaco and, specifically, Charlie Whiting, the Formula One Race Director these past twenty years, and a man working at the Monaco Grand Prix for a thirty-ninth consecutive year after first arriving here as a mechanic for the Brabham team. 'It is the ultimate case of grandfather rights, isn't it?' admits Whiting. 'If someone came along with the bright idea of running a race round Monaco when it had never happened before, you couldn't do it in the modern day, really.' Whiting adds, pertinently, 'It is the race weekend that causes me most stress.'

In 1967, Lorenzo Bandini died when his Ferrari crashed and exploded into flames. 'I led that race in a two-litre BRM, but I had a problem that caused me to pit,' recalled Sir Jackie Stewart when we met to discuss his Monaco years. 'I knew something terrible was wrong when I saw the smoke rising above the circuit from the pits. Lorenzo never got out of the car.' In 1955, Alberto Ascari overshot the chicane at the exit of the tunnel and careered into the water, as there were not any barriers at that time. He had to swim to safety. Tragically, four days later the two-time world champion was killed testing a sports car at Monza.

Today the immense improvement in trackside security, and the incalculable investment that is made each year to make Formula One cars safer, has granted drivers at the Monaco Grand Prix greater protection than at any time in history. The Automobile Club de Monaco provide a highly trained corps of 650 marshals, with 120 professional firefighters, 8 doctors, 15 ambulances and a helicopter prepped to fly to a hospital with a trauma unit at a moment's notice. It remains the ultimate prize to a Formula One driver.

Niki Lauda, a three-time world champion, who won this Grand Prix twice for Ferrari, tells me: 'To win in Monaco, it is up to the size of the balls and the head of the driver more than anywhere. There is no other circuit where you have this relationship between the possibility of crashing and winning pole position. It is a thin line – and it is the challenge.'

In our Smart car, Coulthard is braking and drifting across the track beyond the swimming pool. 'At the end of the lap is La Rascasse, which has also been opened up,' he says. 'The difficult part here is you are braking while you have lateral load, then have to turn that lateral load into La Rascasse. Again, if you are not kissing that barrier you just don't get a great drive off this corner.' Coulthard reveals how he created a visual aid for himself, in the name of safety. 'As we turn on to the start–finish straight over the race weekend, there will be a cone on top of the last barrier. I sold it to Charlie as a safety measure. I walked round Rascasse with him one day and explained you can't see the next corner. As there isn't a crane positioned there, I argued that any crash would block the race. Charlie agreed to a cone on top of that barrier – because I realised if I could see what I was aiming for earlier I could gain time. I don't know if anyone else picked up on it, but racing drivers will always try to find things that can give them an advantage without necessarily helping their competitors.'

Ahead of our car, a bus driver is pulling out into the traffic, causing Coulthard to brake at a zebra crossing. A silver-haired man steps from the pavement on our left and walks in front of us at a leisurely pace. 'That's Riccardo Patrese!' I exclaim, recognising the Italian who won a crazy race here in 1982. Patrese had spun out of the lead one lap from the end, then, astonishingly, took the chequered flag after Didier Pironi and Andrea de Cesaris passed him, only to run out of fuel. The next leader, Irishman Derek Daly, retired with a seized gearbox – and Patrese reappeared to take an extraordinary victory. It was the second Monaco Grand Prix I reported from, in what became almost an annual assignment.

Coulthard hit the horn. 'Riccardo, ciao.'

Patrese smiles as he spots who is driving. 'You OK, David?'

'Sure . . . but you are walking too slowly!'

'It's my age!' laughs Patrese, who is happy to mock himself a few days short of his sixty-second birthday. As we drive on, the two former drivers offer each other a wave as members of a special club: the winners of a Grand Prix that retains an ageless appeal, a racers' race, where the rhythm of the street is brash, loud and addictive. Even from inside a Smart car, if you are being driven by a man who knows what it means to beat the odds to triumph at Monaco.

Circuit de Monaco, Monte Carlo

Introduction

The Shimmering Jewel in Formula One's crown

Everything in Monaco is unhurried and reeks of an eternal order in a disorderly world – until racing cars descend on this principality each May.

For most of the year, the streets are congested with vans and buses; Ferraris and Lamborghinis; Rolls-Royces and Bentleys; Porches and Maseratis; Mercedes, BMWs and Range Rovers; Minis and Smart cars. The speed limit is assiduously respected. Zebra crossings, manhole covers, kerbing and white lines are as apparent here as in any other major road system. Oil and grease are evident, too. It is an improbable environment to unleash a Formula One car at 300kph.

Around the circuit, apartments reach for the sky, and high-rise cranes have permanent employment as new buildings take root and a plethora of real-estate agents joust to sell or rent the properties. The prices can be eye-watering. One estate agency, Faggionato Real Estate – which becomes a neighbour on race day of the Princely Lodge, where His Serene Highness Prince Albert II and his wife, Princess Charlene, view the Grand Prix seated alongside officials from the organisers, the Automobile Club de Monaco (ACM) – provides a random sample of the market in the spring of 2016. In the window there were details of apartments valued from 10.8 million euros and sliding uniformly downwards to a small property at 1.7 million. One six-roomed apartment – 'With exceptional views of the port and sea' – was listed without a price attached. Instead, potential buyers were advised: 'Prix – Nous Consulter.' Only those who can afford to learn the price should bother venturing to ask, it can be assumed.

Each year the armada of ocean-going yachts and floating palaces that motor into the harbour becomes larger and more ostentatious. These boats are variously registered in tax havens like George Town in the Cayman Islands and Valletta in Malta, or Bermuda, or Madeira. It is rumoured – but never openly admitted – that vast sums of money exchange hands to claim a prime berth on the quayside during the Grand Prix weekend. Lynden Swainston runs a boutique travel agency, LSA, in south-west London, and knows from an association with Monaco of over forty years how much people are willing to spend to be aboard a boat in the harbour. 'We have done several boats in the past and you are talking about having to pay £250,000 just for the rental and getting a boat into the harbour,' she says. 'These boats are meant for four or five millionaires to lounge around in the Mediterranean, but people hiring them at Monaco bring sixty to eighty guests aboard for parties, so tables and chairs have to be hired, then there is the cost of the bar and catering. That is another huge outlay.'

Plenty of Formula One drivers live in Monaco as their tax haven of choice, of course, with attractions including an absence of capital gains, income and inheritance taxes. Yet their nomadic existence means they sleep in their own beds fewer nights than most. Except for the one week each year when they can sleep and work in the same place.

This is a time when the streets are bequeathed to them.

While the circuit, in broad terms, is fundamentally the same track Graham Hill and Jackie Stewart raced, the pits are unrecognisable. In 2004 a modern pit complex was introduced; it was as profound a change in the landscape as an old warehouse in London docklands being transformed into a penthouse apartment. The garages are spacious, covered, and have offices overhead. Importantly, there is storage space within them. Prior to the modernisation, mechanics, tyre fitters, engineers and truckies had to carry all their equipment back and forth to the pits from the paddock on the quayside, a significant distance away. 'We moved everything, each day and night, with a 7.5-ton truck,' recalls Dave Redding, team manager of McLaren, who has also been on the payroll of the Benetton and Stewart teams and who has missed just one Grand Prix since 1989. 'Cars were towed to the pits behind quad bikes,' he explains. 'At my time with Stewart – a new team – we were even further away in a car park we referred to as Alcatraz. Nothing really changed until the new pits were created.'

Brawn and Schumacher operated in close harmony at Benetton, then Ferrari. Each of them embraced the peculiar and often claustrophobic conditions. 'So many people found it hard to carry out their roles because of the environment,' says Brawn. 'They were psyched out or didn't enjoy it. Once I was in a management position, from the Benetton days in the early nineties, I'd sit down with my people and before the Monaco Grand Prix tell them, "Right, logistically, we are going to one of the most difficult races of the year. It is also the most challenging for the driver and most challenging for the engineers. I promise you, a lot of the people [rivals] out there hate

Monaco. So, if you love Monaco you will have an advantage. It is a race to be relished. Absorb the atmosphere. Absorb the fact that you are talking to the spectators because they are all around you. Absorb the fact that it will take you an hour to get across town." If you relish all that, it is a very special place. Michael engendered that mental spirit where he understood that, as this is the most difficult track to race on, he was going to enjoy it and be the best. He thought that by saying how much fun he thought it was to drive at Monaco he would intimidate other drivers. When you flip the coin to believe it to be a wonderful opportunity, not a pain in the backside, Monaco really does become an addictive race.'

Monaco provides another role of immense significance to Formula One. It is where sport and business collide, perhaps like nowhere else. Tony Jardine, whose PR and marketing company ran promotional programmes through the eighties, nineties and into the new millennium for the gigantic tobacco brands John Player, Camel and Lucky Strike, says succinctly, 'Monaco is the glittering prize because everything associated with Formula One is epitomised in Monte Carlo: boats, champagne, success and excess.' It is the shimmering jewel in Formula One's crown.

As a former driver, and now a businessman and broadcaster, Coulthard is aware of the lure of the Monaco Grand Prix to captains of industry as well as to the fans arriving from around the world each year. Men fuelling the teams with sponsorship dollars all want to be there to view how their money is being spent and to entertain their clients and friends; they want to see and be seen. Deals are brokered over the weekend, with some contracts being renewed and new ones being courted. The schedule is uniquely different, too. Drivers have their first free practice on Thursday, and in years past the first of two qualifying sessions also took place that afternoon.

In modern times, the hour-long, nerve-wracking qualifying session is held on Saturday afternoon; but it used to be the case that Saturday afternoon was the second qualifying hour. On these days the sound of high-revving Formula One engines bounces off the buildings like thunder rolling in from the surrounding mountains. Friday is a day of reflection for team management, and it is often the day drivers are required to appear on parade for sponsors. Most definitely, it provides another night of heavy partying for the glamorous, the glitterati and the reckless who, these days, most commonly spill out of bars and restaurants at La Rascasse and drink and dance across the circuit until just a few hours before the track is 'live' again.

Business is never far from Formula One's agenda, though. 'How do you get people to make emotional decisions?' asks Coulthard rhetorically, as we cruise along the start–finish straight. 'A glass of champagne, watching Formula One cars and hanging out with celebrities puts people in a heightened sense of emotion. It's very difficult to sell Christmas in January, but pretty easy to sell in December, isn't it? You just have to get people in the environment, in the mindset.'

Nestling on the fringe of the Côte d'Azur on the southern coast of France, Monaco occupies less than two square kilometres – half the size of Central Park in New York – but, with a population of a shade over 37,000, is the most densely populated country in the world. The Grimaldi family has ruled here since 1338. Prince Albert is a passionate supporter of the Grand Prix, like his parents before him, Prince Rainier III and Princess Grace, who arrived from Hollywood as Grace Kelly and infused the landscape with her glamour and beauty.

Prince Albert's racing helmet, from his days representing Monaco as a bobsleigh driver at five Winter Olympics, is displayed next to a helmet belonging to Coulthard in Stars 'N'

Bars, a burger restaurant bulging with racing memorabilia and occupying a prime site close to the paddock. 'We all [the Grimaldi family] feel the keeper of our racing history,' Prince Albert said in an exclusive interview with Coulthard, broadcast on Channel 4 in 2016. Prince Albert was hooked, he said, from first being exposed to the noise and smell of racing cars in 1965, the year Hill completed a hat-trick of victories at Monaco en route to winning five times on this most celebrated speck of Grand Prix real estate. But it is his mother, Princess Grace, who has been credited with spreading Monaco's appeal to Hollywood. Her presence enticed some of the greatest stars of the age to travel across the Atlantic to attend the race, its royal patronage and penchant for gala dinners assuring the Grand Prix an abiding place in newscasts around the globe. Her son said he remembered Frank Sinatra, Cary Grant, Gregory Peck and Bing Crosby all visiting Monaco at the invitation of his mother when he was a child. He would have been eight when the Beatles attended the race in 1966 at the height of their fame. Sir Jackie Stewart, who won that race for BRM, recounted how the Fab Four reacted to Formula One during our time together at his home. 'John wasn't so keen, as he didn't take much interest in motorsport,' he said. 'Paul was interested, Ringo loved it and George was completely knocked out by it. George became a good, good friend.'

Over the decades, the race has continued to attract Hollywood's most bankable stars, including George Clooney, Brad Pitt, Will Smith and Sylvester Stallone. I interviewed Stallone in the motorhome of then reigning world champion Jacques Villeneuve in the harbourside paddock in 1998. The 51-year-old, who turned Rocky Balboa into a billion-dollar movie franchise, was researching an idea to make Formula One a Hollywood blockbuster, with him playing an ageing driver, 'a guy like Nigel Mansell'. Stallone was amusing company, and clearly liked what he saw in Monaco. 'Just as Rocky wasn't really a boxing film, I don't want this to be a motor-racing film,' he said. 'I want to make a human drama. What I have found is a sport where people understand and respect fear. But it is also a business involving hundreds of millions of dollars and a spectacle.' He got that right. This was a fight too far for Stallone, though, as the scale and cost of producing a film around Formula One proved prohibitive even for him. Instead he starred three years later in a film centred on the CART series in the United States, which was critically panned. Cristiano Ronaldo, a truly startling sportsman, is one of countless footballers who has readily accepted an invitation to attend the Monaco Grand Prix for no ulterior motive than a wish to be entertained inside the inner sanctum of Formula One.

'It is an incredible place to drive,' concludes Coulthard. 'Yes, it is difficult. However, everything you do as a racing driver is by the seat of your pants. You just adapt – and at Monaco it is very clearly defined where the limit is.' No argument there. It is not defined by an artificial border sprayed on a corner with a run-off area large enough to be a car park; it is stipulated by those barriers that cripple a car that goes inches off line. It has broken the spirit of even the greatest drivers: like Ayrton Senna, a record six-time winner of the Monaco Grand Prix; like Schumacher, a seven-time world champion. In 1996, such was the casualty rate here that only three drivers took the chequered flag, the fewest number of men ever to finish a Formula One race, anywhere in the world.

Even before workmen spruced up the paintwork for the 2016 Monaco, it was possible to detect the just-visible markings determining the fourteenth slot on the grid. It is outside the offices of Financier de Monaco Wealth Management, and with the curvature of the road ahead sweeping to our right it seems to be a bus ride to pole position. No one had ever won the Monaco Grand Prix from further back than eighth on the grid – and that victory was achieved in Formula One's Bronze Age by Frenchman Maurice Trintignant in 1955. Yet that record was astonishingly rewritten in 1996 by another Frenchman, Olivier Panis, in a race which is unlikely to be replicated. The narrative of how Panis came to deliver the greatest upset of all time on these streets is relived in these pages, in graphic detail, through the eyes of the Frenchman.

But I am duty-bound to stress that this book is not intended to be a conventional history of the Monaco Grand Prix. Rather it is an exclusive companion of stories and shared memories from some of those most intimately associated with this momentous motor race, men such as Sir Jackie Stewart, Niki Lauda, Damon Hill, David Coulthard, Martin Brundle, Johnny Herbert, Jonathan Palmer, Ross Brawn, Panis, John Watson and 2016 world champion Nico Rosberg. At times, without apology, I have taken a deliberate detour in conversation with these men in order to place their accomplishments and experiences within the broader context of their lives and careers. There is a compelling candour to their testimonies.

Others with decades of involvement with this Grand Prix, like the FIA's Charlie Whiting, and Michel Ferry from the Automobile Club de Monaco, Neil Oatley and Dave Redding from McLaren, as well as John Hogan (Marlboro), Mark Wilkin (BBC, and now Channel 4), PR veteran Tony Jardine, photographer Steven Tee, travel agent Lynden Swainston and caterer Lyndy Redding, provided me with insights that broadened the beam I have attempted to shine on the magic and mystique of Monaco.

As Lewis Hamilton memorably said, 'So many great names become legends around this circuit, it's an honour to fight for your place amongst them. But the coolest thing of all is that they still allow us to race here.'

William Grover-Williams, 1929

1

Royal Beginnings: Prince Rainier, Princess Grace and the ACM

The entrance to the Automobile Club de Monaco is located on Boulevard Albert 1er, barely 100 metres from the first corner of the circuit, Sainte-Dévote.

In the foyer is a portrait of His Serene Highness Prince Albert II and his wife, Princess Charlene; indeed, portraits of the ruling monarchy are omnipresent throughout the principality. Poignantly, before you reach the ground-floor restaurant there is a painting capturing the alluring beauty of Prince Albert's mother, Oscar-winning actress Grace Kelly, which is a reminder that her marriage to Prince Rainier III, in front of the world's media in April 1956, elevated the monarchy of Monaco to the global stage as she became Princess Grace.

Beyond the reception desk is a corridor leading to the library. On the right-hand wall is a photographic gallery of winners of the Monaco Grand Prix. Senna is prominently displayed, as the man who has won a record six times on these streets; another man with a history here is Lauda, a victor twice. The careers of the men overlapped as Lauda neared the end of his pre-eminence in the paddock and Senna made his introduction. Lauda recalls their earliest encounter as though it occurred yesterday. He was in pursuit of his third world championship, with McLaren then, after winning two titles for Ferrari. Senna was in his first season in Formula One in an uncompetitive Toleman. Only Senna knew – knew for certain – that greatness beckoned. It was 1984: in this scene Lauda is Big Brother.

'I was on a quick lap on Thursday . . . and I came round a corner to find Senna driving in the middle of the road,' says Lauda. Back in the pits, Lauda went in search of Senna. His question to the young Brazilian was typically brusque. 'Are you one of us?' he demanded.

'What do you mean?' replied Senna.

Lauda explained the fundamental requirements – and respect – expected from a new arrival on the most elevated stage in motor racing. 'You can't sit in the middle of the road in qualifying,' said the Austrian. He had a manner that did not invite debate.

Senna was unusually self-assured, though. 'Niki,' he said. 'This is the way *I* am.'

Lauda left without another word. In qualifying on Saturday, he knew his moment would arrive. 'I did my lap and stayed out,' he said. 'I was looking in my mirrors and waving drivers through. Then I saw Senna approaching from out of the tunnel. On the way to Tabac, I stopped my car in front of his. I took first gear and went. In the garage I waited for him to come to me this time. He did.'

Senna began to make his feelings known, when Lauda interrupted him. 'Ayrton,' he said. 'That's the way *I* am.' One day Senna would carry the most weight in the paddock, then it would be Michael Schumacher's turn to be the master of this universe, followed by Lewis Hamilton today. But back then Lauda was a man not to be disrespected. 'Senna had a belief that he was right, but I told him that I could do the same if that is what he wants. From this moment, we never had a problem. Actually, we got a good relationship.'

Michel Ferry is a link to this regal past and pragmatic present in Monaco. Beside his desk in the inner sanctum of the ACM is a photograph of him with Prince Rainier. Ferry, aged seventy-two, a silver-haired, debonair Monégasque, who is Commissaire Général of the Monaco Grand Prix, has held office within the ACM since 1962. He recalls with fondness the days of Stirling Moss, who won three times on these streets, and Graham Hill, who wore lightly the epithet 'Mr Monaco' given him for winning five times between 1963 and 1969. 'It was another time, a different way of life, a lot of fun,' says Ferry. 'Every night there was a big party with the drivers. Graham was at the Hotel de Paris on Friday and Saturday nights. Drivers were playing cards and drinking.'

The late Innes Ireland, a British military officer, who raced in Formula One from 1959 to 1966, before becoming a much-liked colleague in the media corps, never thought that driving a racing car should dilute his lust for life. Monaco was his perfect playground. 'I remember Innes being totally drunk two hours before the start of the Grand Prix. Nobody was shocked, it was like that,' says Ferry, his affection for Ireland patently obvious.

Jackie Stewart and his wife, Helen, were an exception, says Ferry. 'The couple were very close with Princess Grace,' he explains. 'They were received at the palace and stayed there, more than once, during the Grand Prix.' In contrast, James Hunt never knowingly missed a party in the seventies. Remembering them was another matter. 'James smoked drugs – everybody

25

knew that,' says Ferry. 'Lots of girls were around. The access to the track was free. You could approach the drivers, you could touch the cars. It is finished like this today: the cars arrive in the pits and the teams close the doors. Today you need to ask ten people to apply for a pass!'

For some years it has been evident that the only people not partying in Monaco until after the flag has dropped are the drivers. With car manufacturers Mercedes, Ferrari, Honda and Renault investing at least $1 billion in Formula One between them, that is the least surprising factor of Monaco over a Grand Prix week. 'There is a professionalism that is totally different,' says Ferry. 'Formula One became professional with Bernie Ecclestone, with money, and with a changing mentality. When I discuss with Formula One drivers living in Monaco – and there are a lot – they have no time to spend with their children during the Grand Prix. They attend press conferences; they have to speak with their engineers. They don't have ten minutes during the Grand Prix weekend to spend time with friends. There is no time for night life.

'Perhaps the first professional was Alain Prost. He had a chiropractor with him full-time and people judging if he has to eat potatoes, or not eat potatoes, and so on. Everyone looked at him and thought he was stupid. But we called Prost "Le Professeur" and now the drivers all have trainers and nutritionists. It is not just motor sport; it is the same in cycling and football. Sport is very professional because there is so much money involved – too much money.'

Money is not in short supply in Monaco. Yet Ferry, and a host of other diligent men working under ACM President Michel Boeri, should not be dismissed as men out of step with today's dollar-driven environment. His sentiments have a currency that is held by a wider constituency tired of money being at the heart of too many conversations in the sporting universe; yet it would require a hard heart to begrudge racing drivers for being well rewarded for participation in a sport where death can arrive at the next corner.

Ferry's role after more than five decades' association with the Monaco Grand Prix is still to act as a force for modernisation. He tells me, 'My programme is to find more safety, to give more evolution. After the Bandini crash, people said, "This is crazy." But it was like this everywhere at that time. We had the first Armco guard rails here, at the chicane, in 1962, which, I believe, is the same time as they were put in place at Monza for the Italian Grand Prix.'

His office is on the left of a corridor which acts as a wall of fame, where the winners of this emblematic motor race are displayed for posterity for members of the club and visitors invited beyond the reception area. The image paying tribute to Panis is different from the others. The Frenchman is illustrated in oil colours at the wheel of his Ligier at Loews Hairpin, in a duel with Eddie Irvine, by esteemed British motor-racing artist Michael Turner. It is as if his win was so unexpected that there were no adequate photographs of him. Or perhaps it was deemed necessary to commemorate this moment of historic significance with a commissioned piece of artwork.

No matter. Panis has a rightly prominent place close to the room where Ferry is expounding the philosophy of the ACM. 'Every year we discuss after the Grand Prix what we can do better next year,' he says. 'We have to prove every year that we are evolving to find a better solution; to change a little part of the track, to change guard rails. Our Grand Prix is limited, everyone knows that. Our track is not as wide as others. You have to prove you are ready to invest not only money, but in men as well, to find a solution.'

Monaco's prestigious importance to the world championship is acknowledged in the ACM's exceptional contract with

Ecclestone, who was the omnipotent Formula One rights holder until January 2017, when the American company Liberty Media acquired Formula One. Under the existing contract, the post-race podium ceremony is always conducted by one of the royal family on the steps of the Princely Lodge, beside the front of the grid, rather than on an elevated platform decorated with the names of sponsors, which is a contractual requirement demanded from promoters of all other Formula One races. 'The podium with members of the royal family is the image of the Monaco Grand Prix,' says Ferry, a man whose contribution to the principality has been rewarded with admission to the two highest offices of distinction, Officier de l'Ordre de Saint-Charles and Chevalier de l'Ordre de Grimaldi.

Crucially for the principality, the ACM retain editorial jurisdiction over the pictures broadcast from Monaco on global television. 'Television coverage is number-one priority,' admits Ferry. 'The glamour is backstage: the harbour, the yachts, the Hotel de Paris. You have the terrace there, where you can have caviar and drink champagne if you have the money, and the cars are three metres from you. This cannot exist anywhere else. This is the story, the legend of the place. You can have the same photo in 1929 as you can have today, except it is in colour and not black-and-white. The Casino, the Hotel de Paris, do not change.'

Ferry is keen to relate how the last ten-year contract with Ecclestone, agreed in 2010, runs to 2021, not 2020 as assumed. 'Bernie is a close friend of mine, of the club,' he says. 'He is very correct with us. With Bernie we do not have complicated talks over contracts. If he says it is OK, it is OK. But this contract is until 2021, because the contract in 2010 was written for ten years, but this makes it eleven years inclusive. A lot of lawyers said this is crazy, but as it is a ten-year contract this makes eleven Grands Prix.' What did Ecclestone say when he was told? 'He said, "Ah",' smiles Ferry. Yet Ferry is just as swift to deny that the ACM is exempt from paying Ecclestone's Formula One Management (FOM) a fee for Monaco's place in the world championship. 'Sometimes we read in the press that Monaco does not pay for the Grand Prix,' he explains. 'But we pay a lot – around the same as Monza pay.' Even so, surely Ecclestone offers Monaco a more favourable deal than the contracts proffered to governments in Azerbaijan, Singapore and Abu Dhabi, for instance? It is consistent for all Grand Prix promoters to keep their ticket receipts – for the BRDC at Silverstone it is their only source of revenue from the British Grand Prix – but Ecclestone's FOM take just a percentage of the trackside advertising at Monaco instead of all the proceeds, as is their custom at most other races.

When all is said and done, Monaco has the best commercial deal in Formula One. This is based on one simple economic criteria: Monaco is the showpiece of the world championship as much now as it was when Hill, Stewart and Lauda were winning in a less-enlightened TV age. Ferry understands the economics in play – yet still insists, 'The ACM is still losing a lot of money each year. Look at what we have to build; it costs a lot, a lot of money. After we pay FOM we do not have a lot of income from our share of the advertising and tickets. We lose nearly 10 million euros from the Grand Prix.'

Of course, it is not a permanent entry into the debit column of the Automobile Club's accounts. The value of the race to the principality means the government readily obliges by writing off the losses incurred. 'The government do give back the money to the Automobile Club,' says Ferry. 'They have the VAT from the hotels and with the image of the principality given worldwide exposure it is in their interest. Our tradition is our heritage. Monaco is a special place. Why do Formula One drivers and other sportsmen and -women live here? For tax reasons, of course; but also because Monaco is safe, because it has good schools, and because it is clean.'

Coulthard, whose eight-year-old son, Dayton, is already having karting tuition in school holidays at Le Castellet, a former Grand Prix circuit, a couple of hours' drive from his family apartment, discovered Monaco on arriving in Formula One in 1994. He acted on advice his father, Duncan, had given him as a teenage karting protégé. 'My dad ran a transport business in Scotland, the second oldest in the United Kingdom, and he recommended that I live somewhere to maximise my earnings when – not if! – I get to Formula One, as the best I could hope for would be a ten-year career. When IMG were my agents, they suggested my options to achieve what my dad advised were the Isle of Man, Jersey or Monaco. On a clear day I could see the Isle of Man from where I grew up and I didn't want to swap living on one small cold island for an even smaller one – fuck that. I'd been going on family holidays to Jersey for years and I didn't see being on that small island made any sense either. So, I thought I'd go to Monaco. I came here for an Elf-sponsored event when I was a test driver for Williams and had a look around. Before then, I'd only ever seen the place on television highlights of the Monaco Grand Prix, listening to Murray Walker and James Hunt.'

In 1994, Coulthard was promoted to a race seat with Williams after the death of Ayrton Senna at the San Marino Grand Prix, a tragedy that impacted on so many lives, as we will learn from men like Martin Brundle, a veteran Formula One driver, and Panis, a 27-year-old rookie competing in his third Grand Prix on the day Senna was killed. 'I was being paid £30,000 a year as a test driver for Williams,' explains Coulthard. 'I was then paid £5,000 a Grand Prix to drive in the last eight races of the 1994 season, taking my salary for that season to £70,000. When Frank Williams gave me the drive on a permanent basis for 1995, my salary rose to £500,000. With my first cheque I came down here with Tim Wright from IMG and opened a bank account with Monégasque Bank. I decided to rent the very first apartment I looked at in Fontvieille (near the heliport in Monaco) – it is in the same building as where my office is now. The rent was a lot of money at the time, but it would be ten times as much today. Thankfully, I have since bought the apartment.

'Coming here, I knew nobody and did not speak a word of French. In 1995 I had tonsillitis and remember returning to my apartment and feeling shitty. I admit I questioned what I was doing. But I knew the answer: I was there to maximise my career; it was not just about money. It was about focus, training and absolute discipline. If I'd gone home to living in the village, and my mummy was making soup and doing my laundry, where was the need to be disciplined? Why do people go to training camps? To remove themselves from distractions, that's why.

'Why have I stayed? I don't see what the alternatives are in terms of lifestyle. When I come back here, I smile. Yes, there can be lots of tourists, but there aren't any where I live in Fontvieille, with its picturesque harbour. I am a village boy – and this is a village. I've got my branch of UBS Bank, a corporation I nowadays work closely with, a supermarket, a chemist and restaurant all within a short walking distance. Nice is just along the coast, with an easy-to-navigate airport and great connections to all of Europe, Dubai and New York.' Coulthard does not deny that the tax advantage offered by Monaco was an attraction. 'There was a fiscal reason for coming to live here to start with,' he admits. 'But lifestyle-wise this is somewhere that just ticks all the boxes for me and my wife, Karen. When I had my house in Chiswick, before I moved down here, it was burgled twice when I was away at Grand

Prix races in Australia and Brazil. I have read that footballers in England have had similar experiences when they have been away. Burglars are not stupid. Here in Monaco we have safety and security.'

His contribution to charities supported by Prince Albert and Princess Charlene was recognised in 2015 when he was made an Honorary Ambassador for Monaco. The immense significance of the royal family to Monaco can never be over-estimated. When Prince Rainier died in April 2005, the family arranged for a ceremonial mass to be held a month later, prior to free practice at the Monaco Grand Prix, at the little church called Sainte-Dévote, situated at the end of the escape road at the first corner of the circuit. Sarah Edworthy wrote in the *Daily Telegraph*:

> In a gesture which emphasised how intrinsic the Grand Prix is to the lifeblood of this community, 600 marshals dressed in Day-Glo orange boiler suits assembled at Saint-Dévote to pay tribute to His Serene Highness Prince Rainier III. Prince Albert, face muscles twitching with emotion, stood facing an outside altar after walking up a red carpet in front of a guard of honour.

On 15 April 1958, Prince Rainier had been accompanied by Princess Grace at the inauguration of the Automobile Club de Monaco's new headquarters – the offices they still occupy today. Their signatures are in the guest book. Edworthy added in her dispatch:

> Prince Rainier's family presence in the royal box bestowed a glamorous cachet to podium proceedings captured in the fashion plates of classic photographs. Think Juan Manuel Fangio in the Fifties (goggles, leather

helmets, fabulous cars), or Princess Grace applauding Graham Hill, Stirling Moss and Jackie Stewart in the Sixties (mini-skirts, head-scarves, cigarettes), through to a coquettish Princess Caroline presenting the winner's trophy to Ayrton Senna and Alain Prost; and on until Michael Schumacher and David Coulthard became the modern claimants to multiple Monaco victories.

The War Hero and the First Monaco Grand Prix

The Automobile Club, with its impressive HQ in a prime location, employing almost fifty people to primarily organise the Monte Carlo Rally, the Monaco Grand Prix and the Historic Grand Prix, began in 1890 as a cycling association, Sport Vélocipédique de la Principauté (SVP), but then metamorphosed in 1907 into the Sport Automobile et Vélocipédique de Monaco (SAVM): Monaco Cycling and Automobile Association. With the changing times, its president Alexandre Noghès, a wealthy cigarette manufacturer and close friend to the royal family, presided over an extraordinary general meeting (EGM) on 29 March 1925, when the name was changed to Automobile Club de Monaco.

Before long his son, Antony Noghès, declared the inspirational if wildly optimistic idea of staging a car race round the streets of Monaco, which had cobblestones and tram tracks as part of its topography. He considered the challenges for a couple of years and then enlisted the aid and intuitive opinion of two men: Monégasque-born racing driver Louis Chiron on the sporting side, and an engineer names Jacques Taffe for his technical expertise.

In 1929, the ACM staged the first Monaco Grand Prix, but Chiron was unable to take part as he was racing in the

Indianapolis 500 and the dates collided. The winner in Monaco was an Englishman entered as 'Williams' – born William Grover – who arrived too late to take part in official practice, but won the 100-lap race in a British racing green 35B Bugatti in a time of three hours, fifty-six minutes and eleven seconds, at an average speed of 80.194kph. His place in history is assured for the daring deeds that followed the end of his racing career, which also included winning the French Grand Prix twice, as well as the Belgium Grand Prix at Spa.

The story of how William Charles Frederick Grover later enlisted in the British Army to become a Special Operations Executive Agent, who parachuted into occupied France, is told in riveting detail in the book *The Grand Prix Saboteurs*, by Formula One writer Joe Saward. 'He led a resistance of racing drivers,' says Saward. 'He was born in England, but grew up in France. He turns up in all kinds of books under different names. It took me eighteen years of research to work it out.' Williams – or Grover – was executed at the Sachsenhausen concentration camp, near Berlin, in 1944. He is named on the headstone at the old camp as 'Capt Grover Williams'. There is also a bronze statue of him in his car in the road-traffic island at Sainte-Dévote, although it is taken away over the Grand Prix weekend. The Monaco Grand Prix would never have such a mysterious winner again, perhaps.

Yet the roll call of honour at Monaco is comprised of legends of motor sport. In 1950, the race was won by Juan Manuel Fangio in the inaugural year of the Formula One world championship. The race did not return to the world championship calendar again until 1955, and it has been a permanent fixture ever since. Fangio won at Monaco for a second time in 1957, the year he won his fifth and last world title. A bronze of Fangio standing alongside the Mercedes he drove in 1955 is sited near the entrance to the pit lane. Other world champions to have triumphed on these streets, in a glossary of outstanding drivers across oceans of time, include Jack Brabham, Graham Hill, Jackie Stewart, Niki Lauda, Jody Scheckter, Keke Rosberg, Alain Prost, Ayrton Senna, Michael Schumacher, Mika Häkkinen, Fernando Alonso, Lewis Hamilton, Sebastian Vettel and Nico Rosberg.

'It's just the most hard-core rollercoaster ride, it's like when you drop off a cliff and you go down,' said Hamilton, in an interview for the Monaco Grand Prix programme in 2015. 'There's that fear-factor moment. It's scary, but it is cool.' Hamilton's verdict, you suspect, would get a nod of approval from all those privileged and courageous enough to drive these streets at racing speeds in a Formula One car; the fruition of the dream Antony Noghès first brought to life against incalculable odds in 1929.

Jackie and Helen Stewart: sweet reflections from
the balcony of their suite at the Hotel de Paris

2

British Invasion: Moss, Hill and Stewart

Sir Jackie Stewart is sitting beside the warmth of his open fire in the Lodge in the grounds of his 140-acre home neighbouring Chequers, the Prime Minister's country-house retreat in Buckinghamshire. The books casually displayed on classic pieces of furniture around the room include a volume entitled *Six-String Stories*. It is a limited edition signed by the author, Eric Clapton. Another coffee-table-sized volume is a collection of glossy photographs from the Monaco Grand Prix. The preface is written by Stewart.

With a tray of coffee and biscuits at his elbow, he is recounting his earliest memories of going to Monaco. It is of a time not featured in the book, in which he is celebrated as a three-time winner on the streets of the principality, looking, as he was, like a global star rising from the Swinging Sixties, with dark glasses, coal-black sideburns and shoulder-length hair. Stewart is travelling back to 1964, when he tested with Bruce McLaren at Goodwood and Ken Tyrrell was sufficiently impressed to offer him a contract to drive his Formula Three car.

'I was quick,' says Stewart. 'Ken offered me the chance to sign for him for £5,000 with an additional 50 per cent of the prize money and 50 per cent of the bonus money. At that time Ken was with Shell and Dunlop, obviously important companies. If I didn't accept that offer, Ken said he would pay me £5 a race. I asked, "What's the difference?" Ken replied, "If you take the money and the bonuses I want to have 10 per cent of your earnings for the next five years." I asked to think about it.' Stewart's innate business instinct – which in later life would make his fortune – was aroused and his conclusion was concise. 'I came to the conclusion that if Ken was offering that deal there has to be more money in this than I realised,' says Stewart. 'I phoned him the next day and said, "Mr Tyrrell, I would very much like to drive for you and I will accept £5." '

So, Tyrrell put Stewart in his car for the Formula Three race at Monaco in late spring 1964. On the eve of their departure date, Stewart and his wife, Helen, came south from Scotland to stay with Bruce and Pat McLaren at their home in Surbiton, Surrey. 'The McLarens were flying down to the south of France,' says Stewart. 'But we needed to save money. I had an MG at the time and we headed off for Dover to travel on the car ferry the next morning. At the port I asked Helen for our passports. She said that I had them. I said that I did not. I called Bruce from a phone box and he told me that I'd left my briefcase on the roof of the car and that it had slipped off as we drove away. Bruce told me, "We were waving at you, but you didn't see us." '

McLaren politely told Stewart that he would leave their passports at Surbiton Police Station, as he and his wife had to leave to catch their flight to Nice. 'After we had driven back to Surbiton and retrieved our passports we didn't have time to return to the ferry port,' remembers Stewart. 'But we only had enough money to buy one-way tickets to Nice.' That is what they did. Tyrrell had booked the Stewarts into the Westminster Hotel in Roquebrune-Cap-Martin, between Monaco and Menton, the last French town before the Italian border. Without the funds to rent a car, they hitched a lift from Nice airport to Roquebrune. Stewart, who won international honours for Scotland as a clay-pigeon shooter, and narrowly failed to make the British team in the trap competition at the Rome Olympics in 1960, had experienced overseas travel, but this was his first time out of the country to compete in a motor race. At the reception desk at the Westminster Hotel he was asked, 'Would you like a view of the Mediterranean or the mountains?'

Stewart says now, 'I opted for the Mediterranean. What I didn't know was the railway line ran right below the window of our room!' Even from his humble – and noisy – lodgings, the speed of his astonishing journey from Dumbarton, where his schooling had been affected by his profound dyslexia, to racing on a street circuit where British drivers Stirling Moss and Graham Hill were legends was not lost on him. Tyrrell's final advice to Stewart before leaving England had been to pack a dinner jacket because, in the event of him winning the Formula Three race, he would be invited to a black-tie dinner with the royal family and the winner of the Monaco Grand Prix. Stewart did not own a dinner jacket – 'but I got my hands on one before I left,' he smiles. Perhaps this might have appeared presumptuous to Stewart as he walked to the circuit the next day from Roquebrune, located some six kilometres from Monaco. But then again, perhaps not. For Stewart, who subsequently shared a car ride into Monaco for the next two days with others staying at the Westminster Hotel, duly won the Formula Three race.

The next day Hill, driving a BRM, won the Monaco Grand

Prix for a second year in succession. 'Graham was seated on the right of Princess Grace at the gala dinner and I was on her left. Bette Hill and Helen sat either side of Prince Rainier.' Stewart's drive, in front of Formula One team principals, was an advertisement that he possessed the necessary talent and judgement to return one day in the not-too-distant future as a candidate to win the main event. 'The first to congratulate me winning the Formula Three race was Juan Manuel Fangio,' remembers Stewart. 'It was a big moment for me.'

He pauses for a moment. 'I carried Fangio to his last resting place; as I did with Senna.'

Death was a reality – *is* a reality – that racing drivers have perpetually accepted as an unwritten clause of their terms of employment. They do so without complaint and, through the relentless pursuit of improving the strength of Formula One cars and making circuits more secure, a collection of fortunate men have in recent years walked away from accidents that would have claimed their lives when Stewart was competing. It was, he says, a mournful age. 'I am not one of those people who think the good old days were the best old days,' says Stewart. 'They were the bad old days.' Although Stewart was invited as a grandee of Formula One to be a pall-bearer at the funeral in Argentina of Fangio, the five-time world champion, who died from kidney failure and pneumonia aged eighty-four, his attendance at other funerals, of friends and rivals, in the sixties and seventies, was testimony to the fact that the sport's governance was appallingly laissez-faire.

Stewart responded by stridently placing himself in the vanguard to make motor racing safer; his was a voice that would not be silenced. He made himself unpopular – but he was fighting to ensure circuit owners made greater investment to lessen the risk to drivers, not trying to win a popularity contest. 'When I helped close the Ring (Nürburgring, in

Germany) and Spa (in Belgium) because safety was inadequate, that was when the big row started,' he recalls. 'People demanded, "How could you close the two greatest racetracks in the world?"'

Perhaps an inspection of Stewart's immaculate garden, at his tranquil home in an undisturbed corner of England's green and pleasant land, can supply in part an answer. Hand-crafted wooden benches, over forty in total, are positioned throughout paddocks mowed to perfection by the four gardeners on his staff. Each bench is commemorated to people with a special place in the hearts of Stewart and his family, Helen and sons Paul and Mark. It is a sobering yet somehow wonderful garden of remembrance that is a reflection of Stewart's life and those he has lost along the way. Many of the benches are embossed with names you would recognise: Jim Clark, Bruce McLaren, Jochen Rindt, Piers Courage, François Cevert, Jo Schlesser, Denny Hulme, Jo Siffert, Roger Williamson, Lorenzo Bandini and Graham Hill. All of those drivers died in a racing car except Hill, who perished in a plane crash months after he retired. Some others are monuments to family; another is placed in memory of George Harrison.

Four men were killed in racing cars in successive months in 1968: Clark, Mike Spence (at the Indianapolis 500 in the car that had been offered to Stewart), Ludovico Scarfiotti and Schlesser. 'There wasn't a mark on Mike,' says Stewart, sombrely. 'A wheel came off and hit his helmet and just disturbed the brain. It was similar to the injury that killed Ayrton Senna.' As he shows me around his barn, housing a fleet of motorised mowers and other pieces of heavy agricultural machinery, all spotlessly clean as he demands, Stewart points out some of the benches presently inside for refurbishing. 'Oh, there's Piers,' he says. 'And there's Jochen over there. When they are out in the garden they are together.' If it appears unusual, it is not the least morbid to Stewart. It is a reminder each day, I suppose, of how fortunate he was to survive and watch his sons grow into men of high achievement and share with them the brood of grandchildren they have produced.

The bench bearing Cevert's name is sited near the fountain which is visible from a window of the Lodge looking across the nearest field. 'François was a sort of protégé, if you like,' says Stewart. 'He was a great friend, and I was closer to him than any other team-mate.' Cevert died during practice at Watkins Glen, in New York State, in 1973, the season Stewart won Monaco for a third time, the season he won his third world championship. That US Grand Prix was supposed to be his hundredth and final Formula One race. Instead it became a nightmare which, truthfully, has never left him. 'I was the last driver on the scene, and there was debris everywhere,' says Stewart. 'We saw something no man should ever see.'

Only months earlier I had seen Cevert finish fifth in the British Grand Prix, the first Formula One race I ever attended as a young reporter based in the London office of the *Yorkshire Post*. By then, Stewart had already told Tyrrell and Walter Hayes from Ford, over dinner in London in April, that he was going to retire at the end of the year. 'François was being approached by a lot of people, including Ferrari,' says Stewart. But with his decision to quit already made, Stewart wanted Tyrrell and Hayes to know that Cevert was his obvious heir apparent. At twenty-nine, the Frenchman was fast at the wheel, a Grand Prix winner, photogenic, charismatic, and possessed a love of life outside the car. He was an artist's identikit picture of a Formula One driver.

At Watkins Glen, Tyrrell thought that as Stewart had already clinched the championship he could ask the 34-year-old Scotsman to sacrifice leaving the stage in victory by letting Cevert win. Stewart tells the story: 'Ken asked me beforehand if I would consider letting François win. I said, "Ken, you want me to lose in my last ever race?" Ken suggested it would be the biggest gesture I had ever made in motor racing. In the end, we decided to leave the decision until after qualifying.' It was a decision which never had to be made. Stewart returned to the pits from the scene of his team-mate's death embittered and sickened by what he had seen. 'I came away so annoyed, so angry, so destroyed. That's what happened to everybody who went there. We have all been affected by it.'

As the savage sense of loss struck them, Tyrrell and Stewart felt they could best honour Cevert by withdrawing from the next day's US Grand Prix. 'We decided not to race out of respect for François,' says Stewart. 'If I had driven, it wouldn't have been too difficult for me to win as I was at my very best as a racing driver. But if I had done, it would have been twenty-eight wins instead of twenty-seven. I never thought that was an important enough reason.'

Across the Atlantic in Lyon, unaware of the tragedy at Watkins Glen, Olivier Panis was six years old and harbouring dreams of being a footballer. Before his son's birth, Philippe Panis had competed in France in *course de côte* – hill climbing – in a Ferrari without complaint from his wife, Monique. But this passionate hobby was to come to an abrupt end. 'In 1966, my father had a proposal to do some tests in Formula One at a time when drivers were getting killed,' explains Panis. 'Anyway, the father of my mum was a pretty strict and pretty tough man. After I was born, my grandfather said to my father, a mechanic, "You are a father now and you have a choice: I buy for you a bigger house with a bigger garage and you stay with my daughter and your son, Olivier – or you fuck off. You do your fucking racing and stupid stuff. And forget my daughter and the boy. You choose."

'At the time, he was really passionate and motivated by his racing and he was really fast. But he chose to be a father and a husband. After that he prepared some racing cars, which he enjoyed very much. So, was motor racing in my blood? I think so. But when I was very young, I am not even thinking of motor racing. I love it, because I am working with my dad. I like the noise, the smell. But I want to be a football player.' That was not an ambition Panis would realise.

Mr Monaco

Stewart celebrated his seventy-seventh birthday thirteen days after the 2016 Monaco Grand Prix, where he was representing Rolex, a company he introduced to Formula One in 1968. 'Arnold Palmer and Jean-Claude Killy and I signed with them at the same moment,' he explains. 'We were all still with them until Arnold's death in September; and I hope I now deliver more for Rolex than I have ever done.' Stewart is unique in the paddock: a three-time world champion, a team owner, a broadcaster, and a tireless businessman still in great demand as a knowledgeable host for the prestigious clients flown to the Monaco Grand Prix by global brand leaders. In Monaco last year, in his familiar Stewart tartan trousers and cap, he was showing around guests from the high-wealth division of Swiss bankers, UBS.

No one before Stewart had fully understood that driving a car fast could make you money even faster, and could continue to do so for decades after anyone had witnessed you race. Stewart's incredible backstory, his work ethic and his connections – including the royal households in the United Kingdom, Monaco, Jordan and Bahrain, as well as chairmen of global corporations – have all made him very much a man corporate guests never tire of meeting.

'I am an extreme dyslexic,' says Stewart. 'When you are a dyslexic like me you can't read or count; you are insecure because you have been told you are dumb, stupid and thick. Then shooting changed my life.' Even so, his opportunities still seemed limited. 'I was a mechanic. There was no chance I was ever going to have real money. I remember Ronald Teacher from the Teacher's Whisky family came in for petrol all the time at our garage. I cleaned the windows on his Bentley. Other big wheels came in, too. I always admired people with money as they had nice things.' Stewart's exposure to such men gave him an understanding of what could be achieved. His mind was set. He would become someone, somehow. 'Everything I have got has always been done with a different frame of mind from anyone else that I know. Yet I am still cautious about my money. I have never spent more than I have earned in a year, ever. That includes buying houses. I still think the strongest element underlying all I have done is this: you under-promise and over-deliver. Do that and you never get the sack.'

For Stewart the road to riches properly began with that Formula Three race for Tyrrell in Monaco in 1964. Yet he received only £5 because, wisely, he had not wanted to sell his future to Tyrrell, who, if truth is acknowledged, can only be applauded as a man of prescient wisdom for trying to secure Stewart on a long-term management contract. After that race, the Stewarts may have tasted the hospitality of Prince Rainier and Princess Grace, and made a first impression that would blossom into a warm friendship with the Grimaldi family that has lasted a lifetime, but they still had to find their way home. 'It was too expensive to fly home,' he says. Stewart scoured the paddock to find someone who wanted a car driven back to England – and succeeded. 'I drove a car and trailer across France to the UK with Helen,' he says, smiling.

The next year Stewart returned to Monaco to compete in the Grand Prix for the BRM team as number-two driver to Hill, winner of the previous two races. Stewart and Hill had rooms at the Hermitage Hotel, favoured by BRM bosses Louis Stanley and Tony Rudd, and regarded as the next most prestigious establishment after the Hotel de Paris. Stewart's room had a view of the Mediterranean . . . and this time there were no trains to disturb his sleep. Stewart intuitively loved the street circuit. But so, too, did Hill. On reflection there was a manic insanity to racing there in those times. 'There were no barriers in front of the pits,' says Stewart. 'Mechanics worked on cars at the side of the racetrack. If someone had gone off the road, he would have wiped the lot out.'

But there was glamour from the beginning; and glamour in spades when Princess Grace arrived from Hollywood. 'Because of the yachts, because of the neighbouring Cannes Film Festival, it's always been a great destination for any fan of motor sport,' says Stewart. 'But when Princess Grace came it changed everything. Prince Rainier was a really shy man, lovely, but shy. But when Princess Grace came she was fantastic. She invited stars who accepted her invitation – men like Cary Grant and Frank Sinatra. My guest one year was Elizabeth Taylor, another time it was Sean Connery, the first and most unforgettable James Bond. I have a lovely picture of Helen walking down the pit lane with Liz and Mrs Henry Ford II (Maria Christina Vettore). I can remember Stavros Niarchos (a Greek shipping billionaire) coming over to sit in my Tyrrell in the pits. He wanted to start it up, but Ken said that we can't do that. I persuaded Ken to let him start the engine, though. He sat there with his foot pumping the accelerator, vroom, vroom.' He laughs at that image of one of the wealthiest men in the universe being granted a privilege that his bottomless bank account could never buy.

Stewart led his first Monaco Grand Prix in the late spring of 1965, when American students at the University of California in Berkeley defiantly burned their draft cards in protest against the Vietnam War, when Muhammad Ali and Sonny Liston met in a rematch to resolve the heavyweight championship of the world, and when Jim Clark won the Indianapolis 500 at a record average speed of 150.686mph. Sixteen drivers had started in Monaco, racing over 100 laps of these streets, demanding, it was estimated, 2,800 gear changes. A blistered right palm was guaranteed for those completing the distance. 'In Casino Square there were street lights on the pavement and there was no Armco,' says Stewart. 'The kerbs were like right angles. Straw bales were all that protected the capstans on the quayside. If you hit one of them it would have been ridiculous. Photographers walked on the pavements next to the track.' So did spectators.

Stewart's lead proved short-lived. 'I spun on oil at Sainte-Dévote – but I didn't hit anything and finished third.' Hill won.

But the baldness of that statement does not begin to do justice to the remarkable events that unfolded on 30 May 1965. If Stewart had the panache and swagger of the times, Hill had the elan of a matinee idol. His impeccably trimmed moustache and swept-back hairstyle reinforced that impression, and his appearances on TV, understated, but droll, added to his allure. He had been a petty officer in the navy when called up for national service, and later stroked the London Rowing Club first eight in the Grand Challenge Cup at Henley. He was an Englishman to the core.

At Monaco, he was wearing the club's dark blue and white colours on his crash helmet that afternoon he got out of his BRM and pushed – yes, *pushed* – his car back on to the circuit after being forced to scurry down an escape road to avoid a huge accident. He rejoined the race in fifth place after losing around thirty seconds. Hill's own account of this win-against-all-odds victory, in a book entitled *Graham* written with Neil Ewart, has a deadpan delivery that neatly encapsulates the self-deprecating character of a man adored by millions who cared or knew little about motor sport. It is worth repeating:

> The car that took me to my third Monaco victory was one of the nicest looking BRMs ever built. The road circuit through the streets around the houses at Monte Carlo is one of the trickiest in the world. When you are racing on relatively narrow tracks with sharp corners it's not easy to overtake. You need to get into the lead as soon as possible and keep there. I started from pole position and got off to a flier without any problems and continued to lead for the first twenty-four laps. Then I came across a back-marker as I came over the brow of the hill towards the chicane. I was doing about 120mph with this other car limping slowly towards the chicane, with some sort of mechanical, and it was obvious he would be blocking the chicane at the precise moment I wanted to go through it. I couldn't get there first and I couldn't slow down in time to let him through ahead of me, so I braked as hard as I could and shot up the escape road. The engine stalled as I came to a halt and I had to get out and push the car backwards up the track.
>
> This lost me thirty seconds or so and dropped me back into fifth place. By now Lorenzo Bandini and John Surtees had their Ferraris in what seemed to be an impregnable position. I was pretty annoyed at this, but there was still three-quarters of the race to go. I broke

the lap record several times as I carved through the field and at about half distance I managed to take Surtees for second place. Only Bandini was ahead and as I gradually closed the gap I had several attempts at overtaking him; but the Italian was giving no quarter. This led to a terrific duel before I finally got him and put the BRM back into the lead with thirty-three laps to run. The two-and-a-half-hour race ended at a new record race average of 74.34mph. It was enormously satisfying to have won a race in which I'd had to stop and get out and push.

In this Formula One era of telemetry, computers at trackside, team headquarters plotting strategy in real time, drivers changing gears by flicking paddles behind the steering wheel with their fingertips, and cars powered by hybrid engines, it is imagery from the Stone Age. Yet what Hill achieved that afternoon was an illustration of innovation at its purest. 'Dad called that the most satisfying win of his career,' says his son, Damon. 'It was amazing. Firstly, because the cars were light enough for one man to push them! That win, though, appealed to his sense of meticulousness. He was someone who liked to break things down. He spent a lot of time on the gear ratios and engineering bits and pieces, setting up his car for the race.'

Graham won five of his fourteen Grand Prix victories on these streets; Damon won twenty-two Grands Prix, but in his eight attempts never succeeded here, for a variety of reasons, and none more heart-breaking than when Panis won in 1996. It was almost as though it was deemed Monaco had been more than kind to the Hill family for a lifetime.

Graham was an institution at Monaco and feted like visiting royalty by Rosie from Rosie's Bar, which used to be found near the top of the hill on the left side of the track on the approach to Casino Square. 'The first time my dad went to Monaco he was in the navy aboard HMS *Swiftsure*,' says Damon when we meet for breakfast to rummage through the good days and the bad ones for the Hills in the principality. 'The first time he went to Rosie's was with mates from the navy. But when he was racing he never talked to me about Monaco, there wasn't any reason to do so.'

He was eight when his father won this Grand Prix for a fifth and final time, in 1969. 'I never went to Monaco when he drove, and my first recollection was seeing him on TV on the way to winning that race. I was somewhere in Kent, I think, and I can remember him going round the gasworks hairpin (now La Rascasse) and waving to the crowd.' His father grasped, he says, the fundamental law that applied to Monaco perhaps more than any other circuit. 'He appreciated that it was a race you had to survive. It was a lesson learned from his first race there in 1958. He had started from last and got up to third or fourth place and was halfway through the race, thinking this is a piece of cake, then a wheel fell off.'

Another man to learn an invaluable lesson at the 1958 Monaco Grand Prix was Bernie Ecclestone. He had entered a Connaught B-Type in his first appearance – but failed to qualify. It is amusing to guess how the history of Formula One might have been radically different had Ecclestone proved successful as a driver! Instead fate intervened and Ecclestone, in time, drove on in another direction to become the most powerful, and richest, force in Formula One; perhaps in all sport.

Hill, in turn, was to recover from the disappointment and metaphorically take the baton from Moss, who won in Monaco for Maserati in 1956, then twice more in 1960 and 1961, driving a Lotus Climax. Moss had finished runner-up four times in the Formula One championship, when he suffered a horrific crash at Goodwood in 1962. He was in a coma for a month. Mercifully, he recovered, but he never returned to Formula One. Even so, his reputation as a fearless competitor of great integrity shines as brightly now as it ever did. His knighthood in the New Year Honours list in 2000 was a belated acknowledgement of his place in the pantheon of the greatest racing drivers of all time. His fame reached far beyond the heartlands of Formula One. It was not unusual for a policeman to ask a driver stopped for speeding on a British road: 'Who do you think you are? Bleedin' Stirling Moss?'

On that fateful day at Goodwood, Hill was on the track ahead of Moss. He witnessed the accident that altered motor-racing history as Moss raced past him. 'When he passed me, he seemed completely out of control,' wrote Hill. 'Just what happened no one will ever know – but I am absolutely sure it wasn't due to driver error. Stirling was one of the greatest drivers the world has ever known.'

Like other wives and girlfriends, Bette Hill acted as timekeeper for her husband just as Helen Stewart did for Jackie. At Monaco they perched on a trackside wall, stopwatches in hand. There was nowhere to evade the public, as spectators could roam freely. Damon suspects that one of his father's hidden strengths was to dial out the commotion. 'I think Dad could go into quite a deep state of concentration,' he explains. 'He was also a competitor, at anything. The need to compete drove him. This is an incredibly technical track. I think he had great stamina as well as a high level of concentration. It is a circuit which just keeps coming at you. There is no moment where you can go, "I've got a bit of a boring straight now." Monza is like corner, corner, straight; corner, corner, straight. You spend a lot of time sitting there not doing anything. But Monaco is like a stroboscope, it just keeps flashing.'

Hill treasures a quote he has read about his father, attributed to Prince Rainier. 'He said, "Graham is very English, but he is also Mediterranean, which is what we like." I liked that. Prince Rainier recognised Dad wasn't cold or austere or imperious. He didn't have any of that. He had almost an Italian kind of feel to him. I thought of Dad as Tom Jones meets Terry Thomas.'

When Graham broke both legs in an accident at the US Grand Prix at Watkins Glen in 1969, he was asked shortly afterwards in a televised interview if he had a message for his wife, Bette. Without hesitation, he replied, 'Just tell her that I won't be dancing for two weeks.' Behind his dry humour, Hill built a monument to his career by becoming the only man to have won the Monaco Grand Prix, the Indianapolis 500 (as a rookie in 1966) and the Le Mans 24-Hour race with Henri Pescarolo (1972). It is hard to imagine such an accomplishment – the Triple Crown – being replicated any time soon.

Graham Hill and Jackie Stewart were men of their time, bold, courageous and courteous. They acted at all times by a code of sportsmanship that was unwaveringly honoured. It is indicative of their standing within the wider community of sport that the foreword to Hill's book was written by HRH Prince Charles, while the foreword to Stewart's autobiography, *Winning Is Not Enough*, was penned by HRH The Princess Royal. Princess Anne wrote: 'When his friends were killed in accidents, it was not enough for Jackie to become world champion three times; he worked tirelessly to make the sport safer for future generations. When he entered into a business association, it was not enough for him simply to fulfil the terms of his contract and bank his salary; he wanted to over deliver and nurture a relationship to last, in several cases, a remarkable four decades.'

Stewart was away on a shooting excursion when he learned of Hill's death in the plane accident that claimed five other lives. 'Graham taught me a lot about relationships,' he says. 'I started him in shooting and golf. He was a great friend.' Stewart accompanied Bette Hill to Graham's funeral; and to the funerals of others killed that sorry night. Damon offers another story of his father that typifies the kind of man he was, beyond the illustration of courage and commitment he portrayed each time he strapped himself into a racing car. 'Dad had a great friendship with Eric Morecambe,' he says. 'But Eric had no idea what Dad really did until he was invited to watch him race at Silverstone. Eric was quite shocked, really.'

After knowing Damon for twenty-three years, and chronicling his father's history, it can be safely concluded that braggadocio is not an element within the Hill DNA. The Hills were the first father and son to have been crowned Formula One world champions, Graham twice, in 1962 and 1968; and Damon in 1996. I was reporting from the British Grand Prix at Silverstone in 1975 when Graham announced his retirement to concentrate on running the team under his patronage, Embassy Hill. He had recently failed to qualify for the Monaco Grand Prix and felt it was the moment to support his protégé, Tony Brise. Hill's retirement announcement was delivered with great dignity. It is an overused phrase, but this truly was the end of an era. From memory, my report ran under the headline 'Hill brings down the chequered flag on his career'. It would not win any journalistic awards, but it summed up tidily the departure of a sportsman recognised as a standard bearer for the nation from the stage.

The 'obituaries' of his career told a story of a modest man reaching the summit of his sport without allowing his ego to rage out of control. Shockingly, just four months later we were reading Hill's actual obituary. He was killed when the Piper Turbo-Aztec he was piloting crashed while trying to land at Elstree airport at night, in reportedly foggy conditions. Brise died, too; along with four other members of the Embassy Hill team. Damon was fifteen years old. He never suspected then that he would race cars, never mind one day become a world champion. As a father of a son, Josh, who explored a racing career himself, Damon tells me: 'The idea that your father passes on his knowledge to the younger generation is questionable. I think the younger generation want to show their fathers what they can do without being told what they can do. That relationship has traps.'

Candidly, Damon admits his own success troubled him more than he could have ever imagined. He summoned memories of his father to help him deal with the psychological fallout from being recognised wherever he travelled. 'I am not someone who actively sought to have a posse of famous people,' he says. 'The people who build their lives on fame make me uncomfortable.'

At fifty-six, he still finds it disquieting to be an identifiable figure because he happened to be outstandingly good at driving a racing car twenty years ago. 'I had to deal with fame – but I didn't know what to do with it,' explains Hill. 'It was like someone gave me this thing and I thought, "What the fucking hell do I want that for?" My dad knew what to do with it. I got a lucky break, I think. I saw what it did from behind the scenes. I saw how it affected people's behaviour. It made me very suspicious about fame, and very suspicious about what it does to your ego.'

Monarch of the Glen: Stewart from Driver to Team Owner

Unlike Damon Hill, Stewart would not deny that he courted fame. At the 1971 Monaco Grand Prix he was trailed by cameras directed by Hollywood film-maker Roman Polanski for a documentary entitled *Weekend of a Champion*. Stewart gave Polanski an admission pass to all areas of his life that weekend. In one clip, he offers Polanski an indication of how a driver must treat the challenge presented on the streets of the principality: 'At Monaco be kind to your motor car and it will be kind to you,' he says. 'You are married, you are great friends, you are having a fantastic affair. I am sure if you spoke to Fangio, he would tell you the slowest way round Monaco is the fastest way. By that, I mean bring the power in progressively; you don't want your car to be an adventure ride. I am happy if I look slow.

'Monaco should be driven smoothly and quietly. On an airfield circuit like Silverstone, or other tracks, if you go over a white line marking the edge of the road it means sweet Fanny Adams. If you do that here, you hit a six-inch-high kerb and you can break a wheel or bend your suspension. Newcomers feel a claustrophobic effect. Then you see the young guy who is going to make it; he's clean, not rushed. A racing car is balanced on a fine knife edge. You have to keep it upright. Between the tobacconist and the gasometer hairpin I rested my head on the head rest because your neck muscles get terribly sore. You are stopping and starting all the time; your head goes back and forward. The G-loads on your neck cause soreness.'

In another clip, he is shown cutting himself shaving in the bathroom of his suite at the Hotel de Paris. 'Good job I have my own doctor with me,' says Stewart, twinkling for the camera. He did as well; for there was no assurance in those years of a qualified doctor being stationed at a racetrack.

At the Lodge, with the fire crackling in the background, he explained how he willingly cooperated with Polanski during the intensity of the Monaco Grand Prix: 'Roman has been a friend since 1966 and I agreed to the idea of the film because it came from him.' The film offered an insight behind the scenes at a Grand Prix for the first time and, while capturing the glamour and the sense of stardom Stewart enjoyed, it also revealed a man under an inordinate amount of stress. All these decades later, Stewart happily elaborates on what it was like to be a professional driver at that time. Formula One was just one aspect of his career. 'In 1971, I did eighty-six crossings of the Atlantic,' he recalls, without need of a diary. 'I was racing in the Can-Am series and contracted to the Ford Motor Company for fifty-five days a year. I had a big contract with ABC television's *Wide World of Sports*. I was with them for almost twenty years. The current F1 drivers don't fully realise that we were doing F2, Touring Cars, Sports Cars and GT cars to boost income. In 1966, my F1 contract with BRM was £10,000.

'By 1971 I was earning £1 million; I was the first to get to that type of number. That was a lot of money then, but I was working for it. In 1971, when I won Monaco with Roman making the film, I had mononucleosis. I got easily exhausted. I was so stuffed at the end of that championship I didn't even go to Paris to pick up my trophy. Helen went on my behalf.' The following year the stress of travel and racing caused him further problems when he suffered from a duodenal ulcer that at first went unnoticed. 'Twice I spun off in the 1972 Monaco Grand Prix for no real reason, though it was wet.' Eventually, doctors discovered Stewart was bleeding internally, and that he had an ulcer that was haemorrhaging. 'I was feeling so poor I thought about retirement,' he says. 'But I decided I'd have one more year.'

That proved to be a year of triumph and tragedy – of a third championship, and the death of his friend, François Cevert. He rejected all offers to come out of retirement and is proud of that decision. Yet he has never ceased to examine or evaluate drivers. His thoughts are illuminating. 'This is not to put anyone else down – and you must treat it that way – but Jim Clark drove most smoothly without ever bullying his car. I knew him and I studied him, as we shared an apartment together in London. I drove the same way. Lauda was the first one to drive in that direction afterwards, but the one who did it properly was Prost, not Senna.

'To this day I think Prost was a finer driver than Senna. Prost was much more sensitive. There was no extra steering angle, no loads of opposite lock. I learned all that from Jimmy and before that from watching Fangio. When you see drivers today, there are few with that kind of precision – maybe Alonso, maybe Vettel. Jimmy never won Monaco, because the Lotus was always fragile there. You are talking about a circuit that has been used by buses and other heavy transport. There were manhole covers and kerbs at 90-degree angles. Jim didn't hit kerbs, and while the Lotus was faster than everyone else, it was just too fragile. Today the surface at Monaco is like a billiard table in comparison.'

Stewart's love affair with Monaco had one last reel to play. Graham Hill was denied the opportunity to become a successful team owner, but Stewart made the transition in the company of his son, Paul. Stewart Grand Prix claimed second place through Rubens Barrichello at the 1997 Monaco Grand Prix in the team's fifth race. 'In those days only the winner went on the podium,' says Stewart. 'Paul and I were walking towards the garage after the race, both in tears at what we had achieved, when we received a message telling us that His Serene Highness Prince Rainier wanted to see us both. It was nice of him to do that.'

The Stewart team won one race when Johnny Herbert triumphed at the European Grand Prix, at the Nürburgring, in 1999. After Ford increased its investment, the Stewarts cashed out, and the team became Jaguar Racing for 2000. 'I put in

£1 million to start the team,' says Stewart. 'Everyone said I was blowing my money and that your reputation will be shredded. Paul was chief operating officer and Rob Armstrong was managing director. I was chairman. We had no equity partners and never had one penny of overdraft.

'One of the things I am most proud of is that we got all the sponsors – wonderful sponsors from the Government of Malaysia, HSBC, Hewlett-Packard, Sanyo, Bridgestone and an American telecommunications company – to pay before the season began. Not the full amount, but three months in advance. When we sold the company to Ford there was zero debt. Stewart reveals, with pride, 'The team we started with £1 million we sold for £130 million.'

Sir Jackie Stewart has his memories and he has his trophies; he has a scrapbook of a life truly spent in the fast lane. And he has those benches in his garden with names that are not just etched on a bronze plaque, but woven into the fabric of Formula One history.

And the streets of Monaco have run through the narrative of his life from that first time he bought two one-way tickets to drive in a Formula Three race in 1964. 'Monaco is the Prince of them all,' says Stewart. 'The Monarch of the Glen.'

Niki Lauda and James Hunt, 1977

3

Rare Breed: Niki Lauda and James Hunt

'When you came here from the wide circuits and drove up the hill, you thought, "Fuck, this is narrow." Then you have to say, "Fuck, this is a good challenge." And you have to show 100 per cent concentration, and then all you have to do is give it arseholes.'

Niki Lauda, Monaco 2016

Niki Lauda never did receive the memo on political correctness. Like Stewart, he seems a man born and raised in the Formula One paddock; as familiar in his baseball cap today as he was forty years ago.

Initially, a variation of that cap became a permanent part of his wardrobe to camouflage the shocking injuries he sustained when he was finally plucked – by other drivers risking their own lives – from the blazing wreckage of his Ferrari at the Nürburgring and given the last rites by a German priest in the summer of 1976. But in the passing decades his baseball cap, along with his denim jeans, has become a symbol of his individuality in a sport that long since surrendered its personality to corporate conformity. Lauda has never been measured for a team uniform.

Yet in this television-dominated age the camera unceasingly finds Lauda during the course of a Grand Prix weekend. One minute he will be on the pit wall as the eyes and ears of Dr Dieter Zetsche, chairman of the Board of Management of Daimler AG as well as head of Mercedes-Benz Cars Division. The next he can be seen offering his opinion on the performance of Mercedes' at-war drivers Lewis Hamilton and Nico Rosberg to a passing camera crew in the pit lane.

Officially his title is non-executive chairman of the Mercedes AMG Petronas F1 team, but, in truth, he is a touchstone from the past to the present. His secretive meeting with Hamilton, at a hotel in Singapore in September 2012, clinched the signature of the British driver from McLaren after the groundwork prepared by Brawn, then the Mercedes team principal. The faith Lauda expressed in Hamilton – already handsomely repaid – was crucial at a period in his career when his relationship with Ron Dennis at McLaren had disintegrated.

Unfailingly, Lauda tells it like it is; but as you listen to him dispensing wisdom in his staccato, to-the-point English, or clipping the wings of those with an inflated opinion of their knowledge of the business, it is easy to forget what a brilliant driver Lauda was. He won the world championship twice for Ferrari before his colossal accident, and then won a third title seven years afterwards for McLaren. In between the second and third titles he also went into retirement for two and a half years, as he had become bored 'driving round in circles'.

An audience with Lauda is always to be cherished. Our rendezvous for coffee on the first floor of the plush Mercedes motorhome in the paddock constructed on the quayside of the harbour for the 2016 Monaco Grand Prix is no exception.

The evening before, he went to a business dinner with Dr Zetsche, but he is sharply on time for our 9 a.m. appointment ahead of qualifying that afternoon. At sixty-seven, he shows no sign of slowing down.

Lauda won pole three times in Monaco and capitalised on that advantage, twice, in 1975 and 1976. Typically, it is the victory that eluded him after winning pole in 1974 that he wants to talk about, a story peppered with frustration and humour, a story that is pure Lauda-esque. 'After I won pole, I chose the right side of the track for departure because you could choose at that time,' says Lauda. His Ferrari team-mate Clay Regazzoni had qualified alongside him on the front row, on the outside and dirtier side of the circuit. On the following morning, a short time from the start of the race, Lauda could not believe his eyes when he spied the grid. 'The front-row positions were the other way round – Regazzoni was on the inside, I was on the outside,' he says, still clearly indignant at the injustice. Lauda stormed into the Ferrari garage to seek an answer to the question eating him up. 'Who the hell changed that?' he demanded.

The culprit, Lauda ascertained, was Luca di Montezemolo, the esteemed apostle of Enzo Ferrari and the man in control of the Scuderia. Di Montezemolo had been responsible for the recruitment of Lauda from BRM at the end of 1973 at the behest of Enzo Ferrari, who, reportedly, liked how the Austrian had driven into third place from sixth on the grid before his gearbox failed at that season's Monaco Grand Prix. That call meant Lauda's riches-to-riches career was on the launch pad.

It was not an outcome that was always assured. Lauda, who was born into an Austrian banking dynasty, had appalled his family by taking a $30,000 loan – a substantial amount of money in 1972 – to buy a seat in the March F1 team. It was a gamble that did not pay off, one that exhausted his borrowed resources, and put him back on the job market. Laden with debt, Lauda reacted to his unfavourable circumstances by persuading BRM boss Louis Stanley to allow him to test over the winter for a team which had triumphed at Monaco only months earlier when Jean-Pierre Beltoise, driving smartly on a wet track, claimed the sole victory of his career. It was to prove to be BRM's last race win, perhaps fittingly on these streets where Hill, three times, and Stewart monopolised the Monaco Grand Prix between 1962 and 1966 for the British marque steeped in history.

Yet when Lauda devoted himself to the BRM test programme over the winter of 1973, he was not so much interested in ancient history as to securing his own future in the sport. His fastidious attention to detail throughout testing, along with his stubborn nature, and native cunning, won him a coveted seat on the Formula One grid again. Ferrari's legal counsel ensured that he could be extricated from his contractual commitment to BRM and his new salaried position allowed him to square his debts. He began the next season impressively for his new paymasters.

By the time the travelling circus arrived in Monaco in 1974, Lauda had won the Spanish Grand Prix, from pole position, and he had been second in Argentina and Belgium. He had also been on pole in South Africa, so when he qualified in pole position on the streets of Monaco he walked into the Ferrari garage on race morning full of optimism. Then Lauda saw his track position on the grid had been exchanged with that of Regazzoni.

Apoplectic, Lauda hunted down di Montezemolo. 'I found out Luca changed the positions over because Regazzoni had argued that because [Ronnie] Peterson was our biggest opposition, in third on the grid, it was better for him to be on the inside to cover him,' says Lauda. To Lauda, it was an argument designed only to benefit Regazzoni. 'I said to Luca, "Are you completely crazy?" I had a fight with him like you will not believe. I was upset, pissed off.' Lauda's rage was in vain. Of course, the start of the race unfolded as Lauda suspected, and Regazzoni drove past him from the inside line, with its greater grip. 'Certainly, Regazzoni did a reasonable start and he was in the lead,' he recalls. Lauda's reaction was predictable and decisive. 'I pushed him so hard that he spun in front of me in the swimming-pool section. Now I am in the lead and I am happy again.'

He sips from his coffee, and he recalls with clarity how that warm sense he had inside his Ferrari of the scales of justice being rebalanced suddenly vanished without warning. 'I lead the race, easy; then my car stops.' He had driven thirty-two of the scheduled seventy-eight laps, leaving Peterson to take the flag. Regazzoni recovered to finish fourth. Still brooding after the race, Lauda let rip at di Montezemolo once more, saying sarcastically, 'Well done, now you have nothing. One car I pushed out of the circuit, making it spin, then my car failed.' It was assumed Lauda's car had been halted by an ignition-related problem. Yet in the debrief Lauda was told news he found hard to stomach. He was informed that when the car had been returned to the garage his mechanics started the car and the Ferrari dutifully fired into life. Lauda was incredulous. 'Are you sure?' he asked. His reaction to this news was to insist that the team transport the car to the following week's scheduled test at the Paul Ricard Circuit, two hours' drive away at Le Castellet, without touching a component on it. Sure enough, the Ferrari was handed back untouched to Lauda at the test. 'I was running in Paul Ricard for the whole day and the car was working,' he says. 'I was really unlucky in Monaco . . .'

Twelve months later, Lauda delivered the first win on these streets for Ferrari since Maurice Trintignant had been victorious twenty years earlier. Once again Lauda had commenced the race from pole position – this time without interference from within the Scuderia. Lauda is adamant to this day that pole position is a treasure without price in Monaco. It is a widely held opinion, but Lauda elaborates with detail. 'Getting pole is essential,' says Lauda. 'Because there is no room to overtake. If you know what you are doing here, there can be a car behind you who is potentially five seconds a lap faster and he can never pass as long as you accelerate properly past the swimming pool, as long as you come out of the tunnel at top speed and stay in the middle of the road. No one can pass. This is the way it is: fact.'

In 1975, Lauda won four more times, in Belgium, Sweden, France and the United States, securing the first Drivers' World Championship for Ferrari since Britain's John Surtees had taken the crown eleven years earlier. In fourth place in the championship was James Hunt, who had arrived that season in Monaco in the company of an eccentric British nobleman, Thomas Alexander Fermor-Hesketh, the 3rd Baron Hesketh. Lord Hesketh's entry into Formula One the previous year had enlivened the paddock with his penchant for lavish parties, while Hunt's approach to his work, outside of his racing car, showed a deep dislike for conventional onstage behaviour; he was more Jagger than Gielgud.

At twenty-one, Lord Hesketh had inherited the family fortune, which included a 3,200-acre estate in Northamptonshire and a racecourse at Towcester. He identified motor racing as the perfect playground to create a name for himself. Together with his friend, Anthony 'Bubbles' Horsley, a fellow bon viveur and would-be racing driver, Hesketh competed in Formula Three events around Europe, at his expense. They were not rewriting the record books, but they were hooked on the opportunities this sport afforded them. Once they decided to expand their ambition they looked for another driver. Hunt, who was the son of a stockbroker, and attended Wellington College in Berkshire, was the natural choice.

His over-exuberant driving style in Formula Three had led to him becoming known as 'Hunt the Shunt', but he was available and met the criteria Hesketh and Bubbles looked for in a driver. If his driving was uninhibited by fear or caution, Hunt's lifestyle might be construed as even more reckless. He was just the type of chap His Lordship and Bubbles wanted to be involved with. So, bankrolled by his private equity, Lord Hesketh, Hunt and Bubbles, who was now team manager, went from Formula Three to Formula Two and then to Formula One as though it were an end-of-term party after the first year at university. Champagne flowed and women were in abundance.

It was perhaps no coincidence that they made their entrance into the big time at Monaco in 1974 with cars painted red, white and blue – and devoid of sponsorship, as Hesketh felt the independence of the team was more valuable than tobacco money. Indeed, Hesketh was the only Formula One team owner attended by footmen during lunch at his stately pile. With grateful thanks to the archive of *Classic Car*, I am reminded that for Monaco the team opted for a Rolls-Royce Corniche and a Porsche Carrera as their transport of choice from England to the Côte d'Azur. Naturally, Lord Hesketh had moored his 162-foot yacht, *Southern Breeze*, off Monaco for purposes of rest and relaxation. Hunt had the look of a dishevelled Adonis and wandered about barefoot in shorts and little else. He raced hard and partied harder.

According to *Classic Car*: 'The team attracted a few similarly well-bred kindred spirits – the van driver was Charles Lucas, grandson of the architect of London's Albert Hall; catering was by Tom Benson, a successful Chelsea restaurateur, and Christopher Simon Sykes (later a top society photographer) captured the whole, jolly affair on film.' More critically, Harvey Postlethwaite was brought to the team from March to be chief engineer. Postlethwaite later achieved success with Ferrari during a much-respected career with various Formula One teams before his premature death from a heart attack, aged fifty-five.

If the F1 fraternity was amused, if not faintly embarrassed, by the gauche behaviour of the new arrivals, they had to take them rather more seriously when Hunt rose to sixth place in the Monaco Grand Prix before the driveshaft failed on his Hesketh-Cosworth 308. It can be assumed no team consumed more champagne that night. Hunt instantaneously became a fixture in diary columns of newspapers across the land. Hesketh Racing was here to make a statement – until the money ran out.

The next season, when Lauda won Monaco during his route to the world title, Hunt was involved in a race-ending collision at Mirabeau with Jochen Mass, driving for McLaren. But six weeks later Hunt delivered the maiden – and last – victory for Hesketh Racing at the Dutch Grand Prix. On the face of it, Lauda was a more circumspect man than Hunt. Yet the reality was that Hunt and Lauda had become friends before they reached Formula One having shared a flat in London for a time, as they fought to gain recognition in the lower leagues of motor racing. Their passion for life, as well as speed, ensured their lives would be spent in parallel once Hunt joined Lauda on the Formula One grid.

At Monaco, it was a ritual in those days for the drivers, as well as mechanics, journalists, and motor-racing fans, to congregate for a drink on Thursday night at the Tip Top Bar, an unremarkable-looking watering hole on the left-hand side of the track on the run down from Casino Square to Mirabeau.

With Friday anointed a rest day, the crowd from the narrow bar spilled beyond the track barrier into the street until the early hours of the morning. Taxis for those trying to return to accommodation outside Monaco were at a premium. On one occasion a couple of mechanics – we will keep the identity of their team a secret – left a Mini precariously balanced on four bar stools while the owners were inside having a drink. Even the most sober of men could become intoxicated by the amount of alcohol being ferried from the bar to the street. Brawn, who would taste so much victory champagne over the years in Monaco, mostly in celebrating another Michael Schumacher victory, tells me that his first visit as a mechanic with the March Formula Three team ended with less decorum than he became associated with in Formula One. 'I had a bit too much to drink and woke up on the beach,' reveals Brawn. In his defence, his bender came after the Formula Three race had been held.

'In the old days, I'd go to with James and stand around the guard rail and have a couple of beers,' smiles Lauda, as we talked in the Mercedes IIQ. 'But I always went home in time – James did not!' His face reveals the affection he still feels for Hunt, twenty-three years after his death from a heart attack aged forty-five. When Hesketh effectively ran out of funds by the end of the 1975 season, Hunt's own fortune soared. He was chosen to replace the outgoing two-time world champion Emerson Fittipaldi at McLaren. The intensity of the rivalry that developed between Lauda and Hunt for the 1976 world championship drove each of them to the limit. And it almost cost Lauda his life.

After winning at Monaco for a second consecutive year, Lauda, with fifty-one points, led the world championship by thirty-six points over Regazzoni. This was an era when only six drivers scored points, which were awarded like this: nine, six, four, three, two, one. After Monaco, controversially, Hunt had just six points, because even forty years ago the technical regulations, then as now, were interpreted by engineers as a challenge to circumnavigate or exploit in any way they could find. But during a tumultuous and controversial season that 1976 championship went to the wire – after Lauda astonishingly returned to the track following the accident that scarred him for life when his Ferrari crashed and burst into flames at the Nürburgring. At the final race in Japan, Hunt became world champion for McLaren when a violent rainstorm transformed the track at Mount Fuji into a tarmac river seething with danger. Lauda parked his Ferrari after a couple of laps and only the blind, or the stupid, challenged the wisdom of his decision. Lauda had no reason or need to prove his courage to any man. Hunt, who finished third to win the title by a point, was unwavering in his admiration for his rival and friend. 'I feel awfully sorry for him,' said Hunt later. 'Niki's decision was the bravest of all. None of the rest of us had the courage to stop racing in such ridiculous circumstances.'

Less than three years later, Hunt declared his own career over almost as dramatically as Lauda had removed himself from that Japanese Grand Prix. After a career total of ten wins – nine of them for McLaren after the riotous days at Hesketh – he walked out of the sport after failing to finish the Monaco Grand Prix in 1979. He was by now driving for Wolf, an uncompetitive team who would depart Formula One after three seasons, just months after Hunt quit. 'I don't feel I can win in this car and the risk is too great to drive for sixth place,' said Hunt. For all his flamboyance, Hunt never forgot that he was engaged in a sport of ever-present danger. And for unfathomable reasons he failed to record one memorable result at Monaco. What can be said without much fear of contradiction is that as Hunt left the paddock beside the harbour for the last time as a driver, an extraordinary chapter in Formula One had closed behind him.

Hunt returned shortly afterwards as a broadcaster with the BBC. Mark Wilkin, nowadays Formula One Editor for Channel 4, recalls with fondness and some trepidation his initial assignment with Hunt, which occurred at Monaco in 1989 when he produced the BBC's Grand Prix coverage for the first time. 'I hadn't seen James all weekend,' recalls Wilkin. 'We were in the commentary box ready to go "live" when, walking down the middle of the road in a pair of shorts, without a shirt or shoes, and carrying two bottles of wine, was a weaving James Hunt. As James came in, I took the wine out of his hand and replaced it with a bottle of water. He sat down and promptly fell asleep. It was maybe fifteen minutes before we got the first sensible words from him!'

The blond-haired Lothario was the antithesis of Murray Walker, the incomparable voice of motor racing for armchair fans first drawn to the sport on the small screen. Walker did his homework with impeccable dedication – even if the facts he mined sometimes surfaced during commentary in a form that won him the affectionate epithet of Muddly Talker. In contrast, Hunt approached broadcasting as a high-wire act. Eventually, they gelled to form a compelling double act. Hunt spared no driver's blushes. He would deliver a coruscating verdict on those he did not rate, yet could be complimentary of those deserving of praise, and by the time of his shockingly premature death in 1993 Hunt was much respected for his unique delivery at the mic. 'To be fair to James, long before his death he had completely cleaned up his act,' explains Wilkin. 'There were some difficult times, but he became a very responsible broadcaster.'

Wilkin provides an anecdote to illustrate his point. 'James rang me up once and said, "Mark, I have found this marvellous place."

'I asked, "What's it called?"

' "I think it's called the Press Room . . ." '

'Oh,' said Wilkin, playing along. 'I think they have one of those at every race.'

Hunt continued, still enthused: 'It's amazing. You can go in there and they have all these statistics.'

'I sort of knew about it,' said Wilkin.

'But you don't understand, Mark. It's brilliant. I can now prove that Patrese is a wanker.'

Wilkin laughs at the memory. 'It was absolutely hilarious,' he says. 'But this was so typical of James – this little exchange showed how he was taking his role ever more seriously.' After his death Walker broadcast a tribute to Hunt which concluded: 'After enthralling viewers with his wit and wisdom, James Hunt's absence will fill the worldwide followers of Formula One with sadness. I am really going to miss him very much indeed.'

Two decades later, Oscar-winning film director Ron Howard made a film called *Rush* which depicted the climax of the rivalry between Lauda and Hunt in 1976. The two men had been the fiercest of rivals, but also the greatest of friends and partners in a host of adventures unknown to drivers in the corporate world of Formula One today. 'Of course, James died too young,' says Lauda. 'But James saw more of life than most men who live to be ninety.'

'When You Are Thinking of Winning the Monaco Grand Prix the Next Day, You Don't Want to Be Talking to the Chairman's Wife about Boats'

Lauda reclaimed the world championship in 1977, but his relationship with Ferrari was diminished as the team hierarchy never fully forgave him for withdrawing from that race against Hunt in Japan. He signed for Ecclestone's Brabham team for 1978 – and delivered another adrenalin-pumped drive at Monaco early that summer. 'I had a puncture ten laps into the race and after changing tyres I came back out last,' he says.

His natural instinct prevailed. 'I had nothing to lose. I touched guard rails front end, rear end and drove all the way through the traffic to finish second to Patrick Depailler in a Tyrrell. I had the freedom to enjoy this race, I remember it well. It's all up to the balls and the head of the driver at Monaco, more than anywhere else. For sure, a good car helps, but it is the driver who is the big difference here.'

Lauda grasped from the beginning of his career that Monaco had to be afforded an independent mindset to elsewhere. 'When you start to drive on Thursday, you have maybe twenty centimetres to the guard rail. For pole position, you have to be no more than three centimetres from the guard rail. You don't try to understand the lap or go slowly into it, because then you are always behind. You have to go out and say, "Fuck, this is a good challenge, and show 100 per cent concentration; then all you have to do is give it arseholes." When you nail it right from the beginning – and the others don't – you are always ahead. When you have done the quickest lap, then you get confidence, then you can find another two-tenths, and this is an ongoing development by taking more chances and not crashing.

'Concentration is everything. Even if you are in the lead you cannot afford to lose concentration for one second. It is easy to look away at something, or brake a little late. Then, bang! Your race is over. Jack Brabham fell asleep [lost concentration] at the last corner and crashed, which let Jochen Rindt win [1970]. Ayrton Senna went home crying after he crashed, allowing Alain Prost the victory [1988]. When I was leading here I told myself I had to go quick otherwise I can make a mistake. So, what I did if I had a twenty-second lead was to reduce my revs and change gear earlier. You had to be very precise with your gear change. If you missed a gear, you over-rev the engine and the whole thing is over. I still went like shit through the corners, though.'

Monaco is unlike anywhere else when plans do not go to script, because the scope of the global coverage means that no one's blushes are spared. Lauda experienced the indignity of failing to qualify for the Monaco Grand Prix in 1983, the only time in his life that such a fate befell him. Neither McLaren's wealth nor their manpower could spare Lauda and his number two, John Watson, from the humiliation of being unable to make the twenty-car grid out of an entry list of twenty-eight cars. 'On Thursday we were slow and had no grip,' explains Lauda. 'We got the car better and we would have been quick in second qualifying, but unfortunately it was raining on Saturday.'

The dreadful conditions meant that neither McLaren driver could improve their poor times from the first qualifying session on Thursday. 'I will never forget this,' says Lauda. Guests from Marlboro and Unipart had been flown to Monaco for the weekend at vast expense, and all they witnessed was the McLaren garage being packed up. 'Ron Dennis was unhappy,' recalls Lauda. 'But I said to him, "It's not my fucking fault your shitty car is not working on Thursday."'

John Hogan, who, as account director for Marlboro, bankrolled a substantial proportion of McLaren's budget, still views the failure of Lauda and Watson to qualify as a low point of his career thirty-three years after the event. 'The worst thing was flying to Monaco in the company plane with all the heavy hitters,' he explained. 'On Thursday, when I saw the times, I am thinking, "Oh, fuck." Yet after speaking with Ron he assured me it should be all right as he felt that they easily could do the time needed in the second qualifying on Saturday. What he could not legislate for was the weather. As we were coming into Nice on Saturday I could see it was raining. On the way into the airport I could see both cars on the track and I sensed that they were not quick enough!

'It was a good car, but it was not as quick as the front runners as they had a Cosworth engine which was not turbo-charged like the engines Ferrari, Renault and Brabham had. In their heart of hearts, Niki and John would probably admit they were not going to stick their necks out in a car which they didn't think they could put high up the grid.' On Sunday morning, as their rivals prepared to race on the streets of Monaco, Lauda and Watson flew to the Austrian's home in Ibiza for a training session, relieved to have escaped the gloom that descended over the McLaren team. It was the worst place in the world to be humbled in such a manner.

Over the years, Lauda came to understand that a driver at Monaco is expected, more than anywhere else, to spread his workload beyond the usual parameters of setting up his car with his engineers. In Monaco, a driver is in perpetual demand by team sponsors to attend functions or dinners. Lauda resisted these overtures as much as possible, establishing a tone that others following him, like Prost, Senna, Schumacher, Alonso, Hamilton and Vettel, would imitate. The Austrian had the clout to be resolute in striking a balance between fulfilling obligations for sponsors and guests while being able to command the necessary calm and focus to do a complex job to the maximum of his ability. 'I told Ron my job was to win the race, not drink champagne,' says Lauda. 'The only time you can be alone in Monaco is when you are in the car, or in your hotel room.

'I tried to reduce what I had to do to the minimum, but a driver here has no freedom. This is hard because drivers must always be polite and go to dinners, which are boring on a Saturday night. When you are thinking of winning the race the next day, you don't want to be talking to the chairman's wife about boats, or whatever. If you come here as a tourist it is fine, but as a racing driver to win this race, with so much distraction, it is hard.'

He pauses to rewind a file from his memory. 'When I was leading the race in the mid-seventies, I picked up people in the crowd as I came to Rascasse. I could not believe it when I came round this fucking corner and there were two ladies, champagne in hand, not even looking at me. I thought, "What the fuck am I doing here? I am driving my balls off and there are people who don't even look."'

Lauda shakes his head at the absurdity of it. He tells me, as we are readying to part, that the day before he and Stewart had gone to have their photograph taken together with a BRM in the paddock. 'Olivier Panis was there as well,' he says. 'I thought, "Why in the hell is he here?" Then I remembered Panis won in Monaco, too.' He did. Against all odds, in some style, in a motor race that is unlikely ever to be dislodged from Formula One history.

Lauda has one more anecdote to share. His third world championship had been his hardest. Prost was the coming man and won seven races in 1984, compared to the five won by Lauda in an identical McLaren TAG turbo. The Austrian's strength was his calculating race craft when it most mattered. And he knows that fortune smiled on him when Prost's victory in the Monaco Grand Prix was rewarded with half points – 4.5 – when the clerk of the course, Jacky Ickx, stopped the race after thirty-one of the intended seventy-seven laps as he judged it too dangerous to continue racing in atrociously wet conditions. There was no safety car to call on then. 'I look at that result and know it made me champion and not that little —' says Lauda. In truth, the partnership with Prost, which Lauda had approached with suspicion, ended with the two men's mutual admiration of one another. Yet Lauda knew that from the next season, Prost was the future for McLaren; he was the past. After eleven retirements in the 1985 championship – won by Prost – Lauda quit Formula One for a second time – but this time it was for good. He had already created his own airline – Lauda Air – and frequently flew the aircraft himself. He was also a TV pundit. But these days he expresses his contentment with his role at Mercedes alongside Head of Motorsport Toto Wolff.

Breakfast with Lauda at Monaco is over. For him there is work to do ahead of the qualifying session to determine the grid for the 2016 Monaco Grand Prix. For me, there is one impression that remains in the mind, and will do so for ever: men like Niki Lauda are a rare breed.

Martin Brundle: Great Escape, 1984

4

1984: Senna and Brundle

In his thirtieth-floor apartment at Nine Elms, Martin Brundle has a view of the Houses of Parliament, the London Eye and Canary Wharf, and can just about make out the dome of St Paul's, dwarfed beneath the capital's skyline. He was also able to watch the night-time shooting of the James Bond movie *Spectre* from the armchair where I am now sipping an espresso.

These days, since he succeeded Murray Walker, Brundle is *the* voice of Formula One in the English language. His commentary and analysis for ITV, BBC and now Sky have a ring of authenticity thanks to his appearances in 158 Grand Prix races and his status as a former World Sports Car champion and winner of the Le Mans 24-Hour race. His raft of awards for broadcasting reflects the status he has acquired behind a microphone and in front of a camera, too. In his apartment there is not a shred of evidence of his success in either career.

At heart, Brundle remains a petrol-head, albeit one with insight, intelligence and wit. He thinks deeply about his sport, and he concludes that some of those drivers with multiple victories at Monaco, such as Moss, Hill, Stewart, Lauda, Prost, Senna and Schumacher, had a greater mental dexterity than other fine drivers, which gave them their distinctive edge.

'A very good driver might need 80 per cent of his capacity to drive round the streets of Monaco, which leaves them 20 per cent to work out what else is going on,' said Brundle. 'Whereas the greatest drivers need just 70 per cent to drive the car, which leaves them 30 per cent to work out what is going on with strategy, tyre and brake wear, radio messages and traffic, for instance. Of all places, Monaco will punish you if you need 100 per cent to drive the car, as the chances for making a mistake and hitting something rise incrementally. The great drivers have extreme skill, maturity, confidence and that extra capacity to handle the challenges of Monaco. That's why they were multiple winners. The biggest thing about Monaco is that from the first lap on a Thursday until the last lap on a Sunday you are just as susceptible to making a mistake, or have your car fail. You have to get to another mental level. The concentration levels needed are phenomenal.

'In which other sport do sportsmen or -women compete for two hours with a pulse rate at around 180 beats per minute, deal with repeated G-forces, and abnormal heat because of the clothing you are wearing and the fact that on a sunny day there is little air circulating round the track, while maintaining extreme levels of concentration? I imagine downhill skiers and boxers have that sort of mental and physical challenge – but not for two hours. In my view, nothing else challenges a sportsperson mentally and physically for such an endurance test as racing at Monaco.'

Brundle made his debut in the Monaco Grand Prix in 1984, the same year as Ayrton Senna made his entrance for the Toleman Hart team. Remarkably, Senna finished second behind Prost's McLaren during a rainstorm so violent that it caused the race to be stopped after thirty-one laps – less than half the distance. Senna's legend had a birthplace.

Yet Brundle, who had been narrowly beaten to the British F3 championship by Senna in an epic battle the previous season, had reason to deem himself more fortunate, having survived a horrendous crash at over 170mph. His car flipped over during pre-qualifying as twenty-seven cars competed for the twenty places on the grid. It was a heart-stopping moment – for those watching from the grandstands, never mind for Brundle inside the car.

There was a potential madness to Monaco in those times, as Brundle acknowledged. 'Without a speed limit in the pits you relied on mechanics to move a leg out of the way if they were working on a car when you came barrelling in,' he said. 'It was a ridiculous situation. When I look back, I don't know how or why we did what we did, it was just the norm. You came in and went out of the pits as fast as you could.'

To heighten the tension, the subplot to the Grand Prix for the teams at the back of the grid was an all-out skirmish to win one of the coveted twenty places on the start line. 'There was massive pressure on teams like Tyrrell,' said Brundle. 'You have all your sponsors coming, as well as family and friends, so getting in the race was the first requirement. But you put that to one side – you don't go out in a Grand Prix car in Monaco and think about anything other than the car. Information overloads there like nowhere else. You are not thinking, "That was a nice apex, that will be a good shot for the sponsors."'

Earning the right to be paid 'start money' was a more pressing ambition for those teams in the nether regions of the grid. Perceptibly, Brundle added, 'They were basically analogue cars. You had to press the pedals, throttle, brake and clutch, and shift the gears manually. The cars broke as well. It wasn't a package generated from a computer and a simulator. It's just the way the world has evolved, but I am just reminding people of how it was.'

His detailed recall of his accident, on the entry to Tabac, is testimony to the fragility of the engineering of the time. 'On the Tyrell, we had a brake bias adjustor, a mechanical cable and rod,' explained Brundle. 'The cable went to the back of the brake pedal, so you could change the bias from front to rear brakes. They do it electronically now, but then it was a manual thing. The cable went in front of the throttle pedal, which had a horseshoe curve where the cable went through. It was a time when the harbour-front chicane was just a fast flick, more or less flat-out. So you arrived at Tabac at 170mph to 180mph. I don't know if I had knocked the brake pads on the kerbs through the chicane. If you clipped the kerbs just right it was fine, but if you hit too much of them it would knock the brake pads back.

'When I got to Tabac, the brake pedal plunged. The pedal went to the floor; worse than that, the harder I pushed the brakes, the more the cable pressed the throttle. My head hit the barrier, then the car overturned and my head hit the track. There's one shot of where my arm is dragging down the race track because my upper body was outside the car. I don't know how I didn't lose my arm. Then the marshals arrived and flipped my car back over. I can remember to this day the crowd cheering when I got out. Everything in a crash like that goes in slow motion, which is why I think important moments like that get etched in your memory.'

Weirdly, Brundle instinctively knew his way back to the pits, through the crowd by the swimming pool, because he remembered that was the area where the nearest toilet was to the garages. 'Sometimes, as a driver, you had to queue-jump to use those toilets!' he said. 'I knew if I got to the toilets I would make my way back to the pits.'

Brundle peered through the triple-glazed windows of his apartment and smiled. 'The spectacular accidents, where bits fly off and the car rolls, look terrifying; but as long as you don't actually get hit, it doesn't hurt as much as it looks like it should, because the energy is being dissipated. It's like jumping out of here – it's not the fall that is going to kill you. It's the sudden stop. I think it's the same with a big crash. But I recognise I was really lucky that day.'

Undoubtedly, Brundle was a talented racing driver; his pulsating duel with Senna in Formula Three illustrated his verve and nerve when he recovered from losing the first nine races in the championship to take the contest down to the wire. On one occasion Senna's desperation was apparent in a late round at Oulton Park, in Cheshire, when he chose to try to pass Brundle in a gap that would never accommodate his car. Brundle told me: 'They had to lift his car off my shoulder, before I could get out of mine. Senna was prepared to have a crash with you to establish precedent and authority. Quite clearly, this was one of the traits we would see from him later in Formula One. Sure, there was a sense that here was a man who was unique, in my experience. But the car control I saw from him, especially in the rain, was just extraordinary. He had a sixth sense where the grip was.'

In his Formula One career, Brundle drove for championship-winning teams: Tyrrell, Brabham, Benetton and McLaren. Unfortunately, those times never coincided with the teams being at their zenith. He tells it how it was without wishing to solicit sympathy. 'Your primary role through that era, certainly with a lot of the cars I drove – and people think I am joking when I suggest this – was to stop it from crashing, not eke out the final half-tenth of a second in collective braking zones like they do now.' Brundle is not the kind of man to glance in the rear-view mirror of life to summon the hindsight of a disaffected old warrior of the track. He is simply testifying to the circumstances of those days, his days, with an account that is trustworthy and accurate.

After his crash at Monaco he had only one thought: to get back to the pits as fast as possible to claim the spare car, an asset all teams, large or small, had at that time. Ken Tyrrell, who had an extraordinary backstory at Monaco, having won the race both with Jackie Stewart (twice) and with Patrick Depailler, observed Brundle being buckled into the spare and informed him: 'You've got to hurry up, you are only in twenty-second place and you have eight minutes of qualifying left.' It was at that point that Brundle, his mind befuddled by concussion, asked Ken, 'Which track are we at?'

Brundle's race weekend was over as Ken gently ordered him to get out of the car. Tyrrell made instantaneous arrangements for his 25-year-old driver to be seen by Willi Dungl, who worked under the McLaren team umbrella and was Lauda's personal trainer. 'I have a confession: at that moment I had never had any physiotherapy in my life,' said Brundle. 'It sounds utterly laughable, but it's true – and Willi was not a conventional trainer. He taped magnets all over me to draw out toxins. I had to keep them on for a couple of days. I do remember that I couldn't sleep for a time.' And Brundle chuckled at a lasting memory. 'Ken got a £3,000 bill from Ron Dennis for his man looking after me,' he said. 'Ron's special, let's put it that way!'

After three visits to Monaco, Brundle had still not completed a race. Let him explain: 'On the way to compete in an F3 race at Monaco in 1982, I stuck my car on the front row of the grid in Dijon. I was a very unwelcome racing driver! The French tried to have me thrown off the front row, while trying to have my team-mate in Dave Price's team thrown out because the numbers on his entry sticker didn't comply, or something like that. Unfortunately, in the race I crashed in a straight line, so I didn't have a car for Monaco. When we got there, we discovered James Weaver, another British driver, had been excluded from the race for not signing in on time. I tried to get in his car – in vain. So, my first job in Monaco was to be up before 5 a.m. each day to drive Pricey and the boys in and out of the track in an old VW combi van. It was purgatory.

'The next year I should have been on pole for the F3 race, but I spun in Casino Square. Then in the race I damaged the car's suspension. That's Monaco for you. It's quite hard to get to the end of a weekend there without some kind of adventure you didn't want. I was always mighty fast round there, though.'

Enter Prost to Herald Dawn of Golden Age for McLaren

Prost's victory in 1984 was a matter of personal satisfaction for John Hogan as well as for Ron Dennis and the McLaren team, as they triumphed at the iconic street circuit for the first time. It was a prelude to McLaren's monopolising the Monaco Grand Prix for a golden decade, when cars produced in Woking, Surrey, under Marlboro sponsorship won the race nine times between 1984 and 1993.

Hogan had orchestrated the original Marlboro sponsorship deal with McLaren for 1974, the year Emerson Fittipaldi won his second world championship. 'We split that $15 million deal with Texaco, as Emerson was a Texaco man,' said Hogan. 'Besides, Philip Morris, the owners of the Marlboro brand, was a relatively small company in those days. We didn't have that sort of money.'

But as both Marlboro and Hogan's ambition grew, he became impatient with McLaren's decline after James Hunt delivered the world title in 1976. Hogan worked ceaselessly behind the scenes to put in place a plan for Dennis, then running an admired team called Project Four outside of Formula One, to replace American Teddy Meyer at McLaren. Dennis, with an astute mind for organisation, detail and forward planning, took control of an amalgamation of Project Four and McLaren Racing to form McLaren International for the 1981 Formula One season. At his side was John Barnard, an innovative designer who pioneered the construction of a carbon-fibre monocoque in Formula One. By the summer of 1981, McLaren's rebranded image was sharpened further when the team moved into new premises in Woking boasting a state-of-the-art machine plant and plush offices. Cleanliness and order were bywords of the Dennis style of management.

Around that time, Dennis told me: 'I can visualise something bigger, better, than anything that has existed in Formula One. The ultimate team hasn't existed. It's not the desire or the ability that has hindered people – but money. We are trying to evolve something at McLaren International where there is no figurehead. We want the team to portray character and style. The closest example I can give is Ferrari. Any driver would want to drive for them, yet they know if they fall out they become immediate history. It's that sort of mystique, that intangible thing, we want at McLaren.'

Hogan shared and believed in Dennis's vision. McLaren was going to surpass all that Ferrari and Williams could throw at them – and if Dennis failed to win a popularity contest within the paddock, in his own domain he was Caesar. 'Honestly, I just can't praise Ron highly enough,' said Hogan. 'He was just one step ahead of the game all the time. He has huge integrity, too. He might not be everybody's cup of tea, but he has integrity. He is a complex character, but within the world of motor racing he has no equal.

'When I say that he has no equal, I mean good and bad. If I had to identify a weakness in Ron – and I have discussed it with him – he has never been able to handle the political, Machiavellian shenanigans that go on in Formula One. His mind doesn't work that way. It is why Ron has always had a problem with Ferrari.' Those thoughts proved to paint a fatally truthful picture. In November 2016, barely a month after my conversation with Hogan, Dennis was forced out of McLaren by his own partners, Mansour Ojjeh and Bahrain's Mumtalakat investment fund.

It was a sorrowful end to what had been an astonishing journey by Dennis. He went from being a race mechanic to a business mogul with an addiction to winning in Formula One by assuming total control. This strength became his weakness in the end. He created enemies, and this time he could not point to the success of McLaren on the track as justification for his methods. McLaren had stopped winning a long time ago.

His ambition can easily be traced from his earliest days in Formula One. In 1983, Dennis had already identified the need to get a younger driver with star quality in a car alongside Lauda for the following year. As luck would have it, fate intervened in the final race of the season. Prost's failure to win the world championship for Renault at Kyalami, outside Johannesburg, was seized on as a gilt-edged opportunity by Hogan and Dennis. Renault's management were still heaping opprobrium on Prost – who lost the title to Nelson Piquet by two points after his Renault turbo engine let him down – when Hogan tracked him down by telephone. Hogan knew, Prost knew too, that his days with Renault were at an end.

'Not putting too fine a point on it, we needed a top-flight

driver,' said Hogan. 'I had heard on the grapevine from South Africa that the French had become, well, French. They had imploded. They were blaming everyone but themselves. Their car was the best in the field, but, somehow, they had not managed to win.' Prost's first experience at McLaren had not been wildly successful, but, older and wiser, he understood from what he had seen that Dennis had dramatically modernised the team – his exit from Renault could have a silver lining.

'I managed to get Alain on the phone down in South Africa,' said Hogan, a man with an enviable contacts book. 'He was living in Lausanne, in Switzerland, which was where my office was located. I had already been in contact with Ron – we used to chat on the phone three or four times a day – and with his approval I asked Alain to call into my office on his way home.'

Dennis made his way independently to Lausanne as well. Before Prost arrived at his office, Hogan instructed his secretary not to put through any calls – particularly from anyone at Ferrari. The fourth person in the meeting was Julian Jakobi, who managed Prost. Hogan and Dennis began the meeting by telling Prost and Jakobi how they were being given the chance to join McLaren at the outset of an odyssey that would alter the balance of power in Formula One. 'We were telling Prost how wonderful it was going to be, but the truth was we didn't have a budget to pay him,' explained Hogan. 'This went on all day – trying to get a deal together. But we didn't have any money!

'Halfway through the day, Ferrari had worked out where Prost was and Marco Piccinini, the Motor Sport Director, was ringing and ringing.'

Ferrari were about to enter into a sponsorship deal with Marlboro in 1984, but at that point McLaren were indisputably the main focus for the American tobacco giants. So, the calls never reached Hogan until after Prost had agreed to sign for McLaren for 1984 as team-mate to Lauda. 'We signed Alain for one year for $250,000,' said Hogan, knowing that it was a steal. 'However, I knew in the background that Renault was obliged to pay off Alain's contract, and that was big money. I told him that it would be all right for him to keep the Renault money – so, that's how it worked out.'

Dennis had another ace to play. He had approached Mansour Ojjeh, whose family company, Techniques d'Avante Garde (TAG), were already involved in Formula One as co-sponsors of Frank Williams's team. The dialogue proved profitable. Dennis and Ojjeh formed a new alliance to create the TAG Porsche Turbo. 'Ron being Ron managed to come out of left field by persuading TAG and Mansour to fund that engine made by Porsche,' said Hogan. 'Basically, Ron robbed Frank, which they laugh about now.' It was an undoubted masterstroke. The McLaren team were primed to take owner-ship of the drivers' championship and the constructors' championship in '84 – just as Dennis and Hogan had planned. Prost and Lauda had won two races each when the teams arrived in Monaco. The Frenchman clinched pole – the first one for the TAG Turbo – from Nigel Mansell's Lotus-Renault by nine-hundredths of a second. Lauda was eighth.

On race morning it was raining hard – and to Lauda's mind that created a problem unique to Monaco. He argued that the spray being carried from their tyres on to the road surface in the tunnel, which was completely sheltered from the rain, of course, would make this a fifth-gear skid pan. Lauda success-fully pleaded with Bernie Ecclestone to have the tunnel flooded by a fire engine. The start was delayed by forty-five minutes to complete the task.

'One important thing to consider was that I always thought the tunnel was the biggest worry at Monaco,' Lauda told me.

'We went from the sunshine into the dark and I argued that we needed at least to see the road. If there was some oil in there you are going to crash and kill yourself. They listened and started to light the tunnel – which, at the beginning, was a joke. But now it is like daylight for many years. It was an important change. In that year it rained hard I got Bernie to hose the tunnel down for safety.' Lauda's voice resonated louder than most drivers.

Mansell dramatically led the Grand Prix – the first time he had ever been out in front in Formula One – but on the sixteenth lap he was powering up the hill towards Casino Square when he drifted marginally off line at full speed in fifth gear. A rear wheel of his Lotus touched a white line and the resulting wheel-spin caused his car to snag a barrier, breaking the rear wing. Lauda spun out when he locked up his brakes at Casino Square.

Rain began to bounce off the track; yet, in a manner that was to be the hallmark of his driving, with each lap Senna kept taking precious seconds out of Prost's lead as the Brazilian maintained wondrous control of the Toleman he was commanding for just his fifth Grand Prix. But this breathless exhibition from Senna proved to be ultimately fruitless. Clerk of the course Jacky Ickx, a wet-weather specialist in a racing car himself, stopped the race after thirty-one laps with the Brazilian closing so fast that observers calculated it was only a matter of time before he would pass Prost. Obviously, Senna was infuriated the Grand Prix had been halted.

Prost subsequently had reason to feel peeved, too. Due to the limited distance the cars had raced, the regulations demanded that only half points could be awarded. Prost received 4.5 points, not nine – a matter of critical importance by the end of the season when he lost the world championship to Lauda by half a point. 'Because of this half-points result, Monaco was not a win, it was a bad memory,' Prost told me at his sumptuous apartment in Paris twenty-four years later.

'If you think, one lap, or two more laps, we would have had full points and, even if Senna had overtaken me, I would have had at least six points for second place. But no one knows what would have happened if we had kept racing. When the race was stopped, it was raining more and more. Nigel had crashed. Niki had crashed. I slowed down a little, but I had more and more trouble with the brakes. I always thought the race would be stopped.'

Senna thought it was a conspiracy. He said to Toleman boss Alex Hawkridge, 'Well, what do you expect? This is the Establishment we are taking on.' What we knew from our observations was that we had witnessed the opening scene in what was to become Formula One's greatest drama, an enduring and, at times, deadly rivalry. And for ten years the Monaco Grand Prix would be contested by just two men: Senna and Prost.

On the evening of 3 June 1984, Prost and the McLaren team partied the night away, with Hogan delightedly meeting the bill at Jimmy'z, the self-proclaimed rendezvous for the international jet set on the Riviera. 'Being a sponsor and an F1 enthusiast, winning Monaco was what I always wanted to be involved in,' said Hogan. 'I always loved Monaco as an event, but as well as an event I think it is the most prestigious motor race in the world. When the broadcast opens on the race, the camera always focuses on the harbour. It is hard to beat.'

Hogan added a little history behind the origin of the broadcasting contract, which uniquely gives the Automobile Club de Monaco overall control of the pictures that are shown around the world. He explained how Princess Grace played a decisive role: 'In America, the ABC network always had a jaundiced view of Formula One. Princess Grace intervened, I believe – not in the actual negotiations but through other channels to make her feelings known.'

To this day the pictures shown from the Monaco Grand Prix are determined by the host broadcaster, a privilege denied at any other race. 'The broadcasts improved and no one has a problem that the principality want to retain the dignity of Monaco by controlling the TV coverage and manage the advertising around the circuit,' said Hogan. 'I didn't have a problem with that and I don't think other advertisers do either. You wouldn't want to swamp natural landmarks with advertising signage – nor would the TV companies like it either.'

And the after-party, at that first, game-changing win for Marlboro McLaren in Monaco? 'It was monumental!' said Hogan. 'I can remember Alain dancing the night away. He also sang some French songs and I must say he is a great singer. By the end of the night he was as pissed as a fart, but then so were most of us. What is extraordinary – and what none of us could have predicted – winning at Monaco was to become almost routine.'

Photographer's Tale

Steven Tee has photographed every Monaco Grand Prix since that rain-halted race. Thirty-two years, and more than 570 Formula One races later, he insisted: 'It's the wettest I have ever been.'

He was exposed – no pun intended – to a tough baptism. His grandfather, Wesley Tee, was the publisher of *Motor Sport* and *Motoring News*, but he did not offer his grandson a passport to the world before he had proved himself through a traditional apprenticeship. 'I began as what is known as a dark-room scumbag!' he said cheerily. 'To begin with I photographed national motor races at the weekend, then worked in the dark room all week, for three years, processing film from the guys who were at Grand Prix races. We sent a pack of pictures out a week after each race – just imagine that compared to the instantaneous supply of pictures today.'

Tee, now fifty-five, is these days managing director of LAT Images, which has a motoring and motor-sport picture collection of over 12 million images. He remembers without much prompting the first day he arrived in Monaco, having covered just one Grand Prix, at Imola, a fortnight earlier. Monaco is a culture shock to all – drivers, engineers, caterers and, as we are collectively called nowadays, the media.

'I stayed at one of the little hotels up at the back of the town,' he said. 'When I went to collect my accreditation at the makeshift cabin near the old railway station, it was closed. When I returned, the queue seemed a mile long and it took the best part of the day to get my press pass. Then I later found that I needed to have gone back on race morning to get a little sticker to get me access to various vantage points. I was hamstrung. I couldn't go to the first corner, I couldn't go to Casino Square.

'I went to Tabac and stood there for ages before the start, only to be told at the last minute that I didn't have the necessary little sticker. I ended up going to the outside of Rascasse, which is pretty rubbish really. But because the race was so wet everyone else's cameras were packing up and I was kind of sheltered. The whole weekend felt too much, almost overwhelming. The fact that they stopped the race early meant I had to get from Rascasse to the podium, a fair way away, at little notice. By the time I got there, the podium ceremony was done and dusted as they locked the place down.'

Tee is now an old hand, if not the oldest, prowling Monaco with camera in hand, looking for a standout photograph in an ultra-competitive business. Photographers were the original messengers at Grand Prix races, portraying the glamour and the extravagant excess at Monaco long before television networks latched on to the sport as an arena of great commercial possibilities. Tee's remit to provide photography beyond the cars on the circuit began, he says, when he started to work with Benetton in the nineties.

One story still amuses him. 'Patrizia Spinelli from the team suggested we get some stuff of Jean Alesi playing tennis on Friday, a day off at Monaco,' said Tee. 'We met Jean on his boat at Fontvieille, the other side of the Rock. He'd driven for Ferrari and there were two Ferraris of his parked on the quayside. Jean was on board with his glamorous wife, and we all had coffee before we cruised off in the Ferraris along the Côte d'Azur to a mega-hotel at Juan-les-Pins. We did a little photo shoot of him playing tennis, with everyone giving him their full attention. I guess that's Monaco at its most glamorous.'

He regularly partied on boats, always with a camera to hand; but not for use paparazzi-fashion. 'On the grid there are always girls who seem six foot two inches tall, with low-cut dresses and passes round their necks. No one seems to know where they come from, but they still get photographed, as they have always been. Girls on boats will always pose, it's all part of the game.'

At Monaco in 2016, Tee headed a team of six photographers from LAT with an unjaundiced eye and undiminished enthusiasm for his profession. 'We need classic pictures – anything with cars and the harbour, anything around Casino Square,' said Tee. 'But I have always said that if you want to show someone how impressive Formula One is, the place to take them is the tunnel. Considering we are living in a twenty-first-century nanny state, I still find it extraordinary that you can wander through there with your camera and take pictures of a car doing 190mph within yards of you. But it's not just the speed the cars are going, or how close you are to them; it's the noise that assaults your senses even with ear-plugs. Taking a picture, a tingle goes up your spine.'

Of course, the natural landscape and the waterfront make Monaco picturesque on a scale rarely equalled at any sporting location. 'The backgrounds in Monaco are so gorgeous that if the sun is shining you can't fail to take good pictures,' he said. 'But it's knowing where to be, when to be there and how to get there that makes all the difference.'

Being a veteran of Monaco since the day Prost first won in 1984 gives a man like Tee – and his team – an edge.

Romance of Monaco

5

Tobacco Road: Money No Object for Cigarette Companies

'Right, Mr Jardine. Monte Carlo. I want an apartment above the start–finish line and I want two boats in the harbour. Can you manage all of that?'

Lester W. Pullen, chairman of
R. J. Reynolds Tobacco, 1987

The second race of the 1985 season – at Estoril in Portugal – will be for ever remembered for the brilliance with which Senna recorded the first Grand Prix victory of his career. In driving rain, just as in Monaco the previous spring, Senna was imperious.

At the end, the Ferrari of Michele Alboreto was the only car Senna had not lapped in his Lotus-Renault, the team the Brazilian had signed for over the winter. The degree of difficulty was further endorsed by the fact that seventeen of the twenty-six cars that started failed to finish. Later, Senna confessed to his own moment of great anxiety in the midst of the mayhem. 'On one occasion I had all four wheels on the grass, totally out of control,' he said. 'But the car came back on to the circuit.'

Not by chance, it is fair to speculate. But there were undeniable rough edges to Senna that could not always be compensated by his exuberance behind the wheel. At the next race in Imola he commanded the San Marino Grand Prix until he ran out of fuel four laps from the chequered flag. The cars were restricted to 220 litres of fuel, and there was a need for drivers to manage the consumption of gas-guzzling turbo engines. Prost was an expert at preserving fuel, tyres and brake wear. In France they created a name for him: Le Professeur. Prost was to dominate the season, a mission in part aided by a series of technical difficulties experienced by his team-mate, Lauda.

At Monaco, Prost won for a second time after Senna had put his Lotus on pole; the first of five pole-winning laps he would deliver on these streets. It is a record that remains unparalleled. Senna led the '85 Grand Prix but his engine expired relatively early in the afternoon. Hogan had been prepared for just such an outcome – by Prost. 'Alain was one of those people who always had the funny little habit of letting you know when he was going to win,' explained Hogan. 'You'd be having a general chit-chat with him at the circuit and he would say something like, "It will be all right." That was it: you knew he was going to win. I was on tenterhooks then. I'd get paranoid about which rooms I was staying in at a hotel. I wanted to make sure the room didn't have the number 13 in it, but Alain would tell me not to worry about such things because, for example, Prost said that the number 13 was lucky for the French. I never troubled to find out if that was true or not. It was enough Alain said, 'It is all right"!

'In this race Alain showed his real race craft. Senna had the legs of him in his Lotus-Renault, but Alain knew he just had to wait until something went wrong. Alain was a driver who could always wait. James Hunt described him once in commentary as "the best strategic driver in the field". He was right – Alain knew how to win by waiting, if necessary.' Once more, Prost had the privilege of being the guest of honour at the gala black-tie dinner hosted for the winner of the Monaco Grand Prix by Prince Rainier. Hogan was to go to several such occasions in the years ahead. 'I loved those occasions . . . I never did make a good Communist,' he chuckled.

For Hogan the Monaco race was a canvas to make the Marlboro brand globally recognised beyond the parameters of trackside advertising. 'We held a press party at the nightclub at the Loews Hotel on Thursday evenings, and a press lunch at the Hermitage on Fridays,' he recalled. Later that evening Marlboro threw a party in the Sporting Club for 300 guests. 'We would spend a couple of million dollars,' said Hogan. Each year, that is. 'As a company you quantify that because, eventually, you have ownership; you were the principal sponsor in Monaco. Everybody knew it was our show. By this, I mean you become synonymous with the event; and that is all you want.'

Prost's second win in Monaco was one of the five victories that accelerated him to his inaugural world championship, and the first ever by a Frenchman. He tells a sweet anecdote in his autobiography *Maître de Mon Destin*, published in 1988. 'In 1981, my mother had come to see me race at Monaco and had managed to worm her way in without a ticket by the simple expedient of brandishing her ID card and kicking up a little fuss,' he wrote. 'Getting into the stands in Monaco without a ticket is quite an achievement, by the way, but my mother has all her wits about her. She may even have bragged a little about it. At all events Prince Rainier got to hear of her exploit and he mentioned it to me *en passant*. Enough said!'

He clinched this much-coveted world title by finishing fourth at the European Grand Prix at Brands Hatch – a race where Nigel Mansell entered the winners' circle in Formula One for the first time. 'I didn't gesticulate wildly, but I do remember my eyes misted over in my visor,' Prost recalled as his mind travelled back to the afternoon he fulfilled his child-hood dream at a racetrack separated from his homeland by the small width of the English Channel. They created a fourth step on the podium at Brands Hatch for Prost to be anointed to public acclaim. The party, he said, lasted until the early hours of the next morning. At the end of the year, French president François Mitterand conferred on Prost the Légion d'Honneur.

When Prost returned to Monaco twelve months later he had a new team-mate, Keke Rosberg, the 1982 world champion. For this race the chicane on the harbour front after the tunnel had been redesigned to significantly slow the cars down. The kink in the track, beside the waterfront, was enlarged to make the drivers brake harder and shift down, thereby reducing the speed they could attain before arriving at Tabac. Rosberg had been one of four names on a shortlist Prost had compiled when McLaren boss Ron Dennis asked him to suggest a replacement for Lauda, who had confirmed his intention to retire when he held a media conference at his home Grand Prix in Austria in the summer of '85. At the time, that was Formula One's worst-kept secret.

Prost's quartet? Rosberg, Michele Alboreto, Elio de Angelis and Senna. Prost declared his frustration that commentators at the time felt he had blackballed Senna, when he insisted in his autobiography: 'Some of the less-informed press would report that I had been opposed to Senna, the bright new star on the horizon, because Ron eventually went for Rosberg. As discreetly as I could, I pointed out to the rumour-mongers that, instead of asking me why I didn't want Senna as a stable-mate, they would be better advised asking Senna why he couldn't join McLaren. In effect, his various contractual obligations were such that he could not have joined McLaren in 1986, or in 1987.'

Senna also had a new team-mate for Monaco in '86: Johnny Dumfries, the 7th Marquess of Bute, styled the Earl of Dumfries at the time. With respect to Dumfries – who later won the Le Mans 24-Hour race – a man born into one of the oldest aristocratic families in Scotland had not been anyone's nominee to replace Elio de Angelis, an Italian bound for Brabham. Certainly, Dumfries was not the first choice of the Lotus management. That was Derek Warwick, an outstandingly talented driver. He began his career in stock-car racing, financed by the family trailer business in Hampshire, and graduated through the lower echelons of motor racing to Formula One without acquiring an ounce of pretentiousness. Warwick, who years later became president of the British Racing Drivers' Club, and more recently provided inspiration with his dignified, courageous and successful fight against cancer, would tell you that he could not spell the word, never mind act pretentiously. He had taken the seat at Renault vacated by Prost at the end of 1983; so, when the French team withdrew from Formula One at the end of 1985, Warwick's unexpected position on the driver market seemed to make him an ideal candidate to step into the Lotus team alongside Senna.

The Lotus management thought this to be the case. The team's tobacco sponsors, John Player, relished the prospect of having a British driver of such immense popularity on board. Only Senna thought otherwise. He vetoed Warwick from getting the drive with Lotus. At twenty-five, this was a measure of the power that Senna held within a team that had won seventy-five Grands Prix and created five world champions: Jim Clark, twice; Graham Hill; Jochen Rindt; Emerson Fittipaldi and Michael Andretti. 'I think it was a compliment to me, but at the time I didn't see it that way,' said Warwick, when we discussed those times years later. 'Nor did you guys in the British press.

'It was seen by you all as a selfish act that destroyed a promising British racing driver's career. No matter how you analyse it – and I bear Senna no malice whatsoever – he destroyed my career as a top Grand Prix driver. I never got myself back into the eyes of the people that mattered. What stands out to me is that through the whole episode Ayrton was selfish enough, focused enough, thick-skinned enough not to give a shit what you wrote, I said, or what everybody else thought. All he knew was that Lotus couldn't build two equal cars – which was right. He wanted the spare car – which was also right. He also knew I was quick, and he didn't want me in that car. He also knew I was British and that I would get the team behind me no matter his own reputation.' Astonishingly, Warwick opened his mail in December to discover a Christmas card from Senna offering his best wishes for 1986. It was sent to Warwick without any sense of irony or meaning to cause offence. As they say today, Senna had moved on. And he had done so without a backward glance.

Later, Brundle witnessed, in his position as a team-mate to Michael Schumacher, how the German extrapolated the lessons learned from Senna and took his demands even further. 'I think this type of behaviour is unquestionably a defining point of the great champions: they have all been selfish bastards,' Brundle told me, in one of countless interviews I have had with him. Look at them: Lauda, Prost, Senna and

Schumacher. All of them got their elbows out, galvanised the team around them, demanded all the best aspects of the resources, then, on top of that, they wanted to disadvantage their team-mate as well.

'And it's right, isn't it?' Brundle continued. 'Well, in a way – and perhaps if I had my chance again I'd try to do the same. But that extra step of trying to minimise the chances of your team-mate, so that you had the whole team focused on you, just didn't cross your mind then. Schumacher took it to another level, didn't he? Michael was like a man with his own test driver.'

In Monaco in 1986, Senna was on the second row with his Lotus-Renault. Dumfries's fastest lap in his Lotus was almost ten seconds slower – and he failed to qualify. The race was won for a third consecutive time by Prost, with Rosberg second to give McLaren a perfect one–two finish. Senna, who had been on pole at the first three races of the season, in Brazil, Spain and at Imola, came home third; a commendable performance yet again. Dumfries had just that one season in Formula One, but two years later illustrated his talent by winning the Le Mans 24-Hour race alongside Englishman Andy Wallace and Dutchman Jan Lammers in a Jaguar XJR-9.

For the second occasion in three years, Brundle was relieved to depart Monaco in one piece. Eleven laps from the end, Frenchman Patrick Tambay lunged down the inside of Brundle's Tyrrell in his Beatrice-Lola and ran out of road, unsurprisingly. The cars collided heavily and the Lola became airborne and somersaulted across the track. 'Tambay's car touched me on the head,' said Brundle. Both men walked away shaken but unscathed. Four days afterwards, de Angelis, renowned as being smooth and stylish, outside a car as well as inside, was not as fortunate. The Italian was killed during testing when the rear wing failed on his Brabham at the Paul

Ricard Circuit at Le Castellet, a two-hour drive from Monaco. He was twenty-eight.

Five months later I was in Adelaide to report how Prost had narrowly won a three-way fight with the two Williams-Honda drivers, Nigel Mansell and Nelson Piquet, to become world champion for a second time by taking victory in the Australian Grand Prix. The death from cancer of his brother Daniel a month earlier had reinforced what Prost already knew: triumph and tragedy can be too easily twinned to take anything for granted. He retreated for a long holiday with family and close friends.

Greasing the Wheels: Tony Jardine and Jonathan Palmer

In 1987, Tony Jardine was running the PR campaign, through his own company, for the Camel Lotus team in which Satoru Nakajima had replaced Dumfries, because Honda had become partners with Lotus instead of Renault and wanted a Japanese driver as a foil to Senna. Jardine's role within Formula One had not always been this enviable, however. He remembers first going to the Monaco Grand Prix as a member of Bernie Ecclestone's Brabham team in 1978. 'I started out as a truckie and team co-ordinator with Brabham,' said Jardine. 'Chris Robson, who became part of the senior management team at McLaren, was the tyres man and I was the spares man. We drove the truck and I did the paperwork. We had a pit-trolley that kept breaking down. We had put a motor on the back and fitted a seat to it – and when it worked it helped us move all the spares, tyres, etc. from the paddock to the garage. The pit lane then was the most dangerous place in Formula One.

'I can remember when we had the trolley loaded and one

of my mates from the Fittipaldi team jumped on the back. We had just got from the paddock to Rascasse and there was Bernie coming towards us. "Who's he?" demanded Bernie, looking at my friend on the trolley. "What the fuck's he doing on there?"'

'I don't know, Bernie,' replied Jardine, sheepishly.

According to Jardine, Ecclestone gave a two-word instruction to the employee from a rival team: 'Fuck off.' Jardine never took such rebukes, to himself or others, as personal. Teams were run on less than twenty personnel; no one with a thin skin need apply. So, typically, for the race Jardine became part of the pit crew responsible for maintaining as smooth a passage as possible for the drivers, Lauda and Watson. 'We had to operate in a little walled section between some trees; it was like a narrow lay-by,' said Jardine. 'Brabham designer Gordon Murray had got us new air jacks with a proboscis on them.'

Lauda soon needed them to come to his aid after he acquired an early puncture. 'When Niki came in I had to find the little hole in front of his car and get the waggly bit of the proboscis into place,' explained Jardine. 'The puncture was on the right rear, but a decision was taken to change all four tyres. We were also going to give him a splash of fuel, which at the time was applied by gravity feed. I got the car up waiting for the fuel. Niki didn't switch off, he was just blipping the throttle: *wow . . . wow . . . wow . . . wow . . . wow . . . wow*. He was looking straight at me, his eyes bulging. The right rear gun came up – that was the signal I waiting for – and I let the car down. But the guy with the gun had come off because the thread was crossed. I could hear Lauda's voice above the engine cussing us. Niki must have been in the pits for thirty-five to forty seconds due to the crossed nut and me getting him up, down and up. I think he rejoined the race very angry.'

Angry, yes, but inspired, too. He came from the rear of the

pack to second, but this clearly did not appease Lauda's frustration. 'The first person Niki came to see after the race was me,' said Jardine. 'He grabbed me and swore at me. I kept apologising, but Niki was not listening.' Jardine is a naturally gifted mimic and he opted to detail the final exchange by offering a very passable imitation of Lauda. 'What happened last night?' said Jardine, his voice as clipped and sharp as Lauda's when animated. 'Were you people drinking? Fucking shit, useless.' Jardine's lasting memory is depicted in a photograph taken around 9 p.m. that night. 'The picture shows me still clearing up,' he said. 'I am covered in dirt, in pieces, knackered.'

Two years later, Jardine returned to Monaco as an assistant team manager with McLaren. 'Just to make it clear, Teddy Meyer and Tyler Alexander were running the cars for Prost and Watson, then there was me running everything else!' Jardine said, smiling. 'Prost, in his first spell with McLaren, was a young man feeling his way into Formula One, but one with very obvious potential in the car. He was pissed off because Teddy kept asking him to come to the team's small headquarters at Colnbrook, near Heathrow. I became used to Alain calling me to ask me to collect him as he didn't want to stay with Teddy. I'd ask my wife, Jeanette, to pick Alain up in her Citroën 2CV and we would get him a room at a little hotel near us. There was a nervousness about Alain's demeanour and he could never concentrate when you were talking to him; his eyes darted all over the place.

'In the car he was different. In the first two races of the season, in Argentina and Brazil, Alain was sixth and fifth in the McLaren M29C, which was a shit box. In Monaco, Prost was tenth on the grid, while Wattie didn't even qualify. It indicates how fast Prost was already developing. The team had little mopeds to get around Monaco and Wattie wanted me to go down to the pits with him on race morning. We were terrible. We'd tell him: "Wattie, we don't want to be seen with you." Well, imagine: Wattie crashed his moped and tore his shirt. He was given so much grief by the team!' Only a man of Watson's unflappable nature would not have taken umbrage.

The spirit of the McLaren team was further dampened shortly after the race started. Derek Daly and Jean-Pierre Jarier, driving identical Tyrrell cars in the middle of the pack, close to Prost, had a frightening collision at the entrance to Sainte-Dévote. Prost became part of the shunt. 'Daly appeared to lose his braking point and took out Jarier . . . and with the cars flying around Prost lost the rear wing of his McLaren,' said Jardine. To the dismay of the McLaren crew, Prost got out of his car. 'If he had just driven on and come round to the pits we could have fitted a new rear wing,' said Jardine. 'If you keep going round Monaco you can get into the points. We were all upset when we got the car back and it was pretty much pristine.' It was another tale from a catalogue of what-might-have-been stories woven into the streets of Monaco. As for Jardine, he took the decision to take the experience he had gained from working inside Formula One teams to work in PR, finally establishing his own company; and later became an accomplished broadcaster, too.

By 1987, Jardine's PR business had captured its biggest client: R. J. Reynolds, an American tobacco conglomerate based in Winston-Salem, North Carolina. He pitched against two American agencies in the company's headquarters to win the contract to publicise and promote the cigarette brand on Lotus cars: Camel. At the moment when R. J. Reynolds's chairman, Lester W. Pullen, confirmed Jardine's appointment in his office in Winston-Salem, he said, 'Right, Mr Jardine. Monte Carlo. I want an apartment above the start–finish line and I want two boats in the harbour. Can you manage all of that?'

Unhesitatingly, Jardine replied, 'Yes, sir.'

In reality, Jardine had just three months to meet those demands. 'We went down to Monte Carlo and began bribing anyone who could be helpful,' admitted Jardine. His business depended on the success of his mission, because men like Lester W. Pullen do not expect to be disappointed. 'I did a really good deal for the apartment. I got that for around £14,000 for four days by giving the people who had originally rented the apartment cash to make them go away. Moné-gasque police helped us plan routes to get the R. J. Reynolds party in and out of the apartment. We had to also arrange jets, limos, boat taxis and exclusive dinners on beautiful boats hired for the duration of the Grand Prix. Money was no object.'

The stage was set for Senna to star with his new paymasters in attendance. Prost had reached a significant milestone at the race before Monaco, when victory in the Belgian Grand Prix enabled the Frenchman to score his twenty-seventh win, equalling the record held by Stewart. The Scotsman was con-tent to endorse Prost's claim to greatness in a TV interview broadcast from the principality. 'Alain Prost, in my opinion at the present time, is the finest Grand Prix driver in the world, probably the finest racing driver in the world,' said Stewart. 'And therefore I am happy that it is him who will be taking the record and not someone I would not be proud to have it.'

However, it was Mansell who put his Williams-Honda on pole ahead of Senna. This was a potential tinderbox, for a fort-night earlier the two men had squabbled at high speed over the same piece of tarmac during the Belgian Grand Prix. In that race, Senna's Lotus went no further than the sand trap that he had been catapulted into. Mansell coaxed his Williams back into the race, but not for long. He had to retire on lap 17. Each thought the other was to blame. It is the default psyche of most racing drivers, but none better reflected that mentality than Senna. In his eyes, his driving was beyond reproach at all times.

Mansell felt unequivocally that he was the innocent victim of this particular collision. And his blood was still at boiling point when he climbed from his car back at the Williams garage with the race going on without him. He marched angrily in search of Senna. The Englishman found him in the Lotus garage. Before anyone could react, Mansell grabbed Senna's neck and had to be dragged away from the Brazilian by three Lotus mechanics. When asked later what had happened, Senna replied sardonically, 'When a man holds you round the throat, I don't think he has come to apologise.'

Two weeks on, calm heads prevailed on the grid at Monaco. Mansell took the lead, with Senna in pursuit. But the Englishman's luck deserted him once more when he slowed to a halt on lap 30 with a loss of turbo boost from his Honda engine. Senna drove untroubled to the chequered flag in his active-suspension Lotus to take the first of what would become a series of victories on the streets of Monaco. Behind Senna came Piquet, Alboreto, Berger and Jonathan Palmer, who was awarded the Jim Clark Trophy for the best-placed driver in a normally aspirated car: a Tyrrell.

Palmer assessed his fifth place as a job well done within the limits of the disadvantage he experienced against the turbos of Lotus, Williams and Ferrari. 'It was a good effort, I suppose,' said Palmer. 'Getting round Monaco is quite a skill in its own right. You had to avoid other people's accidents, find that balance of going flat-out while looking after the car. There is also a need to be patient in traffic, but having the judgement to go for a gap when it presented itself.'

Palmer had qualified as a doctor, but motor racing was his passion. His intellect never precluded him from taking risks and he liked the precarious challenge of Monaco above all else. 'It was somewhere you always felt you were earning your money as a racing driver,' said Palmer. 'I remember the first laps I did round here in a Formula One car felt like you were doing a million miles an hour. On all circuits, the more laps you do, you think about it overnight and when you come back the same lap time seems far less a trauma the following day. And that was very much the thing with Monaco: you get in a groove and what seemed like a crazy circuit with these kinds of cars feels totally normal. It slows down in your mind. As days pass, you get more and more grip and go quicker and quicker. The track evolves unlike anywhere else.'

Palmer was at the Monaco Grand Prix in 2016 to oversee the performance of his son Jolyon, racing alongside Kevin Magnusson for the Renault Formula One team. His younger son Will was also competing in a support race. 'Watching from the outside you are obviously helpless,' said Palmer. 'Jolyon doesn't want to talk to me about my experiences here – and he is right. There's nothing I can really tell him that would be helpful from twenty-five years ago.'

Yet Palmer, now sixty, is a man who still lives on the precipice as the chief executive of MotorSport Vision, which owns Brands Hatch, Oulton Park, Snetterton, Cadwell Park and Donnington, as well as the Bedford Autodrome, used for track days, testing and PalmerSport corporate days. He is developing a plot of land in France for his motor-sport business, too. He totally comprehends the level of pressure on his son, Jolyon.

'Jolyon is in a Renault factory team which has a huge investment in Formula One,' said Palmer. 'There's probably 500 people working on the engines, and another 500 working at the factory in Enstone on the cars. By the scale of the operation that presents a huge amount of pressure on the drivers. In contrast, when I was at Tyrrell there was a total of seventy-eight people, or thereabouts, in the team. Jolyon won at Monaco twice in GP2, but those times of that kind of elation happen no more than 5 per cent of your career in motor racing. Most of the time it is 50 per cent disappointment, 30 per cent so-so and perhaps 20 per cent when it is good. It's just the way it is.'

Formula One is a hard arena to survive, no doubt. And that's before you dial in the political undercurrent that influences if not every deal, then most of them. By year end, Jolyon learned he had kept his seat for 2017 at Renault; and doubtless Jonathan had played some unseen role in the background. Knowing how to keep the wheels greased is a speciality he developed in the embryonic stage of his own driving career.

It was a simpler time, as Palmer remembered. Less corporate governance existed and there was not the colossal investment from car manufacturers with shareholders to consider. Even so, Palmer was constantly looking at the next deal. Racing was always a means to an end. But that is not to deny that he was ferociously competitive in a race car. He took an instant liking to Monaco. 'When we raced, we had manual gearboxes,' he said. 'Half the time you would be driving round here with just one hand on the steering wheel. There would be sections when you didn't bother taking your hand off the gear lever; it was up a gear, down, up, up, up, up, down, down. It would have made a spectacular shot for an on-board camera with a driver's hands moving around so much. Today, you can barely tell fingers on the paddles behind the steering wheel.

'I think one of the reasons I used to go quite well here is that if I had a fault in my driving it would be that I would over-analyse it. I was at my worst at places that had long straights like Monza. I could spend so long thinking whether I should brake, let's say, at ninety-seven metres or eighty-six metres. By the time I had thought that through five times, I had screwed up my braking! Here there is no time to think. There are no corner boards; everything a driver does is instinct-ive. It is just one frantic blur of activity and you just get into a rhythm – almost trance-like. Most qualifying sections you'd find tyres had got white paint marks down the side because you had been glancing the barriers and didn't realise it.'

Palmer, who drove in eighty-three Formula One races, joined McLaren as a test driver at the end of the 1989 season and at times worked closely with Senna. Ask him whom he deemed to be the best driver around the streets of Monaco and he'll give an unequivocal response: Senna. 'Ayrton had an aura about him, an immense self-confidence,' said Palmer. 'He just knew that he was better than anyone else – to the extent that it baffled and complexed him if anyone was quicker, in a manner that was not the least bit affected. He just couldn't understand it. To Senna, it was changing the natural order of the world and there must be something to cause that. Just watching him in the car, it was artistry.' Yet with his profound comprehension of motor racing and the intricacies of the business, Palmer looked at the cars being driven last spring at breakneck speed through the streets he so loved and said, smiling, 'But the point, surely, is that they are all bloody bril-liant, aren't they?'

His fifth-place finish in 1987 would in all probability have passed unnoticed by Senna. The Brazilian had been busily spraying champagne from the ground-level podium and accepting the congratulations of the Lotus team when Jardine approached him. Senna was wanted across the track at the request of the high-powered party from R. J. Reynolds. It tran-spired that a wife of one of the board members in Monaco was Brazilian and she specifically wanted to meet Senna. Jardine recalled Senna's reaction to this invitation as succinct and barbed. 'Ayrton just looked at me and said, "I don't go to any apartment." I pleaded, "Ayrton, please." Senna replied, "Fuck off, no." And he left.'

All Jardine could do was spin the rejection from Senna by concocting an excuse that the Brazilian was unwell. 'Is Ayrton being funny, Tony?' enquired Pullen when Jardine arrived alone at the apartment. Jardine told him that was not the case at all, and that Senna was sick and sent his apologies. 'It was a bare-faced lie, but what else was I to do?' said Jardine. 'Ayrton was very difficult when it came to PR and appearances because, in his view, he thought that if he delivered on the race track he had given the team all the exposure they needed.'

At the Italian Grand Prix in September, McLaren announced that Senna had signed to drive for McLaren for 1988 when the team would switch to Honda engines: the engine that powered Nelson Piquet to his third world championship in the 1987 season with the Williams team and the engine that had brought Senna victory at Monaco. Senna's signature on a McLaren contract represented a statement of awesome intent by Dennis, a succinct piece of business which, among other things, would have a defining impact on the history of the race.

In the paddock at Monza, Dennis stood beside Prost and Senna, one a two-time world champion, the other craving to conquer the planet, and smiled at the prospect of an era of unbridled domination for McLaren. What could possibly go wrong?

Travel Agent's Tale

Lynden Swainston has been caring for motor-sport spectators in Monaco since she was a courier with Page & Moy in 1977, when that company chartered three jumbo jets to Nice.

Nowadays she runs her own highly regarded travel service, LSA, from an office in Mortlake, south-west London. Over the years she has reserved the rooms worldwide for drivers and their families and friends, but as a symptom of the sport's expansion the landscape has changed. 'Twenty years ago teams had a secretary dedicated to booking hotels and flights,' said Swainston. 'They would work with travel agents with specific knowledge of their needs. Now McLaren, for example, have ten people in their own travel department; most teams do.'

She is recognised within Formula One, and within the travel and hotel industry, as an expert in finding rooms, race tickets and hospitality on yachts or apartment balconies, through corporate packages or bespoke-managed luxury group deals. Swainston works in collaboration with one of her old employers, Travel Places, based in Sussex, to incorporate flights.

Her experience has been hard won. Her temperament is unflappable. Her stamina through a race weekend – and none is more tiring than Monaco – is inexhaustible. 'You do get problems that can only occur in Monaco,' said Swainston, who started LSA sixteen years ago. 'One year we had a boat of twelve people in the harbour who all suffered from seasickness. I had to find them hotel rooms at no notice. Another time we were looking after the bosses of Hamleys, one of the sponsors of the Williams team. We had a beautiful boat in the harbour for them – but the boat started to take on water and the whole lower deck flooded. We asked all the guests to pack their bags and organised for them to have a dinner and party on the roof at the Stars 'N' Bars restaurant near the paddock. I had to find them another boat – on the Thursday of the Monaco Grand Prix.

'I went to Patrick, the wonderful concierge at the

Columbus Hotel. Somehow Patrick got a boat from Italy; he can do anything. By the time the guests had finished dinner, and with the help of quite a lot of people from Formula One who saw me standing in shock beside the harbour, we managed to transfer their entire luggage from the quayside on to the new boat. We put all the suitcases in the right cabins, all the stereos in place. When they got back they didn't even notice it was a different boat. However, at 2 a.m. one of them rang me and demanded, "Where have you put the CDs?"'

Doubtless, she smiled and told them. 'Really there isn't a problem at Monaco that cannot be fixed with money,' she admitted. 'If people want a table at a specific restaurant and the restaurant is full, you go to the hotel concierge and give him 100 euros and a table materialises. The society of concierges within Monaco is tight.'

In her office there is a fish-eyed lens shot of Monaco on a wall. Lynden knows the geography of the place like few others. She can sell accommodation at the high end of the market, where clients in 2016 were asked to pay 28,000 euros for a four-night stay in a small suite at the Hotel de Paris, in Casino Square. Or she can cater to the 'budget' market, where a two-star hotel charges 4,800 euros for the same length of stay. Outside of the Grand Prix dates, a room at such a hotel can usually be reserved for 150 euros a night, or less.

Such is the demand for rooms at the most sought-after hotels that Swainston's staff secures bookings for the following year within twenty-four hours of a race ending. Bernie Ecclestone has an interest in his own agency, Formula One Travel. 'We work happily with them,' said Swainston. She has bailed out drivers and journalists without rooms by calling in favours or knowing of an unexpected vacancy that no one else has heard about. 'One of our guests in 2015 was a guest of the Monaco royal family, so someone was sent from the palace to meet me and pick up tickets,' she said. 'I have sat next to Prince Albert in a restaurant, because that is what happens in Monaco. It is the greatest motor race in the world, and though pricing is exorbitant it still lures people from everywhere around the globe.'

She still remembers the occasion when it was her responsibility to look after a titled chief executive whose company sponsored one of the teams. 'We were told he drank specific champagne and smoked Cohiba cigars,' said Swainston. 'We had a bit of trouble securing his champagne before dinner on the first evening, but we sorted it out. Then at the end of dinner he called out for a cigar – and they didn't have any Cohiba. One of the girls who worked for me was dispatched to run round Monaco looking for them – but she had only eighty euros! I think in the end she found some at the Hotel de Paris.'

An even greater challenge was presented by the CEO on race day. 'At about 3.45 p.m. he took a call to tell him his plane was going to land in Genoa, not Nice as we had planned for,' said Swainston. 'He asked if I could get him to Genoa and thought a boat might be a good idea. I thought that through for a few minutes, and remembered my friend Rebecca at Ocean Vision. I called and requested a speedboat to transport a party of six from Monaco to Genoa in about twenty minutes. She came back and said she had available a Mangusta 80, a splendidly smart speedboat. She named some horrendous price, but I was told by the CEO's secretary to book it. Just before the race ended we had a Jaguar underneath the apartment we had secured for him on the start–finish line to take him to the port, and the Mangusta was waiting to whisk him to Genoa.'

Flowers arrived on her desk on Monday morning. 'I come back absolutely shattered – because it is such hard work,' said

Swainston. 'As people pay such a high amount for their rooms they expect a lot more. If a shower doesn't work properly, or there is a scratch on the walls, they are on my case! However, there is always a tremendous sense of achievement when you come back from Monaco, even if there is the odd horror story!'

Alain Prost: Le Professeur, 1988

6

Ayrton: From Hero to Zero beside the Sea

In 1988, McLaren was untouchable. If Prost didn't win, Senna did. In a sixteen-race season, McLaren took victory fifteen times. Absurd as it sounds, it was not for a second boring. How could it be, with Senna on a mission not just to defeat, but to deconstruct the career of Prost? How could it be, with Prost refusing to yield to the younger man's whim?

Senna's first competitive appearance in the McLaren MP4/4 at the Brazilian Grand Prix in Rio de Janeiro resulted in him claiming pole position. The script demanded nothing else, of course. In Brazil, it was carnival time without the need for street floats.

But this was to prove to be Prost's race, not Senna's. For the Brazilian's version of the McLaren – a low, sleek racing machine of imposing menace – jammed in first gear on the parade lap. Once back on the grid, Senna waved his arms above his head to signal he was in difficulty . . . while Ivan Capelli's March began exhaling smoke from its Judd engine. An aborted start was the call from Race Control. As Senna's car was pushed from the grid, he sprinted to the garage to get buckled into the team's spare car.

Senna started from the pit lane, knowing the potential that his car had shown at a belated winter test meant he could salvage much from the afternoon. Tens of thousands of Brazilian fans cheered him for mile after mile. By lap 20 he had passed every car apart from the other McLaren being driven by Prost. However, a less than perfect pit stop dropped Senna to sixth place; but that was the least of his problems. After thirty of the scheduled sixty laps, Senna was shown a black flag to disqualify him as he had breached regulations by changing cars when the race had been only delayed, and not stopped and restarted.

Prost took his fifth victory in Brazil in seven years. At the next race, Senna extracted revenge and won the San Marino Grand Prix at Imola. Prost was a close second, a mere two seconds behind. Every one of their rivals had been lapped by them; and the season had taken a direction that would not be altered.

Inside the McLaren team it was already evident that Senna had his mind set on the downfall of just one man: Prost. McLaren team manager Jo Ramirez told me: 'From the beginning Ayrton had only Alain in his sights. Whenever we talked to Ayrton, he asked, "What tyres is Alain using? Which springs?" If you told him Nelson was coming quicker, he wasn't interested. Alain was his goal.'

Two weeks later at Monaco, Senna provided us with a qualifying lap of such mesmerising speed, of such uncompromising commitment, of such sublime sweetness, in such a violent manner, that he made time stand still. It was a lap of the gods.

Senna took pole . . . and he took your breath away as he drove the 3.328 kilometres of these streets in 1 minute, 23.998 seconds. Prost's best lap, enabling him to join Senna on the front row for the race, was 1.427 seconds slower in an identical car; Prost's best lap left him in another postcode from Senna. Third fastest was Gerhard Berger, whose Ferrari was 1.2 seconds slower than Prost. Senna's qualifying lap had breached a new frontier.

Neil Oatley, who these days is the director of the design and development programme at McLaren, was race engineer for Prost at that point of his career. In this age a driver has access to a timing monitor whenever he is in his car in the pits during qualifying, but then they had the times that rivals were posting handed to them on a piece of paper. Oatley remembers Prost looking at Senna's lap time as he sat in his car. 'Alain was stunned, as you can imagine,' he said. 'If you are half a second down, a driver will think, "I can make a bit of time here, a bit there." But how the hell do you counter that? You couldn't.'

According to Oatley, Prost and Senna liked a similar set-up on their cars at Monaco. 'To be honest, there was very little difference between their needs,' he said. For Monaco, McLaren, in common with other teams, made subtle differences to meet the specific demands presented on these streets. 'It's a relatively bumpy circuit, so you would run the front wing higher than anywhere. The cars would be a little softer sprung to give them more compliance. Of course, this is all relative; to you and me the car would still feel very stiff. We'd run soft compound tyres and because of the lack of straights you don't need an aerodynamically efficient car. The more downforce you could pile on to the car, the quicker it is going to be. We had an extra stand-alone wing stuck on the engine cover halfway between the driver and the rear wing. We put in special steering racks, which meant the driver needed less steering-wheel movement to steer the car quicker. At Loews hairpin you needed more steering lock than anywhere, at any other track, and the steering racks gave three or four more degrees of lock. Then we also used to make special wishbones that allowed the front wheels more movement.

'Although it is never exceptionally hot for engines at Monaco, because of the slower speed, and the enclosed nature of the circuit, water temperature is always a problem. To deal with this you have maximum openings on the bodywork. Visibility for the drivers is an issue as well. Quite often we jack up their seats ten to fifteen millimetres to suit them. There are special mirror positions for Monaco, as a driver needs a wider field of vision. The other technical challenge was that calliper temperatures tend to get very hot because there are so many braking points round the track. You had to be very careful keeping the callipers cool, with special ducting. It's probably less of an issue now, because we know more about brake cooling; even so, it's always a worry that the callipers will start boiling at Monaco.'

Oatley, an inherently shy man, joined McLaren from Haas Lola at the end of 1986 as John Barnard left for Ferrari. 'It was a time of transition, with turbos going to disappear to be replaced by V10 engines. Steve Nichols, who had been with the team for some years, carried on with the turbo-charged car while I was looking at the V10 car for 1989. In 1988, I was on Alain's car and there was a good atmosphere across both sides of the garage.'

Yet would it not be only a reflection of the human condition if Senna's speed, exemplified by that stunning qualifying lap at Monaco, began to dominate when emotions were at their most vulnerable over a race weekend? 'Ayrton was the new boy on the block and I could detect there was a migration in the way the team dealt with the drivers,' said Oatley. 'It's not a conscious decision. It just happens.'

It happened in Prost's favour when he was with Lauda; it would happen this time in reverse for Prost as Senna's immense dedication to winning became apparent. 'Alain was very, very good,' said Oatley. 'But Ayrton's arrival took dedication and single-minded attitude to another level. Alain still had time for a bit of fun – that was way down on Ayrton's list of priorities.'

Senna's qualifying lap that afternoon in Monaco was a case in point. His analysis was as mesmerising, in parts, as his performance. 'Sometimes, I think I know some of the reasons why I do things the way I do in the car,' he said. 'And sometimes I don't think I know why. There are some moments that seem to be only the natural instinct that is in me. Whether I have been born with it or whether this feeling has grown in me more than other people, I don't know. But it is inside me and it takes over with a great amount of space and intensity.'

These words – and those that follow from Senna – were recorded a couple of years later by Canadian journalist Gerald Donaldson, who lives in England, and published in his book *Grand Prix People*. I am indebted to him for permitting them to be reproduced here. 'When I am competing against the watch and against other competitors, the feeling of expectation, of getting it done and doing the best and feeling the best, gives me a kind of power that, some moments when I am driving, actually detaches me completely from anything else as I am doing it . . . corner after corner, lap after lap. I can give you a true example and I can relate to it.

'Monte Carlo, 1988: the last qualifying session. I was already on pole and I was going faster and faster. One lap after the other, quicker and quicker, and quicker. I was at one stage on pole by half a second, then one second . . . and I kept going. Suddenly, I was nearly two seconds faster than anybody else, including my team-mate with the same car. And I suddenly realised that I was no longer driving the car consciously. I was kind of driving it by instinct – only I was in a different dimension. It was like I was in a tunnel, not only the tunnel under the hotel, but the whole circuit for me was a tunnel.

'I was way over the limit, but still able to find even more. Then, suddenly, something just kicked me. I kind of woke up and I realised I was in a different atmosphere than you normally are. Immediately my reaction was to back off, slow down. I drove back more slowly to the pits and I didn't want to go out any more that day. It frightened me because I realised I was well beyond my conscious understanding. It happens rarely, but I keep these experiences very much alive in me because it is something that is very important for self-preservation.'

Senna never achieved another lap quite like that again.

Prost's interpretation of that lap was prosaic, more pragmatic, as he told me: 'Ayrton's pole time was fantastic. But you have to take risks for a lap like that and I was not prepared to do that so much any more.' Hogan described it thus: 'Certainly, Senna went into an almost hypnotic trance before he went out of the garage for qualifying, as he always did. You could see his eyes glaze over. That lap in Monaco is the most extraordinary piece of driving and focus and concentration you have seen in your life. He just doesn't fucking lift his foot from the throttle.'

Yet in Hogan's mind, Prost was not rattled. 'In Monaco, it doesn't matter if you are on pole by one-tenth of a second or one-hundredth; you are in front, and that will do,' he said. 'Senna was always likely to do that to Prost, but all it did was gain him seven metres' advantage on the grid at the start.'

When the Grand Prix began, Senna drove into an untroubled lead. Prost lost second place to Berger when, briefly, he could not engage second gear. The order did not change for a long, long time. 'If you look at the opening laps of that race, Prost was so careful,' said Hogan. 'He didn't want to get sucked in; he let Senna have his head.' It was not until lap 54 that Prost surged past Berger after passing the pits on the start–finish straight. Even then, he was some fifty seconds back down the road from Senna. But with clear air, Prost began to drive visibly faster. His lap times had been in the low 1 minute, 29 seconds, or high 1 minute, 28 seconds, but he was now setting fastest laps. Senna reacted as you would expect: by going faster himself. On lap 59, he set a new lap record: 1 minute, 26.321 seconds. He cared not that he still held a monumental advantage. His state of mind, remember, was controlled by an obsession to break Prost's spirit. On the McLaren pit wall, Dennis was growing alarmed. He wanted his drivers to deliver a one–two finish and he did not need Senna to be unnecessarily reckless.

Ramirez, a kindly Mexican with racing in his blood, never took sides between Senna and Prost on this day, or any other. He engendered the trust of both of them, but on the pit wall Dennis wanted to call a halt to the machismo driving lighting up the streets of Monaco. 'Ron began to panic,' Ramirez told me. 'He ordered Senna over the radio, "Slow down, slow down, he cannot catch you."' Senna was not really listening. Although he did marginally back off when, briefly, Prost's lap times became slower, as he could see from his pit board. Was Prost trying deliberately to destabilise Senna? It was a game within a game – but Senna was soon driving on the limit again. Prost was calm personified. 'Even if you have one chance in a million you try to exploit it,' he explained. 'I was pushing on purpose.'

On lap 67, the worst fears of Ron Dennis were realised. Senna's car touched the inside guard rail at Portier and slewed across the road into the barrier on the other side of the circuit. The entrance to the tunnel beckoned, but Senna's car was going no further. It was untidily parked beside the barrier separating the track from the Mediterranean Sea. Oatley recalls the radio crackling into life from Senna's car: 'I crash.'

The Brazilian climbed from his car in a state of shock in

front of our eyes on the screens in the media room. He removed his gloves, the fight drained from him by an act of carelessness. Senna took off his crash helmet and walked back along the street, knowing Prost was getting ever closer, but marshals ushered him away from the scene before the Frenchman arrived. There is no visual evidence, but it can be assumed that Prost's reaction was one of disbelief, and that he was as stunned as Senna, as shocked as the crowd in Monaco and as dazed as the millions of viewers watching the TV pictures around the world. He was also elated.

Prost motored to a victory that Senna had assumed was his destiny. In the McLaren garage there were mixed emotions . . . and the engineers and mechanics waited for Senna to return to get an understanding of what had happened. They waited, and they waited. But Senna never arrived. He had vanished from the scene of his negligence, we later discovered, to seek the sanctuary of his apartment in the Houston Palace building, not far from the accident that hurt only his pride.

'The mood in the garage was mixed,' admitted Oatley. 'We had been waiting for a one–two finish with one car a long way ahead. Obviously, it was unusual for a driver not to come back to the pits to talk about things. I suppose there was some concern for Ayrton's mental condition.'

Hogan had a different take on why Senna never reappeared. 'Ayrton was an emotionally selfish man,' he said. 'That was the nature of the beast. Very bluntly, he was a spoiled child and that's how that manifests itself in those sort of *me, me, me* situations. Any other driver would have come back to the pits.'

If it is a harsh judgement, it is one supported by the evidence. Senna's disappearance was unusual and some argued, with justification, it was immature. Ramirez was not one of them; all he wanted to do was to find Senna to try to console him. For some hours, his efforts to speak with Senna were rebuffed. Each time he called the Brazilian's apartment in the Houston Palace, the telephone rang out unanswered.

However, at around 9 p.m., Ramirez's persistence was rewarded. His call was picked up by Isabelle, Senna's loyal Brazilian housekeeper. At first she denied Senna was there, but Ramirez at last persuaded her to pass the phone to him with the message that it was Jo on the line. Senna took the phone. 'Ayrton was crying as he spoke to me,' said Ramirez. He asked him, in a bedside manner, 'Ayrton, why didn't you slow down? Prost would never have caught you.'

Senna claimed he would have lost concentration by slowing down, but wasn't that precisely what happened anyway? 'Ayrton was so emotional,' recalled Ramirez, on that day I spent with him in his Spanish home near Malaga. '"Jo," he said, "I am the biggest idiot in the world."' Later that night Ramirez visited Senna at his apartment. 'Ayrton was blaming himself so much,' he said. There was sadness about the whole incident for McLaren, for Ramirez, and for Senna, a man who wanted to be perfect in a racing car at all times, no matter whom he offended.

Prost had a more objective viewpoint. 'Ayrton was really angry when he didn't win this race,' he said. 'But he didn't know who to be angry against. He was always like this. He wanted to have a fight and his biggest motivation was to fight against me and to beat me.'

In Monaco, Senna beat himself.

One of those in the crowd that weekend was Damon Hill. 'I went down to Monaco as a spectator, to have a look,' said Hill. 'By sheer chance, there is a picture of me in the 1988 to '89 *Autocourse*, a Grand Prix annual. The photograph is actually of Prost about to enter the tunnel; however, if you look closely at the picture you will see there are three guys watching from the sea wall behind the barrier. It's me with two mates. We had special passes and walked through the tunnel for a look.

'I had started racing cars, and I was looking at the Grand Prix from the point of view of someone who wanted to race there one day. I just went to get a taste of Monaco.' He also drew a rebuke from a local policeman. 'I got told to put my shirt on!' he said. 'The rules in Monaco are very strict.'

Hill had been photographed during practice at almost the exact spot where Senna donated the race to Prost. His visit had been so much more than a pilgrimage to the streets where his father had become synonymous with triumph; it had been a reconnaissance to lock away important details for the day he hoped he would return as a driver. '*That* accident was a famous lesson Ayrton taught everyone,' said Hill. 'The moment you think you have cracked Monaco, it is going to bite you. The moment you think you are on top of this place you are vulnerable. You have to pay your respects to the beast, or the monster, or whatever Monaco is, before you get carried away with yourself.'

Senna absorbed this hardest of lessons quite swiftly. He was victorious at six of the next eight races and won his first world championship – an occasion for wild celebration across Brazil – by three points from Prost after the best eleven results of each man were counted, as the regulations demanded. His triumph was sealed at the penultimate race of the season at Suzuka, in the Japanese heartland of Honda, where he had to overcome an atrocious start from pole position, dropping to fourteenth at the second corner after his engine had stalled on the line.

Senna successfully, boldly, navigated his way through traffic to catch and pass Prost, dealing with a less than perfect gearbox, on a treacherous wet and dry track. He had fulfilled a dream that he had fostered since arriving in England in 1981 to drive in the Formula Ford 1600, but in the hour of his victory Senna looked over his shoulder and declared the aberration of Monaco as a pivotal moment in his life, as well as in his career.

'It feels like tons of weight have been lifted from my head, from my shoulders,' said Senna, after becoming World Champion. 'I feel very light and pleased. Many times people ask which was my best race, and up until now it was always Portugal in 1985 in the rain, my first win. But this one is the best now, for sure.'

Then he added, poignantly, 'I can talk about it now. Monaco was the turning point of the championship for me. The mistake I made in Monte Carlo woke me up psychologically, mentally, and I changed a lot. And that gave me the strength and the power and cool mind to fight on critical situations. That was when I had the biggest step in my career as a racing driver, as a professional and as a man. I have to say that it brought me closer to God than I have ever been – and that has changed my life completely.'

Senna won eight races in 1988. Prost won seven. McLaren won the Constructors' Championship and the Drivers' Championship, and the team was at the centre of the Formula One universe. It would remain there the following year, but for entirely different reasons. Civil war – more accurately, uncivil war – was only months away.

How the Relationship between Prost and Senna Turned Toxic before Monaco '89

It is important to understand the differences – as well as the similarities – of the two men who dominated the Monaco Grand Prix for a decade. Senna's success, speed and unyielding application to the science of driving a Formula One car faster than anyone else on the planet had enabled him to establish a foothold within McLaren that proved pivotal to a shift in power. Even the team's testing arrangements seemed to favour Senna; certainly, Prost thought so. While Senna took an extended winter break in Brazil, Prost endured the bulk of McLaren's test programme with their new car, the MP4/5, powered by a 3.5-litre Honda V10, ahead of the 1989 season.

Prost was displeased with the arrangement, as he told me: 'I had an argument with Ron. At times in the season Ayrton had gone home to Brazil while I was testing all the time. Now, he had flown home to Brazil for three months' rest. At this time, we were testing a lot and doing a lot of endurance testing. I was driving, driving, driving and very often I was tired. I'd been in Formula One for almost ten years and I always tested a lot. We had been through such great tension in 1988 . . . and Ayrton was on the beach for months and I was still testing, testing. I was not very happy. I felt we had different jobs.'

During the winter, the Frenchman's doubts over whether he was competing with Senna on a level playing field had caused him to arrange to have dinner, at a golf club near Geneva, with Nobuhiko Kawamoto, president of Honda's Research and Development division and the company's number-one man in Formula One. Again, this was indicative of the changing mood at McLaren. Prost felt Senna was the favoured son of the company, and his memory of that dinner is pertinent. Prost said that to the best of his recollection Kawamoto explained to him: 'We did not do a good job for you. Our engineers were giving more support to Ayrton. They were an after-the-war generation and they liked the nature of Ayrton because he was like a samurai.' Prost emphasised: 'He did not say it in these precise words, but I was seen more as a robot. Mr Kawamoto promised me that the new championship would be completely different.'

At McLaren, Oatley, who designed the '89 car, does remember how Senna had immersed himself with the engineers from the team and from Honda, specifically at the outset. 'By that stage, Ayrton already had a good relationship with Honda from his days at Lotus before he came to us,' said Oatley. 'Effectively, the same engineers came with him to McLaren. At the time, data was at a fairly embryonic stage on the chassis and still done on a more intuitive and subjective way with the drivers. So, Ayrton used to spend a huge amount of time going through the detail of the engine with the engineers from Honda. He was building the engine to suit him and the way he wanted to drive the car. I had not seen anyone before attending to so much detail.'

It is important to understand this background detail, but it would be unwise and inappropriate to assume from this that Prost was not working as hard. Dennis assessed the characteristics of Senna and Prost like this: 'Ayrton was always more animated and therefore came across as a little less controlled. Alain was far more calculating behind the scenes.' Dennis had understood that placing them together had always carried an inherent risk of the relationship imploding, but he calculated the probable reward for the team meant it was a risk he felt capable of managing. As the Formula One circus pitched tent again in Monaco, the third race on the 1989 calendar, Dennis discovered that all pretence at keeping Senna and Prost united was over.

Senna and Prost shared one characteristic: both had the mind of a champion. Beyond that there were crucial differences. Senna's entire *raison d'être* was to be lauded as the best, the fastest driver in the world. For him, this could be achieved not by just beating the man recognised as the number one in

Formula One, but by overpowering him in a way that destroyed him. Prost was not a rival; he was a target. In Brazil, but elsewhere, too, Senna's image glittered like a jewel lodged in the canopy of the rainforests of the Amazon. He had been born into a family of privilege in São Paolo, but his humility, and his success on a global stage, as well as his great philanthropy and devout faith, meant he was also adored by those living in the slums of the *favelas*. His popularity and his fame outreached by far the achievements of other Brazilian world champions Emerson Fittipaldi and Nelson Piquet.

'In Brazil, Ayrton was bigger than Pele,' said Betise Assumpcao Head, as she reflected on her four and a half years of working for Senna as his personal press officer. 'When Pele was achieving greatness, there were not so many people who had television sets. Every Sunday, people expected Ayrton to win in what was by then a TV age. He was the only certainty of some good in the country.' Betise had been hired by Senna, as his stardom exploded, to provide a news service across Brazil for each day of a Grand Prix weekend, and beyond. She had been appointed for her skills, and because she was multilingual, not because she was a fan. Senna trusted her to sift and approve all requests for an interview with him. But once you were with Senna you were alone with him; no conditions were attached to any interview I ever conducted with him, and no subject was ever censored beforehand. He was never less than engaging, but there was little light and shade in his life around motor racing.

'At a race, Ayrton was often intense and stressed,' said Betise. 'He would carry the weight of the world on his shoulders. At the beginning this was because of how important Formula One was to him; as time went by, it was because of how important it was for everybody and he knew how much was at stake every time he went out in the car. Ayrton was not a light-hearted man. He had no natural sense of humour, though he could laugh at a joke even if he could not tell one. I think I made him laugh – that makes me happy – but I did not dare tell a joke once he was in race mode.'

It would have been unnatural, and unrewarding, if Senna had ever tried to engage with Prost outside of an engineering debrief, and vice versa. Prost was a brilliant politician in the pit lane, though. He had never before been disadvantaged by any team-mate, as he was astute at drawing the most important personnel to his side of any argument. His smooth driving style meant he looked after his cars, their tyres and their brakes, and he managed fuel consumption by going only as fast as was necessary to win. He was Le Professeur. Yet, in France, Formula One never attained a greater importance than football or rugby. 'We are living in a country where we do not have stars,' insisted Prost. His world outside of a racing car was not aligned in any shape or form with that of Senna: a global mega-star.

Hogan said of Prost: 'He is one of those drivers who have a sense of history. If he had been British he would be revered in the same way as Jackie Stewart is.' Yet if Prost was not a *star*, he had a sublime, natural talent that assured he was afforded great respect. Beyond that, Prost was a man who understood the value of the press to make a point, or get over an opinion. He had trusted friends within the French media. Dennis came to comprehend this as part of the rivalry between Senna and Prost. 'They were completely capable of presenting a unified front in front of the media in Europe, or at a Grand Prix,' said Dennis, in a Sky TV documentary. 'But then they would fuel their national press when they got home. Which then really provoked a reaction from each other when either of them was on the receiving end of the consequences. So that was challenging.'

At times, it was impossible. The wafer-thin trust between Prost and Senna had crumbled catastrophically before they walked into the paddock at Monaco in 1989. At the previous Grand Prix, at Imola, Prost had been incandescent because Senna betrayed a gentlemen's agreement of his creation. 'At Imola, Ayrton had pole and I was second,' said Prost. In the McLaren motorhome, they decided on an agreed strategy for the benefit of the team after Mansell had surprisingly won the opening Grand Prix in Brazil for Ferrari. 'We were not very confident about the start, so we agreed that we would not race one another until after the first corner, Tosa,' said Prost. 'It was Ayrton's idea.'

Hogan was in the McLaren truck at the circuit when this deal was struck. 'I happened to be sitting in the back and Alain and Ayrton were having a quite extraordinary conversation. Ayrton said to Alain, "Did you ever win the world championship in karts?" Alain said that he had and Ayrton told him that he had not, and it clearly pissed Senna off that he had not won! It was a one-race shot in their time. Then they got round to talking about the start and agreed as to how they would play the first corner. I understood what had been agreed.'

At the start, Senna drove into the lead. 'I let him go, as agreed,' said Prost. What occurred next was unscripted. The race was stopped after Berger's Ferrari thundered at 180mph into the wall at Tamburello. When the drivers assembled for the restart, Prost assumed justifiably that his agreement with Senna was still intact. It was not. Prost led, but Senna overtook him and drove to a victory that blew McLaren apart. Prost refused to attend the post-race press conference, which cost him a $5,000 fine – a pittance in comparison to the real price of the afternoon.

Two days later, Prost and Senna both had to attend a private McLaren test at Pembrey, a small race track near Llanelli, in South Wales, which had slow speed corners similar to some on the streets of Monaco. Dennis changed his plans to be present – because the atmosphere between his drivers was now toxic. All the success Dennis had achieved, all the investment he had attracted, had been built on a willingness to have a team with two strong drivers: Lauda and Prost; Prost and Rosberg; Prost and Senna. Only this time, he had lost control. Eventually, Dennis's hard-line approach, then his softer attitude, found a diplomatic solution. Senna was persuaded to apologise to Prost. It was a solution that did not survive beyond the moment the two drivers arrived at Monaco.

This time it was Prost at fault. In response to a call from a journalist friend at *L'Équipe*, a daily sports newspaper in France, Prost had revealed some of the details from the meeting in Pembrey. In Prost's mind, it had been an 'off the record' briefing, like many he had given before. 'This was my mistake,' admitted Prost. The report in *L'Équipe* was brought to Senna's notice. He took offence, not unreasonably, with Prost being directly quoted as saying: 'At a level of technical discussion I shall not close the door completely, but for the rest I no longer wish to have any business with him. I appreciate honesty and he is not honest.' Prost never denied the comments, but he never meant them for public consumption.

From that moment, Senna vowed never to call Prost by his name, or to speak with him again. Dennis could do nothing to change this poisonous atmosphere within McLaren. His team was split in half. Hogan reckoned that at that time Marlboro paid McLaren $20 million 'for the whole shooting match'. Even so, it was not his place to intervene, nor would he. 'The two drivers were at each other's throats, but that didn't matter,' said Hogan. 'They were competitive, naturally; and no quarter was expected or given. Ron could handle that. It doesn't make for an easy life, but who said life's supposed to be easy?'

Prost generally allowed Senna to make the most noise in

public. 'Senna was an awkward son of a bitch,' said Hogan, chuckling at times past, battles won and lost. 'It took some time before the company [Marlboro] understood what he was about. But my boss was a Swiss-Italian and he said the Italians loved Senna because they think he is absolutely barking mad. Senna was an absolute bloody nightmare when it came to promotional appearances. He just didn't want to do anything at all, zero, zilch. But if he did agree to do something – on the occasion when three men on camels walked past the door! – people loved him. They were intrigued by the mystique about him. It is that mystique and racers' mindset that was reason enough for a Latin country like Italy to love Ayrton. The Italians had loved the late Gilles Villeneuve in the same way; they thought he could walk on water because he would drive a Ferrari on three wheels.'

Senna won the 1989 Monaco Grand Prix from pole position without his pulse rate rising. Prost was second, a distant fifty-two seconds behind. It would not require the mind of Einstein to imagine McLaren's mechanics, and some engineers, being drawn towards Senna's corner, sooner rather than later, by the pull of gravity created by the Brazilian's sheer speed. Oatley remembered this race for the difficulty Senna secretively overcame. 'Ayrton pulled away by fifteen, maybe twenty seconds,' he said. 'Then he started to have a problem with his gear shift. Yet he was fearful of letting Alain get a hint of a problem and maintained the gap by driving every lap as though it was a qualifying lap to compensate the issues he was having with third gear. To him, it was a matter of psychology: never display a weakness. I have seen a picture taken from above the Loews hairpin, looking down into Ayrton's cockpit. You can see that Ayrton is driving, right hand on the wheel, and leaning his left arm across his body to shift gear with his left hand. He was using the wrong hand there to change gear, but he never mentioned it. It was just another way he improvised to make himself quicker.'

Hogan had been around Formula One for a sufficient numbers of years to sense that Senna was gaining the ascendancy within the team. 'Engineers will always gravitate towards the bloke with the biggest right foot,' he said. 'Senna indisputably had that.' At Monza, Prost confirmed he had signed a contract to drive for Ferrari in 1990. The probability of this ugly duel ending in controversy was now exceedingly high. The scene for the showdown: Suzuka, Japan. The race: Prost had command when six laps from the finish Senna drove down the inside of the Frenchman at the approach to a tight hairpin. Senna had gambled and Senna had lost as he had misjudged Prost's mood. For the Frenchman turned to his right to deny Senna any space, as he promised he would. The cars collided and Prost knew that he had the points on the board to be crowned champion. He had the coveted prize of having number one on his Ferrari for 1990.

These vignettes may not be aligned directly to the Monaco Grand Prix, but the line from that race to those that followed in 1989 is drawn to show how the rift that tore Prost and Senna apart in the principality was never fully mended through the rest of their time racing one another. It was the greatest – and the most deadly – rivalry in Formula One history.

Senna Supreme: Mansell Heartache

Senna, who performed in a racing car at times with such artistry, such judgement and at such speed that he appeared to have an unfair advantage, won at Monaco for the next four seasons in a row to establish a record of quite magnificent dominance.

1990: Senna won pole with Prost's Ferrari alongside him on the front row, but the Brazilian's qualifying lap was more than 1.2 seconds faster than that of the Frenchman. 'What Senna does in a car round Monaco is special . . . there is no other word to describe it,' said John Watson from the broadcast booth that day. Yet the hoped-for drama between the two old adversaries never materialised. In fact, Prost was involved in a first-lap collision with Berger at Mirabeau that resulted in the race having to be stopped. Both drivers restarted, but it was another Frenchman, Jean Alesi, driving for Tyrrell, who proved to be Senna's closest challenger. Prost had to retire to his Ferrari after thirty laps, but by then Senna was a long, long way up the road. At the flag, the Brazilian won from Alesi by a fraction over one second. In third place, Berger was the only other driver to complete the full race distance of seventy-eight laps. That season Senna won his second world championship – from Prost.

1991: Senna again claimed pole in his McLaren-Honda just as he had in the first three races of the season in Phoenix, São Paolo and Imola. He won those three races – and he proved unstoppable again on the streets of Monaco. He did have to manage a late technical problem when he was instructed from the pit wall not to use maximum revs through the gears after Honda engineers had detected a loss of oil pressure from on-board telemetry; but such was the lead he had constructed that he could afford to slow his lap times by as much as four seconds. Nigel Mansell was still eighteen seconds adrift of Senna at the conclusion of the Grand Prix. The Brazilian comprehensively won a third world title by winning seven of the sixteen rounds of the championship that year.

1992: A race to be talked about in reverential tones whenever the Monaco Grand Prix is discussed. Senna crossed the finish line with Mansell's Williams-Renault seemingly glued to the rear of his McLaren. As the cars flashed past the pits for a final time, the crowd all around the circuit were standing in admiration and disbelief to acclaim a performance of defensive driving from Senna that was breathtaking to behold. The race had been at the mercy of Mansell for seventy laps, then an unscheduled pit stop by the Englishman allowed Senna to go through into the lead. Without warning, a routine race was transformed into a compelling drama.

For the final three laps Senna safeguarded his position on the road as vigorously as if Mansell was an intruder trying to steal his most treasured possessions from his home. In his Williams, Mansell drove himself to exhaustion in pursuit of the Brazilian. On a set of fresh rubber, he hustled Senna's McLaren, fighting in vain for grip on worn tyres, up the hill to Casino Square, out of the tunnel into the chicane, through the swimming-pool complex, feigning to go right, then left. Senna never flinched. He covered all his angles, and he kept the McLaren under his command with masterful car control impeded by a set of tyres that had so little adhesion.

When the cars came to a standstill, Senna sportingly offered a hand to Mansell to assist him out of his car. Mansell was drenched with sweat. His eyes were fixed on a far horizon. He had failed by 0.215 seconds to win the Monaco Grand Prix. The podium ceremony passed in a blur for the Englishman, who took his champagne bottle and sat down on the side of the track. He had given his heart and his soul for over one hour, fifty-one minutes to win the race every Formula One driver most wants to win, and he had come up short by one-fifth of one second. But his disappointment was not tinged by bitterness. His admiration for Senna was unequivocal. 'I must compliment Ayrton, because he pretty well second-guessed every move I tried to do,' said Mansell. 'He was very fair and he was entitled to do what he did. I think he drove fantastically.'

If Senna had expected to win the 1988 Monaco Grand Prix, he certainly did not believe this race would allow him to equal Graham Hill's record of five wins in the principality. Mansell had won the first five races of the season – an accomplishment unequalled in Formula One history – and he looked to be in line to keep the sequence alive when he took pole position from his team-mate, Riccardo Patrese. Senna qualified third. For the Brazilian, the start the next day would represent a sliver of a chance to place himself at the heart of the race; and not for the first time, on Sunday afternoon he caught out a rival with his willingness to cast caution to the wind. With Mansell driving smoothly off the line, Senna came across the track to mount an attack down the inside of Patrese as the cars approached Sainte-Dévote. His decisive action was rewarded as he edged ahead of the Italian, but there was still the matter of keeping his McLaren under control to complete the pass.

'Monte Carlo is the hardest place in the world for overtaking,' said Senna. 'Even at the start you can't do it unless you are really squeezing it. I went for it at the last moment, so as not to give Riccardo any indication, because otherwise he would have closed the door. I got into second place, but the problem was to stop the car before Mansell turned in, because I was coming so quickly. I thought he might not see me. But it was a good manoeuvre and the only way I had to take second place. If Patrese had been ahead of me out of the corner, I doubt if I would ever have got past him.'

His calculated gamble had paid off. Yet it was soon apparent that Mansell was in an altogether different race from everyone else. The Williams driver was extending his lead each lap. Senna knew his McLaren could not compete with Mansell's car, but through experience he also knew that he had to keep himself as close to the race leader as possible.

'There was no way to catch Mansell,' he said, on reflection some time afterwards. 'Impossible, with the superiority of his car. So, I tried to go hard enough to be in a position to benefit if anything happened to Mansell, but still tried to conserve my tyres – particularly in the early laps on a full tank. I couldn't think of beating him, of course; but you never know what will happen at Monaco.'

What happened of consequence next actually affected Senna detrimentally rather than Mansell. On the sixtieth lap Michele Alboreto spun his Footwork at Mirabeau and moment-arily blocked the track. The next driver on the scene was Senna. He braked barely a metre from the Footwork, he esti-mated. Then he had to be cautious getting round Alboreto's car as the Italian went about regaining the race. By the time Senna was back to speed, Mansell's lead had been stretched to almost thirty seconds. But there was to be a final twist – one that it is unlikely Mansell will ever forget.

On the seventy-first lap, his car went out of shape as he entered the tunnel. 'I almost lost it,' he said, when he relived the incident. 'The back end just went down and I knew imme-diately I had picked up a puncture.' He had to drive almost half the circuit to get back to the pits. Obviously, he lost a huge amount of time. 'The car's brakes weren't working, as I was driving on three wheels,' said Mansell. 'We then had a longer pit stop than normal. As I came out of the pits I saw Ayrton go by.' On lap 72 Senna led by 5.1 seconds. Without warning, a Grand Prix that had seemed to be at the command of Mansell, driving with forceful aggression for the Williams-Renault team, who had stolen a march on all their rivals with their 'active' suspension car, suddenly became a compelling drama.

The race was not much older when Mansell recorded a lap two seconds faster than any other driver had posted. It was a message of intent; it was an indication of how brilliant the

Williams FW14B was handling and the grip that Mansell had attained from the new Goodyear tyres. With three laps remaining, Senna's lead was 1.9 seconds. 'I didn't really know what to do because he was coming so much faster than I could go,' explained Senna. But he was being cheap with the truth. Senna knew precisely what to do. He hogged the racing line where it mattered most and placed himself in the centre of the road elsewhere to nullify any attack from Mansell. 'I knew we would be in a major war for the final three laps. I had no grip to put the power down. It was like being on ice. On the straights it was like a drag-race, you know, wheel-spin in third and fourth gear ... Obviously I was tired, too.' It was a sublime demonstration of his skill, for the slightest error or one fluffed gear change would have opened the door to Mansell.

Senna drove flawlessly, however. As the crowd rose to appreciate the battle between two men driving at the zenith of their powers, even Mansell had to admire the Brazilian's stubborn refusal to yield to the pressure that he had applied. 'Those were probably the hardest few laps I have ever driven,' Mansell said later. 'You have the race under control for seven-eighths' distance, then you pick up a puncture. That's Monte Carlo for you. Then you have to drive at ten-tenths. I think we were both driving way over the limit on the last six laps.' It was like watching two heavyweight fighters from a bygone age: Mansell was Joe Frazier, ducking, diving, trying to force Senna to drop his guard; Senna was Muhammad Ali, mostly staying just out of range, but still landing some concussive counter-punches by never enabling his opponent the opening he so desperately craved. And it was Senna's hand raised in victory. His gesture of helping Mansell extricate himself from his Williams testified to the respect Senna held for the Englishman on this afternoon and stretching back to other magnificent battles they had waged in the name of sport.

So what happened to Mansell's car on the seventy-first lap when he was convinced his rear left tyre had acquired a slow puncture? Goodyear engineers reported that an inspection of the tyre had not revealed a puncture. Was it a wheel-bearing issue, then? No, according to Williams's chief designer, Adrian Newey. What then? 'Difficult to say,' said Newey, as reported in a Formula One blog. 'It might have been a loose wheel nut, per-haps.' Whatever it was, Mansell felt obliged to pit. And we had a climax to a Monaco Grand Prix that will never be forgotten.

Less than three months later, Mansell had the 1992 world championship wrapped up – but he would never race again at Monaco as he could not agree terms with Frank Williams for the following season. Instead he crossed the Atlantic to com-pete triumphantly in the IndyCar Championship. His seat at Williams was taken by Prost, who returned to Formula One after a year's absence induced by his frustration at Ferrari at the end of 1991.

1993: Senna drove his sixth and final year for McLaren on a contract of $1 million a race. McLaren's deal with Honda had ended with their withdrawal from Formula One at the end of the previous season, which meant Dennis had to pay for Ford Cosworth V8 engines. The team admit to investing £6 million in developing Ford's HB power plant. Senna's latest salary demands therefore proved to be a cause for a massive showdown between the Brazilian and Dennis.

Hogan recalled: 'Ron came to us and said, "We need more money." We told him we had a contract that says you don't need more money. That went on for a while. Then I had Ron and Ayrton in my office and said, "The best deal I reckon I can do, Ayrton, is to pay you $1million a race." He mumbled and grumbled, but in the end accepted the principle. Yet what really nailed down the deal was that the next day he drove the McLaren-Cosworth with active ride and said it was fantastic.'

At Monaco, Prost took pole position in a year he won seven times to capture his fourth world championship. Senna qualified third behind a young German called Michael Schumacher driving for Benetton-Ford. Prost's race was compromised, however, after he was given a stop-go penalty for jumping the start. Schumacher appeared in total control of the Grand Prix, but he was forced out of the race after thirty-three laps by a hydraulic failure. This allowed Senna to take his fifth consecutive win at Monaco, and a record sixth victory in total. Behind the scenes, Senna was agitating to get himself a Williams contract for 1994, even mischievously suggesting that he would drive for the team for nothing. His mission proved successful and Frank Williams broke the news to Prost, flying to meet him in Biarritz during the beginning of a three-week summer recess in Formula One. Prost had a clause in his contract that was specifically designed to prevent Senna from driving for Williams while he was in the team. The Frenchman took time to assess his options – but with Renault behind Senna, he knew that the deck was stacked against him even if in law his position was strong.

Prost recalled in a conversation with me fifteen years later how he opted to retire rather than be placed again in the same team as Senna. 'In August I told them, "OK, you want Ayrton, and he wants to drive for nothing, he drives for nothing! Then you pay me my contract for 1994. That is the only deal – you pay me and I go away." I'd had enough of all their stories, of all the politics. I think this was a deal driven more by Renault. They wanted to show they could win a championship with Nigel, with me, then in the future with Ayrton and probably Michael. You know, the funny thing is I talked with Patrick Head from Williams at Monaco this year. Patrick is a racing man and I am a racing man and we had a good relationship, but he explained to me that he was not really aware of all the politics. There were a lot of things he did not know.' Or perhaps chose not to know.

Unwittingly, Senna and Prost, the drivers who had registered a decade of dominance on the streets of Monaco, both drove there for a final time in 1993. While Senna was victorious, Prost drove back through the field from twenty-second place to finish fourth with the artistry that would become his professional epitaph.

With his compelling record at Monaco embellished with his drive in the McLaren-Cosworth in that year, it seems pertinent to ask if Senna was the finest racer of all time on those streets. 'I think that would be the truth,' said Neil Oatley from McLaren. John Hogan responded to the question like this: 'Both Senna and Prost knew they could win every time they went to Monaco. Prost always thought he could out-think Senna round there. Senna always knew he was the quickest. Senna kind of knew that if it rained it was going to be his race; Prost wouldn't play that game. It was very much an even confrontation.' Which man would you want to drive for your life round those streets? I asked Hogan. 'Prost,' he replied. 'On the grounds that he wouldn't make a mistake. Senna might put you in the swimming pool.' He smiled as he spoke.

In that late spring of 1993, there were two men knocking on the door of Formula One by contesting that season's Formula 3000 final championship round: Coulthard and Panis. The title went to Panis, but there would soon, through an awful tragedy, be room for both of these men in Formula One.

Ayrton Senna, 1993

7

Weekend from Hell

O livier Panis shuffled out of the cold wind blowing along Rue Magellan, a side street close to the Champs-Élysées, a short walk from the Arc de Triomphe, to receive a warm welcome from the receptionist at the Hôtel François 1er. Panis exuded an easy charm as he flipped off his beanie to expose a razored haircut and exchanged kisses with a woman who had clearly checked him into the hotel on more than one previous occasion.

He flashed a smile, then excused himself to drop a bag in his room. Minutes later, he reappeared in the small library across the hallway from the reception desk. He ordered black tea for himself with some milk added for me. Panis had arrived in the French capital on this wintry afternoon from his home near Grenoble on business, but also to talk about a racing career that reached a crescendo one afternoon in Monaco. The good times had to wait their turn to be aired, though. For it was impossible to ignore that Panis entered Formula One in 1994, a season that will be for ever remembered as the most mournful weekend in Grand Prix racing since the days of Jackie Stewart and Graham Hill.

His journey on a scholarship through the French motor-racing schooling system, culminating with the F3000 Championship, had been rewarded with a seat in the Ligier Formula One team. Guy Ligier, a charismatic Frenchman, who competed in twelve Formula One races and played rugby for France's B team, as well as winning national rowing championships, had habitually assisted French drivers. Before Panis, other Frenchmen such as Jacques Laffite, Patrick Depailler, Didier Pironi, René Arnoux, Jean-Pierre Jarier, Patrick Tambay, Jean-Pierre Jabouille, Philippe Streiff, Philippe Alliot, Olivier Grouillard, Érik Comas and Éric Bernard had driven for the team from its inception in 1976. Bernard was to be the team-mate and benchmark that Panis, then twenty-seven, would be measured against.

'To come to Formula One was a dream for me,' said Panis, pouring tea into two cups. 'The Ligier team at this time was not on a very good side financially. I get a contract race-by-race at the beginning, because that was the deal with Ligier sponsors Elf and Gitanes Blondes. It was more or less £5,000 per race, I think. It never mattered. And I have a bonus for scoring points – but at this time of the season no one at Ligier is thinking about points.'

Also set to make his Formula One debut at the Brazilian Grand Prix along with Panis was an Austrian called Roland Ratzenberger. He had built his reputation by patiently moving through racing categories in Germany, England and, finally, Japan. He was also professionally fulfilled when he signed a five-race deal with the new Simtek F1 team. Ratzenberger was thirty-three. Panis and Ratzenberger had excitedly flown to São Paolo to make their entrance in the highest echelon of the sport at the Interlagos Circuit, set in the suburbs of a city of extreme wealth and unimaginable poverty. The city of Ayrton Senna.

Yet, in some way, in his home city at the end of March 1994, Senna was a newbie like Panis and Ratzenberger, because after all those years with McLaren the Brazilian champion was making his debut for the Williams team at the dawn of an age of new regulations. Active suspension and traction control had been banned. Refuelling had been introduced to further shake up the sport with an added unpredictable dimension.

'Senna, like Prost, was for me a hero,' explained Panis in the dimly lit library, which reeked of old-world style with that day's edition of *Le Figaro* and the *International New York Times* neatly stacked on a coffee table. 'For me, the two are big champions.' No one could have anticipated what was to unfold over a matter of a handful of weeks.

The first three races of this season, leading to the fourth round of the championship in Monaco, are remembered here in greater detail for one significant reason: the important and sombre impact that they had on Formula One. The voices of Panis, Ross Brawn, Alain Prost, Charlie Whiting, and Mark Wilkin from the BBC, all with a rich connection with Monaco, are brought together to provide a backstory to the misery and heartache that was to devour F1.

In fact, the road to the weekend from hell began during winter testing. 'We had made a strategic decision early in 1993 to focus on the 1994 car,' said Brawn. 'Active suspension was going, which meant the aerodynamic regulations were changing. There was a whole raft of new rules. At the beginning of '93, I said to Rory Byrne [designer] that this was our big opportunity. I told him that I was going to take a small group of engineers away from him to keep the '93 car going, and that he should immediately concentrate with 90 per cent of the engineering staff on the 1994 car. I said I would fiddle with the '93 car and keep it reliable, do a respectable job. But then we are going to make a step change for 1994. We had a brilliant driver in Michael, enough money to do the job and a works Ford engine. We should be up there.'

Brawn's forward-thinking strategy had seen an instant leap in performance in winter testing ahead of the season, as he recalled: 'We were incredibly quick – so quick, we had to keep the speed down.' In the business, it is called sandbagging. Teams deliberately run with higher fuel loads in testing or perhaps disguise the real efficiency of their car's aerodynamic capabilities. Clever men can fractionally slow down cars on a whim. Yet, ultimately, Brawn and his team needed to understand the full potential of the Benetton before it was shipped to Brazil. 'At the Imola test before the season started we did a mock race run – not many people were doing that at the time,' he said. 'So, we did this mock race run and you can't sandbag that because the fuel runs down, the tyres change. Others were coming on to the pit wall and watching the lap times. They were stunning.

'Then the accusations started: "You are running under weight, you have done this, that and the other." It's an easy excuse to make.' Against that background, Benetton headed south to Brazil brimming with optimism; and after Schumacher's win in Brazil, rivals became even more suspicious of the legality of the '94 Benetton. The only thing that travels faster than a Formula One car in Grand Prix racing is the rumour mill.

For Panis, pit-lane politics were as yet unknown to him. He had gained confidence from his performance in São Paolo and his excitement at the next race, the Pacific Grand Prix in Aida, Japan, was heightened by an introduction to Senna in the unlikeliest of circumstances. 'I am going to the toilet before the race, and who came in at the same time? Ayrton Senna!' he exclaims. Panis mimed how he had to make a double take to confirm it was the Brazilian. 'Anyway, I washed

The Monaco Grand Prix has been a permanent fixture on the F1 calendar since 1955.

Right: Mr Monaco – the affectionate nickname afforded Graham Hill, a five times winner of the race.

Below: Only two drivers, Italy's two-time world champion Alberto Ascari and Australian Paul Hawkins, have crashed into Monaco's harbour. Here, Ascari fishes the car from the water; tragically, four days later, he was killed at a private test at Monza.

Above: Argentine Juan Miguel Fangio, El Maestro, approaching Casino Square in 1957.

Below: Stirling Moss accepts his trophy on the podium in 1960, watched by Princess Grace and Prince Rainier.

Above: Jackie Stewart passes the crowd gathered outside the Hotel de Paris.

Below: A BRM mechanic fearlessly steps onto the track with a pit board for Graham Hill.

Entering the tunnel, drivers are temporarily blinded – moving from light to dark in a matter of seconds. Monaco remains the only Grand Prix to feature a tunnel, but the lighting is vastly superior today than it was in the sixties.

Jochen Rindt, hunting down Henri Pescarolo through Casino Square in his outdated
Gold Leaf Lotus 49, stole an improbable victory in the 1970 Monaco Grand Prix when
leader Jack Brabham crashed in the final corner. Rindt wept tears of joy as Prince Rainier
and Princess Grace presented him with the trophy – then Formula One wept when Rindt
was killed four months later. He remains the only driver to be posthumously awarded the
World Drivers' Championship.

Above: Jackie Stewart exiting Casino Square in 1972.

Below: Niki Lauda on his way to win his second, and final, Monaco Grand Prix in 1976.

Above: Reigning world champion Keke Rosberg winning in 1983 for Williams.

Below: Rosberg is joined on the podium by Alain Prost and Nelson Piquet.

my hands and was on my way out when Ayrton stopped me and said, "I want to welcome you to Formula One. Take your time. It is not a mystery why you are here." I was really surprised, to be honest. He was the only one to tell me: "Welcome to Formula One." It was such a good, human action. As it was from Ayrton, it was something important to me.'

As in Brazil, Senna claimed pole position in his Williams. Yet it was a fleeting triumph for the Brazilian as he was beaten off the line to turn one by Schumacher. Worse followed. The rear end of his Williams was clipped by Mika Häkkinen's McLaren and redirected into a gravel trap, and Senna's race was abruptly over when his car was walloped midships by the Ferrari of Nicola Larini. Schumacher won handsomely again, lapping every other driver except second-placed Berger. The German's lead over Senna after these opening two races was an improbable twenty points. But for Senna the return of Formula One to its European heartland, first at Imola, where he had won the San Marino Grand Prix three times, then at Monaco, where the Brazilian was the undisputed master, meant that mentally he could recalibrate the championship. The season for Senna was about to begin afresh.

Senna was a troubled man, though. And he shared his dismay in telephone calls with Prost, his old nemesis. In spite of their bitter rivalry, the Frenchman told me that he took the calls from Senna without hesitation, even if at first they had been a surprise. When they raced one another, Senna had never bothered to acquire Prost's number. 'Ayrton said that he had many problems with the Williams,' recalled Prost, when we had spoken in Paris at great length for my book *Senna versus Prost*. Before the teams arrived in Imola, Prost had taken another call from Senna. 'Each time Ayrton's mood was going down, about the car, about the performance,' said the Frenchman. 'He was also convinced that the Benetton car was outside the regulations. He had a problem with the safety of the sport as well. The week before Imola, he asked me if I wanted to be president of the drivers' association (GPDA), but I didn't want to do this job again. But it is important to know Ayrton was a completely different man and a completely different driver. He was not happy for sure.'

Prost had agreed to a rendezvous with Senna in the paddock at Imola, where he was scheduled to work for a French broadcaster and as an ambassador for Renault. In fact, Senna's first contact at Imola was with another Frenchman: Panis. 'I was coming to the motorhome of Ligier in the paddock for the first time and I saw a lot of people there,' he remembers. 'The first team member I saw said, to my surprise, "Ayrton is waiting for you." Ayrton said he just wanted to have a coffee and a talk. We talked for five minutes – blah, blah, blah – and then he left. It was amazing.'

Then the sport was suffocated beneath a black veil of death.

On Friday, Rubens Barrichello miraculously survived a horrific accident. On Saturday, Formula One ran out of good fortune. In qualifying, Ratzenberger was killed when his Simtek pirouetted against a wall at the Villeneuve Curve at 200mph. Senna watched the accident on a TV monitor in his garages. Suddenly, shockingly, Formula One had to learn how to deal with death at a race weekend for the first time in a dozen years. Senna was profoundly affected by what he saw. After a decade in Formula One without yielding an inch of road, after a ruthless feud with Prost, the Brazilian was inconsolable with grief. 'Ayrton was very shaken, crying,' recalled Betise Assumpcao Head when we returned together to Imola in 2014, on the twentieth anniversary of his death, for my final dispatch for the *Mail on Sunday*. Betise had found him alone, away from the Williams garage. 'He was vulnerable like I had never seen him before. He was lost.'

On race morning the drivers convened for their traditional briefing. One item on the agenda – aside from a sombre minute's silence for Ratzenberger – was Formula One's introduction of a safety car that season. Senna had disliked the fact that it had already been used to lead the cars around the circuit on the formation lap, as he reasoned it was too slow to enable the drivers to warm their tyres to race temperatures, thereby risking the loss of pressure. At the conclusion of the briefing, Senna left to cross the paddock with Schumacher. They were piecing together a plan, it was reported, for the drivers to attend a meeting to discuss safety issues at the next race in Monaco.

It was an appointment Senna never kept.

When the San Marino Grand Prix started, Senna led from Schumacher, but behind them there was chaos as Pedro Lamy's Lotus struck the stalled Benetton of JJ Lehto. A wheel flew into the crowd and injured nine people, and there was debris strewn across the track. Instantly, the safety car was deployed. For five laps, Senna led the procession of slow-travelling Formula One cars around the circuit. In the observer's seat of the safety car was Whiting, a man who would become FIA Formula One Race Director two years later. 'Unlike today, when we have permanent safety cars from Mercedes, and full-time safety-car drivers, the safety car in Imola in 1994 was supplied locally, so was the driver,' explained Whiting. 'I think the Opel something-or-other we used was turbo-charged, but it was hopeless. After two laps the driver – who appeared to be very good – knew the brakes were absolutely shot. We couldn't go any faster than we were driving. Ayrton came up alongside us with his visor up, urging us to go quicker. He was right up to me, shouting, "Faster, faster!" I was telling him, "We can't . . . we can't." Next lap, we came in. That is my last memory of Ayrton.'

Once released to race again, Senna had accelerated hard, but he would not travel a great deal further. His Williams-Renault car leapt across the second of two bumps in the 190mph Tamburello Corner and thudded into a wall. A terrible, terrible weekend was about to dominate the news cycle across the world. Panis recalls driving through Tamburello in the express train of following cars and catching a glimpse from the corner of his eye of Senna's car, stationary off the circuit. He was already pained by the shock of Ratzenberger's death – and the appearance of red flags to stop the race hardly relaxed him. 'On race morning the atmosphere, the ambience was hard,' says Panis. 'I did not feel good. I only knew Roland to say "Hello" at the driver's briefing as we were both new, but the image of a driver hitting the wall like this; I knew straight away that he was dead.

'On Sunday, I did not start like the race before. I feel heavy, because we know Roland is dead. It was really tough to think of racing, but this is our job.' Then he passed Senna's stricken car. 'I think I was in seventeenth place when I passed the crash. Obviously, I did not know what happened, but this is a flat-out corner ... so, you know it cannot be good.' In the confusion, word had reached the Ligier garage that Senna had sustained a broken collarbone. At the BBC headquarters at the circuit, the Corporation's Formula One editor, Mark Wilkin, had little better intelligence, but, instinctively, he knew to prepare for the worst. In the commentary booth, Murray Walker and Jonathan Palmer were briefed to remain circumspect in their language. 'This was the first-ever race we had taken our own production truck and had our own camera,' explained Wilkin. 'In the days when I began in 1989, we used to broadcast some updates into *Grandstand* and then they would go back to the cricket at Lord's or whatever else they were doing that day. If there was a big accident, *Grandstand* would cut away because they never knew what pictures they were going to get. In 1994 we had a live camera in the pit lane, so we had an alternative shot from the Italian host broadcaster.'

For the first time Wilkin had a crew of eight people to upgrade the broadcasting possibilities, including two producers, a driver who doubled as the radio camera operator, a cameraman, and a VT guy, who also was the sound recordist. Wilkin also had the substantial journalistic craft of Steve Rider in Imola. 'As we had the truck and the capability we thought it useful to have the presenter of *Grandstand* out with us,' said Wilkin. 'It proved fantastic to have a journalist of Steve's expertise to seek the truth. In the commentary booth, we had Murray and Jonathan, a former F1 driver and a qualified doctor – men who genuinely understood the process of what would be happening. Jonathan was able to talk us through the medical procedures.

'Editorially, we believe you can never speculate. We had seen the Italians' coverage the day before of Roland Ratzenberger's fatal accident, so we knew what they would think was OK to show. We knew how the Italians would direct the coverage and indeed they lived up to expectation; they just have a different moral view of what you should show on television to a live audience. It is not necessarily wrong, but it is not one I agree with. So, from the Italian broadcaster, we saw Ayrton's accident replayed; we saw shots of Ayrton's body; all sorts of images that I am grateful that we did not show to the British public. We were on air for hours and hours, but we had talked at some length the night before about what we would do if something again happened when we were live. When the race restarted, none of us knew at that stage how seriously injured Senna was.'

By nightfall, the BBC led the *Nine O'Clock News* with

Murray broadcasting from the roof of the truck; it was the biggest story in the world that day.

Schumacher won the Grand Prix, for what it mattered. Hill finished sixth, but no one underestimated the courage and mental fortitude it required from the Englishman even to compete in a race when no one had the faintest clue as to what had caused Senna to leave the road in an identical car to the one he drove. And it must be stressed that the drivers had all raced without knowing that Senna's injuries had proved fatal. Panis returned to his garage, having finished eleventh, to discover the awful truth. 'I saw someone crying,' he said. 'I saw someone else whose face was completely destroyed.' In English, we would probably use the word *distraught* in the context Panis described, but somehow on this miserable day the word *destroyed* felt right. 'OK, we did not do a good race, but what has happened?' persisted Panis. 'I was told that it was not a race problem. "It is Ayrton," someone said. "He died."' The Frenchman was stunned. 'What? You said to me it was a collarbone.' The afternoon, the whole weekend, was cursed and the news stream was unreliable, perhaps dishonest.

At thirty-four, Senna was dead. His three world titles, his record of six wins at Monaco, and the fact that he won 41 of the 161 Formula One races he competed in, secured a legacy that assures him a place for eternity in motor-racing history. His place at the heart of Brazilian life was an even greater accolade. Brazilian president Itamar Franco declared three days of national mourning, and it is estimated that 3 million people lined the route the funeral cortège travelled.

In Saltzburg, around 250 people attended the funeral of Ratzenberger. Johnny Herbert, a driver with Lotus at the time, was one of the mourners at the funerals of both drivers, along with Berger. 'Roland's the forgotten man of Formula One,' Herbert told CNN in 2014. 'Forgotten to many, but not to me.

I always think about Roland, particularly at the European races. Monaco's always one. The year before he died we had a nice dinner there. He was a good friend and we had spoken of our dreams for many years. I'd got to F1 before him, but that season it was great to see him. He had this very happy face, he had that "I got there" face.'

At Imola on that tragic Sunday, Panis felt crushed, like all those connected with Formula One that weekend. 'I just take my helmet, go from the garage to the motorhome to change and leave the circuit,' he said. 'I don't want to be five minutes more at a circuit on a weekend like this. I had my best friend Mickael with me, and he told me that after this weekend he would never come back to Formula One.'

Panis understood that such an option did not apply to him – or any of the others who competed against one another that weekend and would reappear to compete again in eleven days' time during qualifying for the Monaco Grand Prix. 'I say to myself: "I am here to do a job, and I am lucky to be doing this job.' I am passionate about this job. I prefer to die doing Formula One than doing anything else." This helped me to think that Ayrton would have been thinking the same. Maybe he would prefer also to die in a racing car. Roland's death shocked me a lot, and Ayrton's death was another shock. It took a lot of time to absorb. Even now, when I see some pictures of Ayrton, or his helmet, it is tough. This is part of my body now, of my life, these two accidents.'

Drivers' silent tribute to Senna and Ratzenberger, 1994

8

Wendlinger in a Coma: Formula One in a Crisis

Between leaving Imola and arriving in Monaco, Damon Hill made a round trip to Brazil to attend the mammoth state funeral given to Ayrton Senna, where Alain Prost had been a pall-bearer. When they placed wreaths for Senna where they had so often placed victory laurels, the idea that Formula One motor racing, in an enlightened age of ever-improving safety measures, could no longer be tainted by death was unmasked as a fraudulent theory.

'A generation has grown up behind me without knowing the full consequences of the job we do,' said Nigel Mansell when we spoke at his waterfront mansion in Clearwater, Florida, the day after Senna died. 'Complacency breeds contempt. Sadly, this is a very big wake-up call. Stronger cars have meant less breakages and that relates to fewer accidents, which means fatal accidents became a rarity.' Mansell, who was defending champion in the IndyCar Championship, having left Formula One as world champion at the end of the 1992 season after failing to agree a new contract with Frank Williams, added pertinently, 'We've all seen big accidents where drivers have walked away . . . but I am old enough to remember that sometimes you don't walk away.'

Hill understood that because he had known, as a boy, that his father had lost so many friends and rivals in racing accidents. Yet this was a tragedy where he was central to the trauma. When he reached the pits in Monaco, one side of the Williams garage was vacant as the team, rightly, wished to honour Senna's memory by opting to run only one car – for Hill. Even so, Williams's humanitarian gesture came with a price for Hill. 'It's a difficult thing to be in a team where there was an empty slot where the other car used to be,' he explained, when we had breakfast together in 2016. 'There was a ridiculous amount of pressure. I think everyone was just grimly going through the process. The idea that you can reset and just carry on was not an easy one to fulfil. There needs to be a certain joy in what you are doing. It is supposed to be a sport. We are not in the Battle of the Somme here. As racing drivers we are fairly thick-skinned, as we have worked out accidents happen. The best way to cope with any risk is to focus even harder on what you are doing. Clearly, the better job you are doing as a driver the fewer risks you encounter. So, driving wasn't the only issue. It was more the emotional debt we were in.'

Sadly, that deficit increased almost as soon as the cars ventured on to the streets of Monaco, where an 80kph pit-lane speed limit was introduced for the first time. During first free practice Austrian Karl Wendlinger, driving for the Sauber-Mercedes team, lost control of his car as he braked heavily to navigate the harbour chicane after exiting the tunnel at 180mph. Wendlinger, who had shone alongside Schumacher in Mercedes' young drivers' academy, was a passenger as his car hit a wall sideways. His head struck a water-tank barrier between the track and the escape road, and Wendlinger was unconscious when a medical team reached him. As drivers tried to absorb this latest serious accident, he was taken to the local Princess Grace Hospital before being transferred to the intensive care unit of Saint-Roch Hospital, in Nice. Sauber immediately withdrew their second driver, Heinz-Harald Frentzen, from the race.

Wendlinger was in a coma. Formula One was in crisis.

'All of this was a new experience for most drivers,' said Hill. 'Getting back into the cars there was already a lot of trepidation, then Wendlinger had his accident.' Hill truthfully articulated what all felt in the principality, when he said: 'There was a big black cloud over Monaco that weekend. People didn't know how to deal with it.'

Being in Monaco that weekend was joyless. Brave men were going through the motion of convincing themselves that the race mattered, that this is what Senna and Ratzenberger would have wanted. But the reality was different. The reality was that the deaths of two drivers, then the accident which condemned Wendlinger to a life-support machine, had sent a seismic shock-wave through the paddock and beyond. The reality was perhaps best expressed by Panis when he revealed how he had reacted to the chain of events. When he went back to his room at the Beach Plaza Hotel, overlooking the Mediterranean, he closed the door and thought, 'Fuck! Today, it's Karl; maybe tomorrow, it's me.'

Twenty-two years later, when describing his emotional state at the time, his sense of confusion and shock was still apparent. 'I didn't sleep well the whole week,' said Panis. 'It was traumatic. I talked a lot with my wife, Anne. And I remember saying to her for the first time, "Maybe we need to have kids."

'Anne said: "What?" I said I was twenty-seven, and she

was twenty-six, and that it was time for us to have kids. But she just looked at me, and asked, "Why are you saying this now?"

'I can tell you what I told her: "Because I think I would feel better if something happened to me knowing that you are not alone." I felt like this, I remember.'

Panis was at the dawn of the career he had wanted since his teenage years in karting and Anne, who was a blisteringly quick driver during her own days racing karts, understood perfectly the risks attached to earning a living in a Formula One car. But the carnival that had accompanied his arrival in Brazil only a couple of months earlier was over. He was thinking of a future too dark to comprehend, but nonetheless one that he needed to reflect upon. 'For sure, when you drive you are not thinking like that,' said Panis. 'But before you go to the car, the questions kept coming.'

On the drivers' day off on Friday they congregated in a room loaned to them at the offices of the Automobile Club de Monaco to debate and analyse what was happening. They were joined by Lauda, a man of incalculable experience. Brundle played a significant role, too. 'We sat in a room together all day,' recalled Brundle. 'I guess, because I was the only one of the current drivers who had been in business before, I somehow set the agenda. Effectively, I was the de facto chairman, even though there were older and wiser guys than me. What mattered was that we all got together. In Monaco everyone was thinking, "Hang on, what's happening and what's going to happen next?" It was the fear of the unknown. "What *is* going on around here? Is it going to happen to me?"'

Hill recalled: 'The tension existed before Ayrton's accident. He was very much a campaigner – a bit like Jackie Stewart – for what was right. He challenged the FIA, its president, Max Mosley, and Bernie Ecclestone on lots of issues. We had this new development with the safety car being introduced and that became a factor. It was flagged up as problematical by Ayrton. At that meeting there was a sense that out of respect to Ayrton we really ought to be asking key, pertinent questions in Monaco.'

Hill had an area of personal concern that he aired – the siting of on-board cameras on Formula One cars. The cameras were a welcome innovation for armchair fans, but there were critical implications for the drivers. 'Ayrton's accident was the first fatality, if you like, broadcast live on television,' he said. 'Of course, there was no Internet then, but with on-board cameras times had changed. I felt: "I have a family, so I definitely don't want you broadcasting footage from my on-board camera after I have had an accident." My family – any of our families – could be sitting at home watching a race when some potentially shocking news could be revealed to them in such a traumatic fashion. It was a big issue.'

Almost overnight, driver complacency had become obsolete. Before they left the meeting at the offices of the ACM, they had re-formed the Grand Prix Drivers' Association (GPDA), which had been disbanded in 1987. 'We chose three directors, Michael, Gerhard Berger and me,' said Brundle. 'I became chairman, which I felt made me somewhat of a target for Mr Ecclestone and Mr Mosley, because they were not keen on others having a platform or a voice. This was not the way they ran the business. I suppose it could be thought of as a knee-jerk reaction, but we felt a need to take our safety into our own hands.

'Whatever you specialise in during your life, you can see things that are so obvious and wonder why no one else has seen it. I was a car dealer before I was a racing driver. I can price a car to this day. For example, I can ask, "When did you get that door re-painted?" Others may have missed that, but I could clearly pick up on something like that. It was the same as a racing driver – we see things at a circuit that others might not. We decided after the events at Imola, and Monaco, that it was important for the directors of the GPDA to instigate our own track inspections in the future.'

At trackside, before that sombre Grand Prix in Monaco, Hill, Brundle, Lauda, Schumacher and Berger had all talked to reporters like me with an eloquence and truthfulness that was admirable. 'These are sensitive times and I don't want to inflame the position,' said Hill back then. 'But the world is watching Formula One and we cannot let it become a fiasco. People like mock-violence, like *Gladiators* on television, but they don't want to see racing drivers hurt or killed.'

Schumacher, then twenty-five, the winner of all three races of the season, and Senna's heir-apparent, admitted: 'I wondered if I could still drive as I did before Ayrton and Roland died.' A test session at Silverstone a week after their fatal accidents confirmed in his own mind that he could; and during final qualifying at Monaco, Schumacher flicked his Benetton-Ford over kerbs and within centimetres of the metal barriers to claim the first pole position of his meteoric career with a lap time of 1 minute, 18.560 seconds. It was almost a full second under the lap record Mansell had established two years before.

The German drove his slowing-down lap with his arm raised jubilantly outside the cockpit. It was the first celebratory gesture witnessed in those dark hours for Grand Prix racing. Brundle understood this emotional response. 'The last thing I want to do is give an impression that I'm not bothered by the tragic events,' Schumacher said later that day. 'We can justify most things to ourselves, but if Senna can die in a Williams then it can happen to anybody. But what's the alternative? The option is to be standing here retired with a glass of wine, thinking, "I'm glad I don't have to pump myself up to drive flat out through Casino Square." And six months later you would hate yourself. There is a reality to face. The feeling of driving my McLaren-Peugeot round the circuit is incredible. It can frighten the life out of you, but it is the trade-off you make for the feeling of satisfaction when you get it right.'

Lauda's voice in the drivers' meeting was sage and informed, having seen other good men die in a racing car while having personally been extricated from his blazing Ferrari and given a second chance at becoming a champion in the dangerous sport at which he excelled. He was invited to act as official spokesman for the rest of the year. 'I think the Formula One boat rocks in a way that is nearly out of control,' said Lauda, as looked across the harbour to give an insight into the drivers' mindsets in these troubled days for F1. 'But the drivers realise you can't say cancel this race and that race. We had been lucky for so many years with God holding his hand over Formula One; now he has pulled it away. To get control is not to throw down the anchor, though. You can destroy everything that way. To get control is to get the steering back and very gently manoeuvre ourselves out of trouble. It means a lot of thinking; you cannot expect to make this better overnight. Disasters don't get caused by one reason. A lot of things come together and we're right on the edge at the moment with no cushion.'

Some asked: is it a coincidence that these fatalities have occurred since traction control and active suspension were removed from the cars? There was no evidence to apportion specific blame on these latest cars, but Mosley was driving the FIA to make a host of changes. And that in itself posed a threat, as changes hurriedly introduced, without proper testing, could be inherently dangerous, couldn't they?

Brundle testified as to how fast cornering speeds had been driven upwards, when he said: 'The commitment you make for cornering is awesome. I went round Silverstone last week in a pretty competitive time and braked just twice. Once was no more than a brush of the pedal as I changed down from sixth gear to fifth.' Berger added: 'It's unbelievably quick through the corners here in Monaco; and we brake unbelievably late. If you get it right, it's exciting. You are proud of yourself. But when you think about it later . . .' It was unnecessary for him to finish his sentence. Lauda again: 'I think we drove more unsafe cars in the past and in my days we lost one driver a year. Here in Monaco, we seem to have made a good start for improvement. Even so, the boat still rocks. We need a bit of luck and goodwill to get through this weekend and the next couple of races before things naturally calm down.'

Mosley responded to Wendlinger's accident by announcing the formation of an Expert Advisory Group to investigate all matters relating to safety. For Ecclestone, the show simply had to go on. 'We've all got to pick ourselves up,' he said. 'Most people thought that we could not go on after Jim Clark was killed. Or after Colin Chapman died; or this or that. Let me tell you, the sport moves on. And it must do now.'

Ecclestone had long since deleted the capacity to show any emotional public response to tragedy, but, in this instance, there was an essential pragmatism to his statement that could not be ignored. Even so, with the FIA and the ACM, he agreed that the first two places at the front of the grid for the Monaco Grand Prix should be left empty, aside from two miniature painted flags, one in Brazilian colours, the other in the red and white of Austria. Before the race, the drivers assembled at the head of the grid to observe a minute's silence. Senna and Ratzenberger were absent, but not forgotten. However, Brundle disapproved of such a stark reminder of these wretched catastrophes so close to having to race one another on streets where there is no room to make the most fundamental mistake without potentially dire consequences. 'I thought we should have shown our respects at a different time,' he said in conversation for this book. 'It was just not the right moment.' Yet Brundle admitted that those unwanted minutes standing on the grid galvanised the strength of his position in his own mind. 'When I looked up, I saw an opportunity, to be honest,' he revealed. 'All the young drivers looked like rabbits caught in the headlights of an oncoming car. I thought, "I am going to beat you lot today. You are all screwed up." And off we went and raced. I beat them all bar one, sadly.'

He never beat Schumacher. No one had all year – and the German withstood all the tension, and the emotional turbulence, to win the race by over thirty-seven seconds from Brundle's McLaren-Peugeot. No one perhaps fully appreciated it at the time, but Schumacher was granting us an insight into the mindset that hallmarked his career. Inside a racing car Schumacher had no time for introspection.

Hill's race ended when his Williams made contact with the McLaren of Mika Häkkinen as they approached the first corner, Sainte-Dévote. He would admit later: 'I have never been so glad to get out of a place that has so many happy memories for the Hill family.' Even years later, those words had the sympathy of all who had been in Monaco that weekend. Berger claimed the third place on the podium at Monaco for Ferrari with a drive of immense character, as he had grieved as hard as anyone for Senna. Fellow Austrians Ratzenberger and Wendlinger were well known to him, too.

Brundle, who was nearing his thirty-fifth birthday, delivered all weekend for a McLaren team which had failed to tempt Prost out of retirement to drive their Peugeot-powered MP4/9. 'I was on the front of the grid on Thursday,' said Brundle. 'In second qualifying on Saturday, I was knocked back to sixth. But I was feeling very confident, although up until that point my car had been horribly unreliable. The first lap I ever did in it, testing in Estoril, in Portugal, the engine blew up and threw a con rod so hard that it went through the underfloor of the car and damaged the racetrack!

'At the first race in Brazil, I had just lapped Érik Comas and passed the duelling cars of Jos Verstappen – the father of Max Verstappen – and Eddie Irvine when my car inconveniently had engine trouble. I was on the radio to the pits trying to sort out my car when I veered slightly left. Comas came to pass me and at the same time Verstappen, in his first race, and Irvine tried to pass Comas. This was a recipe that all came together like a soufflé – and boom, up it went. As Verstappen barrel-rolled, his car hit my head. I have seen a picture where you can't see my head; it has been knocked down inside the cockpit. As far as I am concerned, that is the closest I have come to dying. Fortunately, I was only knocked out by the blow. When I came round I tried to walk back to the pits and fell over and collapsed. I crawled to the back of the nearest marshal's post, where they were busily waving flags at approaching cars, and I couldn't get anyone's attention. I sat there for a while until I felt well enough to walk back to the pits. I debriefed with the team and flew home that night. About a week later my family insisted on taking me to hospital as I was not making any sense to them. I was badly concussed. These days, when I am doing my Friday track walk for Sky Sport in Brazil, I walk past that point . . . and think how lucky I was.'

Against that early-season history, as well as feeling off-balance like everybody else in Monaco that weekend, Brundle thought his drive to second place had been an exceptional afternoon's work. 'I passed Gerhard down the outside going into Mirabeau towards the end of the race,' he said, a trick easier to plan than to execute. 'I feel I pulled that result out of the bag. The car was practically limping to the line;

how I coaxed it to the finish I will never know. Peugeot were so ecstatic that we cracked open some champagne.' At that moment Ron Dennis appeared – and the mood instantly changed at McLaren. Brundle reported: 'That's when Ron poked his head into the garage and asked, "What's going on here? Don't forget second is the first of the losers."' Some comments defy further comment, don't they?

Wendlinger remained in a coma for some weeks, but made a full recovery. However, his Formula One career effectively ended in Monaco, although he competed successfully for many years in sports cars and touring cars. Panis brought his Ligier-Renault home ninth, two laps behind Schumacher. Flavio Briatore, team principal with Benetton, also owned Ligier, and Panis, in this moment, had occasion to be grateful for a change of circumstance. 'Flavio gave me a contract for two years,' said the Frenchman. Briatore developed a penchant for managing drivers as well as teams. Later the Italian would become a divisive figure in Formula One, but at least Panis had the stability of a guaranteed income for the first time in his career.

And in October his son, Aurélien, was born. It transpired that Anne was already pregnant before Panis began the weekend of the Monaco Grand Prix imploring her that the time was right for them to start a family. 'It was a good surprise,' said Panis. 'I know that Enzo Ferrari said that when a driver has kids he goes slower. But I was really cool – because I knew if something happened to me Anne was not going to be alone.' Yet Panis admits it took time, a long time, to realign his life. 'It was a tough season,' he said. 'For me, it took that long to clear my head out of the car.'

From the heartbreak at Imola, to the apprehension and nervousness at Monaco, through to the final controversy in Australia, it is uncontentious to suggest that the 1994 season will be reviewed for ever as a year of unrelenting anxiety and tension. It is important to include some of the most pertinent episodes in these pages in order to appreciate how Formula One had to journey nervously through its most torrid times since the grim old days that Stewart, and others, had campaigned so hard to eradicate.

Brawn: Chaos and Controversy

Certainly, Ross Brawn felt like a man forever fighting fires as this tragic season became a quarrelsome one for Benetton and Schumacher with their rivals and officialdom. 'I think for a while Formula One was directionless,' said Brawn, as he sat in the conservatory of his farmhouse in the spring of 2016. Brawn savoured a total of seven victories in Monaco, with Schumacher, Jenson Button and Nico Rosberg between 1994 and 2013. He can make a legitimate claim to an eighth triumph on these streets, as he was running the Research and Development Department at Williams when Keke Rosberg won in Monaco in 1983. The Rosbergs are the only father and son to have won the race.

But for Brawn this first win at Monaco in 1994 was not a moment for unbridled celebration. 'As a Formula One generation, we had not faced losing such an iconic character as Ayrton – and no one knew how to deal with it,' he admitted. 'It started to implode and the political battles started, the blame game started. People were looking for the FIA to respond. Max Mosley did respond with changes to the cars, but in the engineering department at Benetton, and elsewhere, there was a definite sense to the effect that if we are not careful, it will be more dangerous than before. In reality that did happen, but we got away with it.'

Rule changes announced by the FIA at Monaco designed to help improve safety included reducing the downforce of the cars with restrictions on the diffuser to further reduce the amount of grip available to drivers. At the next test at Silverstone eight days later, a Lotus driven by Pedro Lamy cartwheeled off the circuit at 170mph and flew through a protective fence before landing in a spectator access tunnel. The 22-year-old Portuguese driver sustained a broken thigh and two broken kneecaps. He was exceedingly fortunate according to his Lotus team-mate, Englishman Johnny Herbert, who arrived first at the scene of the accident.

Veteran Formula One correspondent Derick Allsop reported Herbert's account in the following day's *Independent* newspaper:

I stopped my car and jumped out, but at first I couldn't find Pedro. Then I could see the tub (the survival cell which accommodates a driver) had been thrown on the other side of the fence. I couldn't believe it, he was halfway down the tunnel. The back end of the car was on fire. Even his helmet was steaming. The marshals soon appeared and I helped them put out the fire. I feared the worst after what's happened recently. He was unconscious when I got to him, but gradually he came to. He was breathing heavily and in obvious pain. They put his legs in splints and carried him to a helicopter to be taken to hospital in Northampton. It was as horrifying as any of the recent accidents we have had.

Brawn felt Lamy's accident was related to the hastiness of the changes that were being made to Formula One cars in the wake of the fatal accidents. 'We were implementing changes from race to race without any testing, without any proper evaluation,' he said. 'Lotus had a rear-wing failure because of the way the loads went through the structure change. Luckily, it was testing and there was no one there at Silverstone, otherwise . . . It was a very volatile and difficult year.'

It became a torrid season of rows and accusations, and it is worth recounting how events unfolded because the teams were adapting at furious speed to the regulation changes implemented after Wendlinger's accident and the deaths of Ratzenberger and Senna. News came thick and fast. Benetton and Schumacher were at the heart of a host of controversies; Williams illustrated a lack of faith in Hill to lead the team and summoned Nigel Mansell from America to race for four races in place of David Coulthard, who had been promoted from test driver to fill the vacancy created by the death of Senna. Meanwhile, 23-year-old Coulthard was determined to show – with the time that he did have in the car – that he was capable of racing Hill.

'Damon and I didn't have any relationship when we were team-mates,' admitted Coulthard. 'I was ten years younger and had not grown up with him. He could get quite chippy; and he got chippy with me in Spa when he threatened to punch me.' Barrichello had pole position for Jordan at the Belgian Grand Prix with Schumacher alongside him and Hill third. Coulthard takes up the story: 'I predicted in a Williams team meeting that Rubens would make a bad start and Damon would get a chance to get through. Admittedly I had mentioned it a couple of times, when Damon said to me, "You say that one more time and I am going to fucking punch you."

'I replied, "Come on, Damon, if you are going to do it, do it!" Of course, he never did. I didn't want him to do it either – I am not a fighter. But if someone wants to play the big man in front of everyone, what's the worst that can happen? He hits you, then someone is going to tell him to stop. So it didn't seem a high risk.'

What the episode emphasised was the stress Hill was under as he tried to battle with Schumacher, who had the entire support of the Benetton operation behind him. In just his second season it was Hill, instead of Senna, going head-to-head with the German for the world championship. 'I got thrust into that place,' said Hill. 'Yet I wasn't reluctant. I wanted to be the best as well. At the time Michael wasn't really quantifiable. We all knew he was good, but we didn't know just how good. He was tough to beat; I was up against it. But the challenge brought the best out of me.'

Benetton's win at Monaco, giving Schumacher a clean sweep of the first four races of the tumultuous season, was not universally popular. Brawn had moved back into Formula One with Benetton in 1991 at the instigation of Tom Walkinshaw, who had formed a successful relationship with him as the designer of Tom Walkinshaw Racing's championship-winning sports-car programme with Jaguar. Walkinshaw was the technical director at Benetton – and now in these stormy days in the summer of '94 Brawn and Walkinshaw knew by whisper and innuendo that the legality of their car was under scrutiny. At one point, Brawn confronted Ferrari team boss Jean Todt. 'I said, "Jean, you're upset because you are Ferrari and you have got to explain why this T-shirt manufacturer is thrashing you." It is an easy excuse to say, "Ah, they must have traction control."'

All these years later, Brawn presented a case for Benetton's defence in a calm, measured manner. 'When you ask where is the evidence of traction control, it is simple to answer because there was no evidence. It was rumour, and that's all it was. My defence in the long term was that no one ever left the team and said, "Actually, by the way, we were using traction control." Not one engineer, not one driver ever said that. If you look at almost every travesty in motor-racing history, someone has left the team and spilled the beans. That never happened because we were not doing it. Also, Cosworth and Ford were involved, providing the engines for the team. If we were running traction control, Cosworth would have had to have devised it for us. And Ford would have had to have sanctioned it. They are not the type of people or companies to do that.

'It's a bit like the drug era in sport. Someone could accuse you of something, in this instant the use of traction control, yet they could not produce any proof that you were using it. They demanded proof that we weren't using it. You can't prove a negative other than say, "We are not using it." The political battle did take the shine off the 1994 championship. But, in retrospect, I reflected on that period and I thought that was what toughened me up. This was where I knew I had to learn from these experiences, learn how to keep my team together.'

The punches were coming hard and fast, for sure. In July, Schumacher overtook Hill on the parade lap at the British Grand Prix and was given a five-second penalty. The penalty was ignored and Schumacher was shown a black flag – but he remained on the circuit while Briatore and Walkinshaw discussed the controversy with the race director, Roland Bruynseraede, arguing they had not been properly informed of the punishment. A protracted row led to the FIA World Motor Sport Council deciding sixteen days later to disqualify Schumacher from the British Grand Prix and banning him from the next two races. After Benetton and Schumacher lodged an appeal, he was allowed to compete at the next race, at home in Germany.

More trouble followed Benetton to Hockenheim. During a pit stop the second Benetton car driven by Jos Verstappen caught fire as it was being refuelled. Verstappen disappeared from view as flames engulfed his car and placed some mechanics in grave danger, too. Dave Redding, who is nowadays McLaren team manager, was running Verstappen's car. 'I remember the incident vividly,' he says, but he tells the story without his voice ever letting you know that only the intervention of mates from the McLaren team spared this blighted summer from further tragedy. 'Earlier that weekend we'd had people accidentally dropping glasses from the Paddock Club, which was situated above our pit. When Jos came in, I went to go in on the right rear tyre when I was aware of fluid. I thought some idiot had dropped something from the Paddock Club. I didn't think it was fuel.

'I go into the wheel . . . undo the nut . . . and come out and the car is still on the ground. I thought subconsciously, "Jos is going to go out and the wheel nut is in my socket." I go back in, because I think I need to get the nut on. And as I get back in . . . the whole car goes up in flames. I spun around . . . on fire. I tripped over the rear jack as my eyes were shut. I ran into the gantry as my eyes were still shut.'

The scene was chaotic and frightening. 'I tried to get my balaclava off, which was on fire,' says Redding. 'Perhaps it was not the brightest move to remove fireproof clothing when on fire.' Understandably, the power of logic had deserted him. 'Some guys from McLaren came running down to put us out. I remember hot chemicals coming through my race suit, so I really wanted to get it off. I was burned around my eyes. Next thing I remember I was on a stretcher going down the pit lane in my underpants. We were airlifted to the same hospital that looked after Niki Lauda. But only two or three of the team stayed in hospital, the rest of us were discharged that night.'

Redding's eyes were swollen for days and he was not allowed to drive immediately afterwards, but his bigger con-cern were pains in his chest. 'They were affecting my breathing,' he says. 'Bruising came out a couple of days after I had seen a doctor and I couldn't work out where they had come from. Then I saw the video of the fire, which showed me tripping over the rear jack and running into the gantry. It all made sense. For about five or six years if I went out in the sun I got red marks round my eyes, but it's all fine now. I see Jos quite a bit, we're good mates; but he is barmy!'

The company manufacturing the refuelling equipment for all the teams – Intertechnique – were delegated by the FIA to make an investigative visit to the Benetton factory in England. Afterwards the FIA issued a statement that said 'the [fuel] valve was slow to close because of the presence of a foreign body'. According to published reports, an independent body stated that a filter, designed to eliminate any possible risk of fire, had been removed and that without it fuel had flowed 12.5 per cent faster than usual. Shortly afterwards, Benetton insisted in a press release that there was a fault in the equipment that had been provided. Benetton received no punishment.

In this year of endless friction, Benetton reeled from that scare into another dispute. Victory by Schumacher at the next race at Spa, in Belgium, was followed by disqualification after post-race scrutineering found that there was excessive wear on his Benetton skid-block, a mandatory wooden plank intro-duced at the previous race to maintain a uniform ride-height on the cars. Stewards ruled that Schumacher's car had gained an illegal aerodynamic advantage. Benetton's defence was that the plank had been damaged in the race.

Brawn explained: 'I am pretty good at reading the rules – and for me the rule was pretty clear. The plank was damaged. The regulation was clear: it said the plank cannot wear more than from ten to nine millimetres. But the regulation also said that if the plank is damaged it could be weighed and as long as it was 90 per cent of its original weight it was fine. We had worn the plank to less than nine millimetres, but we had a smashed plank. I asked for it to be weighed. They insisted they had the right to do either – and had chosen to measure it. It didn't feel like a fifty–fifty decision. It was a tough year getting tougher.'

Hill was upgraded from second to victor. Schumacher's discomfort was enhanced when the two-race ban he had received at Silverstone, delayed on appeal, was implemented to keep him out of his car at the Italian Grand Prix and the one that followed in Portugal. Hill won them both. His fight with Schumacher for the world championship went to the final round, in Australia.

We would witness the first title-deciding conclusion to the championship since Prost had denied Mansell the title in Adelaide eight years earlier. Unfortunately, the battle ended prematurely, and cloaked in yet more controversy. On lap 36, with Schumacher leading from Hill, the German touched a wall with his right rear wheel, unseen by the Williams driver. What Hill saw was his rival coming back across the grass. Moments afterwards, Hill tried to pounce, but Schumacher turned in sharply and there was contact between the cars. Schumacher's day was over, but Hill only made it as far as the pits. Schumacher remained at the scene of the accident. Time stood still as he waited to see whether Hill would reappear. When he did not, Schumacher had become Germany's first Formula One world champion. By a margin of one point. In a race that he never finished; nor did his rival for the title. There was an uncomfortable convenience with this script.

For many, the result was a travesty of justice. Herbert is unapologetic for expressing just such a view. 'We had that sad day in Imola and Damon was thrust from being Ayrton Senna's number two to team leader overnight. Bloody hell, did he grab that challenge by the throat and get the best out of himself and the team. He has never had the credit he deserves for that. That was bloody tough. Should he have won in 1994?

Yes! Damon should be a two-times world champion. The result was not fair one iota.'

Brawn admitted: 'It was an unpleasant year. We won the championship but we won it in acrimonious circumstances. I remember the TV coverage was not as good as it is now. What we saw was Michael going off and bouncing back on the circuit and taking Damon off. How much was conscious on Michael's behalf, how much was not? I never asked Michael.'

I did. I flew to Mainz to meet with Schumacher before he appeared on a televised sports show to celebrate his world title. This is what Schumacher told me: 'First, let me tell you that I did not deliberately turn my car into Damon's path. If you look at my past, there was never such a thing. It is not my attitude to sport. But I have seen the video – and maybe know why some people think it has been deliberate – because just before I go into the corner, I start to turn my head. At this moment, I have to say myself, it looks like I try to look in the mirror to find out where Damon is, and then I turn in. But this is not the case. I usually do this. I put the helmet quite far into the inside when I am cornering. But I can see this might confuse people, where they might think I did it deliberately. I did not.

'The point was the car was handling very difficult for the whole race. We had made an attempt to change the settings, but did not have time to check it properly and this was a mistake. It was oversteering. At turn three, I lost control for a moment over a bump. The car started oversteering. I corrected it and got it back. I had to run wide, though, and I touched the wall. I checked the car – you can see that very clearly on television. There was a lot of dust on the tyres, so I cleaned them and drove a bit zigzag. Then I wanted to continue racing; the car felt OK. After I went to the left, everything felt normal. Then I went to the right and I felt something strange. When I looked at the video, the strange thing that I felt was when Damon touched me with his front wheel on the side pods. Immediately after this I was up in the air.

'My first impression at the press conference was that there was something wrong with my car. In actual fact, there wasn't. I wanted to go on racing. Damon, clearly, felt there was an opportunity to pass me. It just got too tight at the next corner for us two and we crashed.'

I suggested to Hill in the winter of 2016 that I was still puzzled by the equanimity he had shown after the race – and for years afterwards. 'That's the way I was brought up,' he said. 'Of course, I have looked at the incident like everyone else. And I have wondered if I could have done anything differently, too. After all, it takes two to tango.' Then with undisguised irony Hill smiled slowly and said, sotto voce, 'I was an appalling overtaker, let's be honest.'

Yet Hill did offer a serious, considered view: 'Inconsistency applied in our sport at that time and that was irritating, but like my dad always said, "Life's not fair." Rather than bitch and moan about it, you choose which way you want to go. In sporting terms everyone wants to be a hero. Yet I understand that different cultures have different attitudes. In some countries, they might say it's a game, and they know how to play the game. We are brought up, mostly, about doing things right. It's a different place in the human mind to approach it like this. Does the end justify the means?

'I have always felt that the way something is done actually transcends the result in the long run. Otherwise the gloves are off and you can do what you like. Well, I don't see things like that. I sometimes wonder if it is an annoyance when we say, "We believe in these rules, we ought to play by them." Then everyone walks all over us and we go . . . curses.'

He smiled slowly again, then added from the soul: 'Maybe that is to our long-term credit.'

Michael Schumacher, 1994

9

How Ferrari Seduced Schumacher on a Boat at Monaco

In 1994, Johnny Herbert was facing an uncertain future in the midst of the turbulence buffeting Formula One. He was driving for Lotus, who by the autumn were at the point of collapse. 'The receivers were called in,' said Herbert. 'At the Portuguese Grand Prix in late September, they were basically running the team without having a clue; accountants strutting about telling the boys what to do! It was just a horrible mess.'

Salvation for Herbert arrived in an unsolicited phone call from Walkinshaw, now running the Ligier team with its close connection to Briatore's operation at Benetton. 'I remember getting a call from Tom telling me that he needed me to come to his house as he had a contract for me to sign,' explained Herbert. Lotus had ceased payment of wages, according to Herbert, and there were no feelings of disloyalty in the mind of the popular British driver when he arrived at Walkinshaw's home in Oxfordshire around 11 p.m. Herbert signed the contract he was presented. 'Tom flew me in his plane the next day to the Ligier team's base, at Magny-Cours. Tom was renowned for being a very astute businessman – and I was deemed as an asset to be traded by Lotus.'

He did a half day of testing, before being entered for Ligier at the next race, the European Grand Prix at Jerez in Spain. His team-mate was Panis. Herbert's recollection of the Frenchman over that weekend, in an identical car, is informative. 'He was an easy team-mate and didn't appear the least bit conniving, a very normal, lovely man. Yes, he had a racing head and he had a desire to do the best job possible in the car. He was naturally gifted and didn't have to really work at driving fast. Outside of the car, he was good fun.' Unconsciously, Herbert was offering a description that could easily be applied to himself.

At Jerez, Herbert finished one place ahead of Panis in the Grand Prix, with the Ligier drivers classified seventh and eighth respectively. The following week Herbert flew to Barcelona for further testing, but when he walked into the Ligier garage the engineers greeted his arrival with surprise. 'What are you doing here?' Herbert was asked. He told them he was there to test for the next race in Japan, only to be informed: 'You are with Benetton now.' Herbert, who these days is a respected pundit for Sky's Formula One channel, still sounded dumbfounded when we talked in the McLaren motorhome in the Monaco paddock in 2016 about the moment he had been transferred without his knowledge to become Schumacher's new team-mate. He was back with Briatore, who had given him his break in Formula One in 1989, then dumped him as he had not fully recovered from a horrific accident in F3000 the previous summer.

Schumacher *was* Benetton and Herbert understood that;

but that did not mask the fact that he did not appreciate being isolated. 'Michael had a particular style of driving,' Herbert said. 'He liked a very sharp front end; I didn't. Which way would the team lean? Michael's way, and I could completely understand that. Flavio – or the team – could only concentrate on one driver. Even so, Flav was good at telling me one thing, then doing completely the opposite. I didn't deal with it very well, I admit. I felt I was banging my head against a brick wall. I didn't bother about qualifying; I just focused on the race set-up. Ross Brawn was good, but his hands were tied because he was there to do a job for Flavio and for the Benetton family.'

When the teams arrived in Monaco in late May 1995, Schumacher and Hill had each won twice. Herbert had been second in Spain to give Benetton a one–two maximum-points finish, while Coulthard had supplied support for Hill and Williams with a second place in the first race of the season in Brazil. Coulthard's first experience of the streets of Monaco in a Formula One car was to prove a puzzle that he had to resolve. And quickly. Coulthard had been chosen by Williams ahead of Mansell to partner Hill after both drivers had driven for the team during those traumatic months following the death of Senna. Clearly, Williams had chosen youth over experience; and a smaller wage bill. At McLaren, sponsors Marlboro found it an irresistible opportunity to sign a world champion, so Mansell was hired to supposedly deliver some gravitas to Dennis's team, which now had Mercedes as their engine suppliers.

Unfortunately, the rumours suggesting 41-year-old Mansell did not fit into the cockpit of the McLaren MP4-10 proved to be true. The 1992 world champion missed the first two races, in Brazil and Argentina, but after a completely new, wider monocoque was built for him it was apparent from his performance in the San Marino Grand Prix, then in Barcelona, that he could not find empathy with the car. In Spain, Mansell had a spin and ultimately parked his car in the McLaren garage. He was reported as saying the car was 'virtually impossible to drive'.

Mansell had driven his 187th – and final – Grand Prix in a spectacular career affording him thirty-one wins. It was never dull with our Nige around. He had lived each episode of his career, triumphant or calamitous, under the glare of public scrutiny, and provided drama, real and imagined, like no other British racing driver since James Hunt – without the sex and drugs element. But with such obvious difficulties between Mansell and McLaren, Dennis had dispensed with his services before the Monaco Grand Prix. Mark Blundell was summoned to join Mika Häkkinen.

While McLaren dealt with such unwanted headlines, Coulthard had issues of his own to contend with in the first qualifying session he had ever undertaken on the streets of Monaco – and a rain-disrupted one at that. 'I think I was eleventh at the end of first practice,' said Coulthard. 'This was shit. I had gone OK on street circuits in the past, but at Monaco there was no one to tell me, "Look out for this, look out for that." Even if I had asked Damon, there is no reason to think he would have told me.'

Hill had been the Williams rookie at Monaco only two seasons before, partnered with Prost. He studied Prost's methods with an eagerness to absorb all he could, as Hill explained: 'You think, "I have to learn something with this guy." I was always a Prost fan. I thought he did things efficiently. He had an economy of style. He was meticulously neat. I thought if I can get close to him, I am doing all right round here. I did not expect him to help, though; and it would have been embarrassing to ask.' He told me an anecdote involving golfing legend Ben Hogan, which resonates with how Hill felt. 'I like the story of Ben Hogan being asked by a young guy, "Mr Hogan, what do I do at this point?" Hogan replied, "What clubs do you use?" The guy tells him he plays Slazenger clubs. So Hogan says to him, "Go and ask Mr Slazenger."'

Hill smiled as he told the story. Yet the point he was making is serious. No one in sport gets a free pass to knowledge, least of all a Formula One driver venturing for the first time on the streets of Monaco. Hill's own first taste of the Grand Prix was memorable for all the wrong reasons. 'I came here in 1992 with Brabham – and didn't qualify,' he said. 'One of the reasons I didn't qualify, perhaps, was that I couldn't change gear. I only had four gears . . . I couldn't get the other two because I was too big for the car!' One year later he was back – this time under the spotlight. He was the number-two driver to Prost in a Williams car that was transporting the Frenchman in the direction of a fourth world championship. He was also the son of a man who had won the race five times. 'I was expected to deliver,' admitted Hill. 'It's very hard to comprehend your circumstances. Your brain goes into meltdown. There is so much happening; it feels like being in a war zone. It was a very cramped pit lane – without a speed limit – and there were people wandering around everywhere.

'Out on the track, you had to make sure you weren't blocking anyone. You are looking forwards, looking backwards, looking sideways; you are trying to find a racing line. The first time you do a lap round Monaco you think that there is no way they can hold a race here. What are they talking about? It's madness. You arrive at the swimming-pool section and think, "Holy crap!" There was a concrete wall staring at you – it's gone now – but then the intention was to head straight for the wall and try to clip it on the left before a blind apex.

'Eventually, you do get a rhythm. It's a bit like dance steps:

left, right, right, right, left, left, right, left. Or something like that. Once you get that right, you start to settle down. But your brain has to get used to editing out all the useless information; there is a lot of it. At Williams, they know the car can be at the front, so you can't be down in the middle of the field. You have to be at the front. People retrospectively have said to me that must have been stressful. Yes, it was. But you want it to be stressful. You like the adrenalin, the heightened awareness. Someone going to race at Monaco in a Formula One car is doing something they have always wanted to do. You get a thrill. You go hurtling down to Mirabeau ... and think, "This is brilliant." You are honking through the tunnel flat; it's very exciting.

'It is the slowest circuit we go to, but you get the biggest impression of speed. You are hemmed in. It looks like a tunnel, because the Armco barriers tower over your head. Obviously, you can see the buildings and stuff. But the things that are level with your eye, in your peripheral vision, are flashing past at 160mph and barely half the width of a car away from you. Think of it like this: when you go on a high-speed train and you look out the window and a train whizzes past in the opposite direction, you jump because the trains are very close. That's the sensation of speed at Monaco.'

If a driver lives on his wits, he must also rely on the information gathered and disseminated by his team. At Williams, Hill always enjoyed a good relationship with technical director Patrick Head – now Sir Patrick Head. 'Patrick was helpful, but he was also a hard taskmaster,' said Hill. 'I liked that. My dad was a hard taskmaster, so I grew up in that kind of environment. Patrick would tell you what you needed to know. He was amazing: he knew what everyone's job was, and what the key element of that job was, and what you needed to concentrate on.' Yet Head was not immune to the creeping nervousness that can raise the heart rate of the most placid of men as the start of a Grand Prix inches ever closer. 'Patrick would famously get quite tense before the start of a race,' said Hill. 'At Monaco, I remember him coming on the radio and saying, "Damon, there is rain coming from the sky." Head's wish to be helpful brought a laconic reply from Hill, cutting through the tension. 'I hear what you are saying, Patrick.'

During practice at Monaco in 1993, Hill had first-hand experience of how the track can bite a driver without warning. 'I came out of the tunnel and the rear wing came off,' recalled Hill. 'I managed to manoeuvre the car up the slip road without hitting anything. A year later Karl Wendlinger crashed at the same spot, struck his head and went into a coma.' Hill's debut for Williams had a serene ending after that initial excursion. He finished second to Senna, in a McLaren. On the podium, Hill had the presence of mind to know the Brazilian had overtaken his father's record of winning Monaco five times. 'I remember I said to Ayrton, "If my dad was here, I am sure he would have been the first to congratulate you." Senna was quite moved by that.'

'At Monaco, That Element of Unpredictability Is Real. There Is No Cheating it'

In 1995, Coulthard found the key to his problems from a source outside the Williams team. He arranged to meet a freelance producer he had come to know during his time at the Eurosport network and who now worked for the Monaco television broadcasters. 'On the day off on Friday, I got hold of the in-car footage and watched it over and over again throughout the day,' said Coulthard. It was homework that brought swift reward. The next day Coulthard invested all the lessons he had learned, and qualified third for his first Monaco Grand Prix behind Schumacher and Hill, who was on pole. It was indicative of how Coulthard would become at home on the streets of the principality, literally and figuratively.

Herbert was seventh on the grid. His first visit to Monaco in a Formula One car had been hopelessly compromised in 1989. 'I couldn't properly stop the car when I came out of the tunnel as I couldn't get hard on the brakes,' he recalled. But he was a fitter, wiser man back in Monaco with Benetton six years later. 'There are drivers who are comfortable in Monaco, not intimidated at all by the barriers,' he said. 'I know others found it fairly uncomfortable to drive here, but I always loved it. It is one of the few circuits – Singapore may be another – where the driver has control of the situation and not the engineers.

'For example, at Silverstone, or Monza, there is a white line, a kerb and an AstroTurf run-off area. Here there is a white line and a barrier that doesn't shift. Your self-belief comes into play and it overrides a lot of the other engineering aspects. Of course, you still need a decent car. If it is a well-balanced car you can benefit much more, as you can place the car on the street and be rhythmic for the whole lap. This is the ultimate qualifying lap, the absolute ultimate, because there is no chance of making a little error and getting away with it. Being precise – that was the whole point of driving a Formula One car quickly round narrow streets. You have to absorb all the information – from your peripheral vision – of the grandstands, the marshal posts, the barriers, the advertising hoardings, and then place the car in the right place on the circuit to gain the optimum speed. I think that's where pure, natural driving talent will come to the fore and stand out. Ayrton and Michael provided great examples of that. You have to use all the information to your advantage without looking where you have to brake, or wondering how to get to the next apex.'

It was, implied Herbert, as though a Formula One driver performing at the limit of his ability at Monaco has a hard-wired satnav system. 'It was all there,' he said, tapping his head. 'I loved that.' Herbert recognises that the surface of these streets is nowhere near as abrasive or bumpy as it was in those times, in 1995, but he insists the Monaco Grand Prix is an examination of a driver unlike any other. 'Today, the circuit is pretty well flat. In the past, there was a camber on the streets, which made them more difficult to drive. At some points, you couldn't go too far left, or in other places too far right. If you did, the camber would just suck you into a barrier. But the biggest change to the track at Monaco over a race weekend is the track evolution. The rest of it doesn't move, but the track changes so much. To get the maximum out of your car, you feel the track through your hips, through your fingers, through the tips of your toes. In the car, the barriers are an enemy to a degree, but the challenge is to erase them from being an obstacle. You mustn't see it as a wall or a three-row barrier. Elsewhere at other circuits on the calendar we had a kerb and grass, then gravel traps. Now, it's a bit of Astro and about three kilometres of tarmac. I absolutely hate that. Formula One is too safe. There is no penalty for going off. At Monaco, that element of unpredictability is real. There is no cheating it.'

Hill claimed pole position in 1995 with a lap that was clean, yet bristling with hostility. He was a massive eight-tenths of a second faster than the next man, Schumacher. 'It was,' Hill said at the time, 'the nearest to a perfect lap I have ever produced.' On the fourth row was Brundle, who had switched from McLaren to join Panis and Aguri Suzuki in the Ligier Mugen-Honda team.

'Tom Walkinshaw wanted me in the car, but because of the Mugen-Honda link he had to put Aguri in for many of the races,' explained Brundle. Little entailing Briatore or Walkinshaw was straightforward. Brundle understood all this, but accepted his role as a 'part-timer' – his words, not mine – because he had a strong relationship with Walkinshaw that had been cemented during the success they shared with Jaguar in the World Sportscar Championship. 'Tom trusted me to be his eyes and ears from behind the wheel of a racing car,' said Brundle. 'That was a good car and I really enjoyed working with the Mugen people. I remember I wanted more progressivity on my throttle. It was a cable throttle back then and they came up with this most beautiful piece of engineering that would have looked nice in a Swiss watch. Basically, you want your throttle to be quite slow, then quick towards the end. You want more driveability in slow corners. I enjoyed the Ligier gang as well – even if it was a bit uncomfortable with Aguri.'

Panis was guaranteed to race at every Grand Prix. 'Ollie was the darling of the team,' said Brundle. 'He used to travel with mechanics and played cards with them. Importantly, Ollie was a very good driver, a really nice guy and a good team-mate, although I think he struggled a bit as I was quite quick and I had been round the Formula One block a few times.' Brundle's conversational French was decent, as he had driven before for Ligier in 1993 and then spent the following year speaking the language with engineers from Peugeot during his season with McLaren. At Ligier in 1995, his role required him to travel frequently to the team's headquarters at the Magny-Cours circuit, a location which enabled unlimited opportunities for testing. 'I was there every other week, because we tested relentlessly,' said Brundle. 'I had the code to the entrance to the hotel, so I could let myself in at whatever time I arrived.'

For Panis, Brundle's presence accelerated his comprehension of the business side of Formula One: the side of the street where deals are peddled and political skirmishes can lay waste to the weak and lame. Not for nothing had Formula One been called the Piranha Club. 'Before I didn't have any clue about politics; it's a sport, I thought,' said Panis. 'In 1995, we are 200 people at Ligier. I know all of them because I was there all day long. It's part of my family. I travel with the plane of Ligier with the mechanics, and when there was time we would jet-ski or do other things together. I lived in Grenoble, but for much of the time I stayed in the hotel at Magny-Cours and, like Martin, I had my own key. You changed your room every night if you wanted! It was like it was your house.

'At this time, the boss of the team was Briatore, but the team principal was Walkinshaw. Tom was a tough guy – and at the beginning I did not think he liked me. He pushed me hard on many, many things. Martin was very good friends with Tom and, I admit, I felt Tom was doing this to kill me. One day I spoke with Martin and told him how I felt. Martin said to me, "You are wrong." I said I thought it was easy for him to say that, but Martin explained, "If Tom pushes you, it's because he likes you and feels you have something to give him. If he doesn't say anything to you, then you are on the way out." I learned a lot with Martin, a lot. OK, motor racing is motor racing, but there is politics and games towards everything else in Formula One. This I learned. Martin was a team player, and he was scouting on the circuit for the team when he was not driving. I learned much about setting up the car, about approaching the race. I take a lot from him.'

At Monaco in 1995, Hill and Schumacher made textbook starts, but behind them Coulthard and the Ferraris of Alesi and Berger were involved in a hefty collision at the first corner, Sainte-Dévote. Berger had challenged on the outside while

Alesi charged down the inside of Coulthard. 'There wasn't any space for Alesi and he hit me,' said Coulthard. His Williams subsequently collided with Berger and was launched into the air, spinning through 180 degrees as the two Ferraris made contact. The race had to be red-flagged. Coulthard walked back to the Williams garage to get the spare car readied for the restart, which had been set up for Hill, a taller man than his team-mate. 'At that time we usually had twenty to thirty-five millimetres of throttle travel – from nothing to 800 horse-power,' said Coulthard. 'On the way from the pits to the grid for the restart, I was getting 100 per cent throttle in twenty millimetres.' The throttle's behaviour played to Coulthard's paranoia – a feeling of suspicion and distrust familiar to all racing drivers at some point in their careers. Inside the car, Coulthard thought, 'The bastards. Now I know why Damon has more power than me.'

What had actually happened was that a Renault engineer had reset the pedals from those favoured by Hill to those required by Coulthard; however, in the haste to get the Scots-man on to the grid the engineers did not reset the software on the throttle to accommodate the changes of the pedal set-tings. 'This lack of travel on the throttle pedal meant it was really difficult to control the car,' explained Coulthard. 'In the first few laps Michael and Damon were getting away from me. Every corner was, "Whoops!"' He mimed wrestling a steering wheel at high speed first one way, then the other, to reinforce the scale of his predicament. 'But once I became used to its behaviour, I started to catch them up.'

Coulthard's first Monaco Grand Prix was to be denied a decent ending, however. 'Because the throttle settings were out, the driveshaft broke after sixteen laps,' he said. Yet the lessons of that afternoon stayed with Coulthard when he crossed the Rubicon from driving to punditry. 'From outside the team there were murmurings of disapproval of my driving in that Grand Prix,' remembered Coulthard. 'Don't get me wrong, I fucked up plenty of times in my career, but I was not to blame for all the mishaps, as that example illustrates. Now, in commentary, when guys go off, I am careful to say, "There are a number of things that might have cause that. It could be a straightforward driver error or it could be a technical problem." The reality is, it is not always what you think.'

Schumacher won the race, his second in a row at Monaco, with Hill finishing over thirty seconds behind. Herbert was fourth. 'I can be content that I finished in that position and fourth in the championship at the end of the year,' he said. 'Benetton won the Constructors' Championship, so I fulfilled the job I was brought to the team to do.' Did Briatore express his gratitude? 'I heard nothing from Flavio, but I never expected to if I am honest,' said Herbert. 'Did I underperform? In many ways, yes, I feel I did. But then I wasn't given the same ingredients you needed to succeed. It's hard enough as it is, but to have things against you, and a car where the back end was always moving around, something I never liked, but Michael did, made it harder still. There was no way I was going to stay on with the team after the end of the year.'

Herbert's contribution stretched to two Grand Prix wins, at Silverstone and Monza. His maiden victory at the British Grand Prix – accommodated in part when Hill and Schumacher collided on lap 46 – brought the house down at the old airfield in Northamptonshire. Herbert was not the only one committed to leaving Benetton. Schumacher was courted and seduced that summer by Ferrari. It was a natural move from the Scuderia, who had lost the art of winning. When Schumacher won his second Grand Prix in Monaco, Ferrari mechanics were packing up to head home across the Italian border, still wondering when their fortunes might change. The team had won just once in almost five years. It was an intolerable existence that could not be permitted to remain unchallenged within the corridors of power at Ferrari or their parent company, Fiat. The recruitment of Schumacher, on a no-expense-spared contract, was a bold statement of intent. The fastest, most calculating and most obsessed driver of his era had at the stroke of a pen given Ferrari a priceless endorsement that the team was on a mission to reclaim old glories.

For Schumacher, the switch made huge sense, too; not simply because Ferrari were prepared to make him the highest-paid driver in Formula One history. He had clearly exacted promises from Ferrari president Luca di Montezemolo and team boss Jean Todt that Ferrari would be radicalised to suit him. The swoop for Schumacher illustrated how far and how high he had journeyed since Eddie Jordan had given him his debut at the Belgian Grand Prix in 1991, where he had replaced Bertrand Gachot, who was imprisoned in England after an altercation with a London taxi driver. Schumacher qualified in seventh place – an astonishing performance from a 22-year-old driving at his first Grand Prix. Yet not everyone was surprised.

Two men who had instantly recognised Schumacher as a star-in-waiting, a man with the feel to be untouchable on his day at Monaco, as well as uncatchable at super-fast circuits at Suzuka, Spa or Silverstone, were Brawn and Walkinshaw. They had first witnessed his driving prowess in the Mercedes junior team in sports-car racing. 'I'd raced against him with Jaguar for two years at that point, and Schumacher stood out like the balls on a dog,' said Brawn. 'It was so obvious he was far ahead of the other guys. If you remember, he was racing in the same team as Heinz-Harald Frentzen and Karl Wendlinger, and they both went to Formula One. Michael was miles above them.

'At the time of the Belgian Grand Prix, Tom had just got involved with Benetton, in a pretty much kick-arse mood. He was telling me he was going to change everything and the drivers were useless. Tom set out in a bid to get Michael into the Benetton team there and then. My recollection is that Michael had a one-race deal with Jordan which Mercedes had paid $250,000 to secure. But Eddie didn't know what this kid was like; Tom and I did.

'Of course, after he raced at Spa, Eddie had seen what they had, but I don't think Eddie had his claws tight enough into Michael. He had some options on the contract, but they were vague. It took a 24-hour legal battle, but, sure enough, Tom secured Michael to drive for Benetton.'

Now with Ferrari showing their hand in 1995, it was Benetton who did not have the wherewithal to keep the German, even though he was heading for back-to-back world titles with the team. After initial soundings had been taken with his manager, Willi Weber, Schumacher met with di Montezemolo and Todt on board the yacht of Fiat president Gianni Agnelli, moored off the coast of Monaco. Business deals have historically been sealed in Monaco; this was one of the most critical in Formula One. According to Italian journalist Umberto Zapalloni, who wrote the officially sanctioned 2004 publication *Formula Ferrari*, Agnelli personally broke the news of Schumacher's impending arrival. Zapalloni writes:

On the Thursday prior to the Hungarian Grand Prix, Agnelli spilt the beans about Schumacher's imminent signing. It had been rumoured in three Italian daily papers, but the Fiat patriarch pre-empted any official announcement when he let slip the news to journalists in Villar Perosa, scene of the traditional pre-season football match between two Juventus squads. Official denials were the order of the day, but they fooled no one and a few days later the agreement was confirmed.

Schumacher was bidding *arrivederci* to one Italian-owned team to join another – the most famous motor-racing team in the world. Agnelli had his man. Hogan worked on the contract with Todt, as Marlboro were about to become the primary sponsors of Ferrari. 'Michael's first contract with Ferrari was for $35 million a year, which Marlboro paid,' said Hogan. Pertinently, he added, 'Michael earned a lot of money outside the team, too. Weber was a bright manager. As soon as you win a world championship, every bugger comes out of the woodwork with sponsorship offers. In my experience with other drivers and managers, 99.9 per cent of them are rejected. Weber was different. When I asked him what his criteria were, he replied, "Simple, I take everything. Otherwise they won't go away."

'Michael lived in Switzerland, and I would go into a supermarket near my home there and, for the sake of argument, I would see Michael Schumacher-endorsed spaghetti. If you went down another aisle there could be Michael Schumacher dog food. Willi took everything – and he controlled it. To me, there wasn't a lot wrong with that. Michael always gave great value to us. The people in the company loved him, really loved him. It was a pleasure to work with him. Michael was – *is* – a very nice man. You asked him a question, you got an answer. As a bloke, he was always very curious about what you did as a job. For instance, he always asked me about currency exchange rates, things like that.'

For Benetton, Schumacher's second win at Monaco, and the subsequent other victories that enabled him to win another duel with Hill during a successful defence of his world championship, had come at the considerable cost of his departure. 'I didn't see it coming,' said Brawn. 'We were winning races and winning the championship again. There were some issues in the background between Michael and Flavio over contracts and so on, which were getting a bit bumpy. How much that had to do with it, I don't know. Obviously, the magic of Ferrari was attractive and special to Michael. For him, there was also the fact that he had known Todt from his days driving sports cars.'

Schumacher had a grand design in mind. In time, he intended to create a team in his image within Ferrari. Brawn was high on the list of those he respected. 'I think, slightly apologetically, he asked me that summer if I would be interested in moving,' explained Brawn. 'At that stage, I didn't see there was an opportunity, as John Barnard was there as technical director at Ferrari; besides, I had a lot of loyalty to Benetton. I was very much looking at the situation in these terms: we're losing someone very special in Michael, and that will be to the detriment of the team, but it is imperative for us to knuckle down and try to build something new.'

Benetton reacted to the loss of Schumacher by signing Alesi from Ferrari as his replacement. 'We always felt Jean had a great deal of talent,' said Brawn. 'In the right environment, he would have the chance to flourish and blossom. That could have been the case. Everyone was mentally recovering from the disappointment of losing Michael and thinking ahead to the future, and building a car to suit Alesi, to giving him everything he needs, when suddenly Berger came on the scene as well. Gerhard was a late call.

'Alesi went absolutely ballistic when he heard Berger – his nemesis – was coming, because he had been promised Benetton was to be his team. Todt told me later that Gerhard had been determined, at first, to stay at Ferrari and see how he stacked up against Michael. But at some stage he got cold feet and didn't want to stack up against Michael. I liked both Alesi and Berger. They were both good fun and very, very good racing drivers; but the two of them together was a bad mix. Gerhard's primary objective was to beat Jean and there was a psychological battle between them, which is such a waste of energy in a race team. They had so much previous, you couldn't stop it.'

The colours of Benetton, so dominant with Schumacher at the wheel, with Brawn and Byrne an axis of excellence, and Briatore managing team affairs without fear of whom he offended, were doomed to lose their lustrous shine. Further bad news was waiting for Benetton down the road, too: Ferrari would be back for Brawn and Byrne.

An Act of Faith Panis Will Never Forget

Hill's victory in the final race of the 1995 season – the last Formula One race on the streets of Adelaide – somehow encapsulated a frustrating year. He had lapped every other driver at least twice in the Australian Grand Prix, yet caught the flight home aware that he had to substantially change his attitude if he was ever to get the better of Schumacher, a man demonstrating that he was destined for greatness. The following testimony from Hill may not be entirely focused on Monaco, but there is an intuitive truthfulness about the way that he probes his duel with Schumacher that warrants telling. 'I think I got ahead of myself in terms of working my rivalry with Michael,' said Hill. 'Michael was better at playing mind games. I wasn't quite as savvy, or quite as cunning as the way Michael and Benetton were in operating

Above: Irishman Derek Daly survived unscathed after becoming airborne in his Tyrrell at Sainte-Dévote at the start of the 1980 Grand Prix.

Below: Ayrton Senna navigating the Loews hairpin in first gear in 1987 when he claimed the first of a record six victories.

Each year, more and more yachts squeeze into the iconic Harbour for the Grand Prix, where VIP guests arrive to party.

Above: Joy: Ayrton Senna and Ron Dennis celebrate the 1992 Grand Prix triumph for McLaren – the team with a record fifteen wins at Monaco.

Below: Despair: Nigel Mansell drove himself to exhaustion in vain pursuit of Senna.

Casino de Monte-Carlo: a timeless backdrop to the Monaco Grand Prix.

Above: Olivier Panis jubilantly carries the French tricolour on his lap of honour in 1996, after creating the greatest shock in the history of the race.

Below: In 2001, Michael Schumacher gave Ferrari their most recent victory at Monaco.

Above: The Grid Girls of Monaco.

Below: Ross Brawn showered with champagne after Jenson Button and Rubens Barrichello provided a one-two in 2009 for Brawn GP. Brawn is associated with eight wins at Monaco.

Above: Nico Rosberg celebrating in 2013, the first of his three wins, to emulate the triumph of his father, Keke, thirty years before. The Rosbergs are the only father and son to have won the Monaco Grand Prix.

Below: Daniel Ricciardo's valiant effort for Red Bull in atrocious weather could not prevent Lewis Hamilton from triumphantly taking his second victory at Monaco in 2016.

Photographic evidence of why Monaco will eternally remain the jewel in F1's crown.

in this new era. As a team, Williams were very British, a team with a stiff upper lip, where you do your best and hope that is enough. We were up against a team that was more imaginative and one with more fluid thinkers. Michael was very difficult to beat – because he was so good. He could do stuff I couldn't dream of doing. Yet on my day, I could beat him, yeah. Unfortunately, the 1995 season was a case of getting kicked in the head by a bloke who is not only really good, but one who could expose my weakness to the press. That crushed me.

'I was *exposed* that year. I had to go away and lick my wounds . . . and work out what to do. That was all part of my education. I didn't start racing in Formula One with Williams until I was almost thirty-three – and you can't suggest my career path to anyone! So, I was on a very steep curve early in my career, but late in my life.'

Hill was not alone in leaving Adelaide with a great deal on his mind. Panis also caught a European-bound flight, concerned about what the future held for him. He had finished second in this Australian Grand Prix and received the gleeful gratitude of Ligier mechanics, who were delighted to be rewarded by a podium place at the end of a long, hard season. But when Panis looked around for Walkinshaw, the Scotsman was nowhere to be found. 'I was second in a car where the engine died at the sight of the flag, but when I come to the box, I am told Tom has already left to take the plane home. To finish second and for the guy to leave, this is something strange.'

Panis could not find any peace at home in France. He was hearing from influential friends at the heart of the Ligier team, including from highly placed personnel within title sponsors Gauloises, a French cigarette manufacturer, that his seat was under threat. Panis explained: 'I had heard that Tom wanted two English drivers. The boss of Gauloises Blondes was a good friend of mine and he told me that he would call him and let him know what he thought. He told me he said to Tom, "OK, Tom, no problem. If you don't want to keep Panis, don't keep him. But if you don't keep him, we go with him." Tom said that he was keeping me.' Panis paused, 'I know the politics now,' he said, smiling.

Regardless, Panis still wanted personal confirmation that he was integral to the team for 1996. 'It was the holidays, but in my mind I needed to speak to Tom,' he admitted. 'I called him and said that I would come to England to meet him. Tom said to me, "Why, Olivier? I am busy." I told him that it was important for us to meet to decide if I continue with Ligier next year or not. He wanted to know what had happened for me to feel this, but I said I would only talk with him face-to-face.'

Walkinshaw relented. 'I went to the manor of Tom,' he said. 'Tom's wife was from Belgium and she spoke French and made me feel more comfortable.' But the niceties of his visit had to give way to a harder conversation. Panis had questions that he wanted answered. 'I asked Tom, "One thing I don't understand is why is it for the whole year long you don't like me?" Tom replied, "Why do you say that?"'

It was not a dialogue Walkinshaw would have encouraged. He was much respected for his abilities within a racing team, but he had little time for sentiment or small talk. In contrast, Panis needed to feel he warranted support. 'I said to Tom that it was difficult for me to understand that when I did the podium in the last race he had left the track before I got back to the garage. Tom just told me he left because he had a business to take care of.' Panis tried to seek further reassurance from his boss, 'I said, "Tell me if you don't like me. I need to make my decision for next year. I spoke with Jordan already, and Sauber." Tom's response surprised me, yes. He said, "To be honest, I love you." ' Was Walkinshaw describing tough love? 'Exactly,' said the Frenchman. 'And I accept this is true, and we start 1996 together as Team Ligier.'

It was an act of faith that Panis will never, ever regret.

Olivier Panis, 1996

10

Hard Day's Night
at Ligier

Early 1996

The first time Panis drove his new Ligier JS43 in testing he sensed that it was a car that offered him an opportunity. 'The car was quick,' he said. But more specifically, he felt the Mugen-Honda engine could be teased and tuned to be a threat for one weekend in May. 'In my mind, I knew with this car it was possible to do something at Monaco.'

He relayed his feelings to Tenji Sakai, an engineer from Honda working inside the Ligier team. Effectively, Panis was telling Sakai that with an assiduously prepared engine the car could be in contention on the streets that Prost, Senna and Schumacher had dominated for the past dozen years, though Panis had no data to back up his ideas. 'I gave Tenji a hard time – "I want an engine like this, a throttle like this" – but I said, "If we do this, I tell you in Monaco we do a good thing. I am 100 per cent sure."' It might have sounded fanciful had he expressed such thoughts outside the tight-knit team around him at Ligier, but his enthusiasm was infectious and the challenge was accepted by Sakai as a matter of honour.

As the Monaco Grand Prix appeared on the horizon, Panis had even greater clarity. 'I told Tenji and the team, "Even if we lose top end from the engine I don't care, provided it is easy and smooth on the throttle."' In reality, the Ligier cars had many of the same characteristics as the Benetton-Renault cars, the world champions for the two previous seasons but now facing life without Schumacher. 'We developed some of our own aerodynamic package because the Mugen engine was not the same as the Renault,' said Panis. 'But our monocoque was the same as Benetton – fantastic, really.' Yet the season was barely three weeks old when Walkinshaw left Ligier along with operations director Tony Dowe and technical director Frank Dernie. Walkinshaw's TWR business had bought a controlling interest in the rival Arrows team. 'When Tom left I was disappointed,' admitted Panis. Flavio Briatore was now effectively in control of Ligier as well as Benetton. 'I had a good relationship with Flavio,' said the Frenchman. 'He was the first guy in Formula One to give me a contract – and if you do your job Flavio was easy to live with.'

Not everyone would agree with this sentiment, though. If Walkinshaw's departure was a setback to Briatore, there was another storm brewing at Benetton. Brawn was frustrated because the promises brokered with Briatore were not being honoured. He can distinctly recall how their union dissolved: 'When Michael left, I thought of what the team needed to make another step forward. I redefined my role in the team, my levels of responsibility. I sat down with Flavio, we wrote out a new contract, with a new role defined. You have to remember, in that team Flavio didn't run the factory – and Tom had moved away. I proposed to Flavio and to the

Benetton family that we needed a restructure of the engineering side. I was team principal de facto, in engineering. Flavio would still do the commercial side; I had no interest in that. That was all agreed.

'I went into 1996 with the new understanding of what my role was going to be. The problem was it wasn't supported. Flavio wouldn't announce it to the workforce. He refused to countenance the changes in the structure we needed to implement. I had a semi-perfect storm. I had lost Michael, I had two drivers that were a nightmare to deal with, and I had this new role I had been promised that wasn't happening.' Brawn's loyalty to Briatore and Benetton was exhausted. 'I was refusing to go to a race at one stage as they wouldn't address the issues I had,' he explained.

Before the Monaco Grand Prix, Schumacher's manager Willi Weber called Brawn, who remembers the conversation as being straightforward and to the point, with one pertinent question at its heart. 'Do you fancy coming to Ferrari?' Willi asked. Like Schumacher, Brawn found the lure of working for Ferrari too seductive to turn down. He agreed to the proposal of a meeting with Jean Todt. Then Brawn told Briatore that he wanted to be released from Benetton.

'I went to Flavio and said, "You have not respected my contract, and I have taken advice and consider I am free of contract." Flavio went into recovery mode and told me I could have whatever I wanted. I responded by telling him that he was only doing this because I was pushing an arm up his back, not because he believed that is what should be done. To me, that meant the chances of success would be minimalised.'

According to the account in the book *Formula Ferrari*: 'Todt met with Brawn for the first time in May in Monaco and the deal was done over the next few months.'

Monaco: 16–18 May 1996

Hill had won four of the first five races of the season – in Australia, Brazil, Argentina and San Marino – by the time the Formula One caravan reached Monaco. The other race – at Nürburgring – had been claimed by his Williams team-mate Jacques Villeneuve, the replacement for Coulthard, who had been signed by McLaren. Schumacher had been on the podium three times for Ferrari. In other news, Panis had finished seventh in Australia, sixth in Brazil and eighth in Argentina, had crashed at Nürburgring and retired through engine failure at San Marino.

For Hill, it was unclear whether it was a bonus or a burden to know that every driver to have won the first race of the season since 1990 had gone on to become world champion: Senna, twice; Mansell; Prost; and Schumacher, twice. After two years' intensive rivalry with Schumacher, he was battle-hardened and determined to seize whatever opportunities arose. His win in Brazil was the fifteenth of his career – one more than his father achieved. Hill once told me in the days when he was a headline act: 'Every driver's first responsibility is to himself. When I am in the car I want to beat every other bastard there. That doesn't mean when I am out of the car I hate everyone's guts. I don't. I just don't want to lose to them. That's the ethos of sport, isn't it?'

His desire to win at Monaco ran deep; his desire to be world champion ran deeper still. He was prepared for the peculiar distractions ahead, though. 'For people who worked in the pits, it's hell,' said Hill. 'The pit lane was never meant to be used this way, simply because it is part of a promenade for fifty-one weeks of the year. Then there is the noise. It is incessant and very loud, even by the standards we are accustomed to. The sound of the cars echoes through the streets, bounces off the buildings and the cliff face and comes at you from all directions. It is necessary to shout and this can wear on your nerves.'

Qualifying on Thursday was never more than an hors d'oeuvre to the main course, while, as ever, Friday was a time for technical staff and mechanics to reflect and make any improvements they could, and for sponsors to make claims on the drivers. The action that mattered took place mid-afternoon on Saturday in the second qualifying session. Thousands of Ferrari fans had travelled from neighbouring Italy and countries from across Europe to pay homage to Schumacher. His fight with Hill was to be central to the hour-long dispute for pole position. In contrast, Panis conducted his business without drawing much scrutiny. His speed was evident, however. 'On my first set of new tyres in qualifying on Saturday I was in the top five,' he said. His optimism did not last long. 'On the second set, I got a misfire. I was really pissed off.'

Panis returned to the pits in the hope his engineers could find a solution. They could not. His team-mate, Pedro Diniz, fared worse: he crashed. The Brazilian hurried back to the garage to get the team's spare car to make a fresh attempt. 'My engineers were still thinking maybe they could find the problem with my car,' said Panis, a bystander with a vested interest in the activity within the Ligier pits. 'I was pissed off, as I was sure I would qualify in the top five.' Without a resolution to the issue, it became apparent that Panis would need the spare car to improve his own grid position, but then fate dealt him another bad hand. 'By the time we decided to call Pedro to come back for me to have the T-car . . . Pedro crashed. Bang! That was it. I was in fourteenth place on the grid.' This was not the scenario Panis had envisaged when he was diligently trying to find an engine and chassis combination to mount a successful assault at Monaco. No one had ever won at Monaco from further back than eighth on the grid – a feat achieved by another Frenchman, Maurice Trintignant, in 1955, in the Bronze Age of Formula One. Panis admitted his emotions got the better of them. 'I said, "We are fucked!" Tenji was crying.'

At the time, each driver was permitted twelve laps in qualifying. Team strategists tried as best as they could to find a gap in the traffic for drivers to exploit. Unlike today, it was an inexact science; there were no real-time traffic indicators monitoring the patterns of rival teams on a raft of computers back at the headquarters of the teams. Drivers prepared themselves by withdrawing into a world of silence. At Benetton, Alesi sat in a chair in the garage, holding his head in his hands. At McLaren, Häkkinen disappeared from the prying lenses of cameramen beneath a white towel. Schumacher preferred to sit in his car at the end of a run and wait for tyres to be changed and data to be inspected before contemplating another lap. He had been reminded in the morning practice session of the capricious nature of these streets when he approached Sainte-Dévote too fast and hit a barrier head-on. Schumacher had been lucky: the only damage his Ferrari sustained was to the nose box of the car, a part easily replaced. Obviously, the incident did not slow him down in the qualifying itself. Nothing ever did, of course.

John Watson, a winner of five Grand Prix races and in 1996 a commentator for the Eurosport network, said of Schumacher's uncompromising attack during qualifying: 'Michael is on the outer edge of grip locking up wheels all round the circuit.' Hill was driving as hard, but with less dramatic effect, his Williams darting between the Armco. 'If you could have got a wafer between Damon's car and a barrier that would have been a miracle,' commented Watson. Williams had not won at Monaco since 1983, when Keke Rosberg triumphed after starting from fifth place on the grid on slick tyres on a wet track. Then thirty-five, he was also the reigning world champion, and that weekend was seriously debilitated by a virus. At the Williams garage, waiting to congratulate him, was a young Ross Brawn. 'I was the eleventh person to be employed by Williams,' said Brawn, who spent a total of seven years with the team. 'I was a mechanic, machinist and even drove the truck sometimes.' When Rosberg won, Brawn was running the Research and Development Department. 'That was a great opportunity in an environment where you could prove your ability instead of being dependent on your academic ability. I didn't have a lot of qualifications in that arena. I had an ONC as a mechanical engineer, but I didn't have an engineering degree. I had no knowledge of aerodynamics, apart from what I picked up as a hobbyist.

'I was keen on model aircraft and I did a lot of private study on fluid dynamics and aerodynamics because I was interested. I was lucky because Williams were testing in the wind tunnel at Imperial College, London, and Professor John Harvey and Professor Peter Bearman took me under their wing. They gave me a hairy-arsed education in aerodynamics – which was all that was needed in Formula One in those days. The one-eyed man is king in the land of the blind, as they say. I was in the wind tunnel on a regular basis. Then, with a team, I built the Williams wind tunnel. They were probably the only team to own their own wind tunnel at that stage. It was a reconditioned tunnel, but was still clever forward-planning by Frank and Patrick. It would be laughed at now, but no one else had anything like it so we were ahead of the game. In seven years, Williams went from eleven people working for the team to two hundred. It was a pretty rapid expansion. I really enjoyed those years.'

At heart, Brawn describes himself first and foremost as an

engineer. He is being disingenuous, because he was so much more than that: team principal, arch-strategist, trusted confidant of the drivers, technical wizard and team owner. For all his success – eight Drivers' Championships and eight Constructors' Championships – Brawn admits to relishing his earliest years at Monaco with Williams. 'It was a marvellous place for engineers. You could walk up and down the pit lane and see the cars properly,' he said. 'It was typical for teams to have tame photographers taking pictures of other team's cars. To fight espionage, you did your best to cover everything up. But mechanics had to service the car between practice sessions – and that was a great time to take photographs of the inside of other people's gearboxes because they would make ratio changes between P1 and P2. You'd have a great chance to see what was going on inside the innards of their gearbox. It was all de rigueur. You had to service your cars and take photographs of other people servicing their cars! You trained your mechanics to try and keep stuff hidden, but in a pit lane like that at Monaco it was almost impossible.'

In 1996, Brawn was a marginalised figure at Benetton as Hill tried to take the pole position that would give him, he imagined, a better hope of providing Williams with a victory at Monaco, the first after Rosberg's triumph thirteen years earlier. Hill found a clear road – and he placed his Williams on provisional pole with a time of 1 minute, 20.866 seconds. The clock was rapidly counting down to the end of qualifying when Schumacher reappeared in his Ferrari. His first flying lap was good enough to steal the pole from Hill, but his second was even faster: 1 minute, 20.372 seconds. It is one of motor racing's truisms: there is only one place that you can gain time in that quantity at Monaco, and that is from the driver. 'Michael was fantastic and confirmed he is the master of this track,' beamed Todt. Little wonder at the excitement within

Ferrari, as the team had not tasted the victor's champagne at Monaco since Gilles Villeneuve won in 1981 – a preposterously long drought for the best-funded and best-resourced company in the Formula One paddock.

Hill absorbed the disappointing news from the data available to him in the Williams pit. He was still computing how Schumacher had gone almost half a second faster as the German drove a lap of honour and waved to the legions of Ferrari fans around the circuit. Schumacher was still in showboating mode when Berger, on a last-minute qualifying mission, arrived at high speed behind him on the exit from the tunnel. Berger slammed on the brakes of his Benetton to avoid what would have been a violent collision and passed Schumacher travelling backwards after a spin took him out of harm's way. An infuriated Berger returned to the pit lane to voice his disapproval at race control. Schumacher's defence was that he thought the session had ended. His offer to apologise to Berger closed the incident and he would start the race the following day from pole position, with Hill sharing the front row.

In the Ligier garage, Panis realised he had a duty to raise morale as mechanics and engineers, his friends, toiled to resolve the riddle of his misfiring car. 'I went round the mechanics and said, "We can still finish on the podium,"' he told me. 'I saw looks from them that said, *This guy is nice, but he is fucking crazy.*' The work continued into the night. Panis stayed as a mark of solidarity to Sakai, and the Ligier crew led by Paolo Catone and André de Cortanze. 'Around 9.30 p.m. my wife called,' said Panis. 'She said that we had a dinner to attend and it was clear she was upset. But Anne was used to me being first at the circuit and the last to leave.' By this time, there was not much more Panis could do and he left to meet Anne at the Beach Plaza Hotel, along the promenade from Portier. All Panis could do to console himself before turning the lights out that night was to convince himself sunrise would be accompanied by a new dawn of opportunity.

1. Michael Schumacher (Ferrari)	1:20.356
2. Damon Hill (Williams-Renault)	1:20.866
3. Jean Alesi (Benetton-Renault)	1:20.918
4. Gerhard Berger (Benetton-Renault)	1:21.067
5. David Coulthard (McLaren-Mercedes)	1:21.460
6. Rubens Barrichello (Jordan-Peugeot)	1:21.504
7. Eddie Irvine (Ferrari)	1:21.542
8. Mika Häkkinen (McLaren-Mercedes)	1:21.688
9. Heinz-Harald Frentzen (Sauber-Ford)	1:21.929
10. Jacques Villeneuve (Williams-Renault)	1:21.963
11. Mika Salo (Tyrrell-Yamaha)	1:22.235
12. Jos Verstappen (Footwork-Hart)	1:22.327
13. Johnny Herbert (Sauber-Ford)	1:22.346
14. Olivier Panis (Ligier Mugen-Honda)	1:22.358
15. Ukyo Katayama (Tyrell-Yamaha)	1:22.460
16. Martin Brundle (Jordan-Peugeot)	1:22.519
17. Pedro Diniz (Ligier Mugen-Honda)	1:22.682
18. Giancarlo Fisichella (Minardi-Ford)	1:22.684
19. Pedro Lamy (Minardi-Ford)	1:23.350
20. Ricardo Rosset (Footwork-Hart)	1:24.976
21. Luca Badoer (Forti-Ford)	1:25.059
22. Andrea Montermini (Forti-Ford)	1:25.393

Olivier Panis, Winner, 1996

11

Panis: History Man

19 May 1996: Race Day

Even before he had drawn back the curtains in their hotel room to greet the new day, Panis felt emboldened by a good night's sleep. 'I woke so confident,' said Panis. 'I told Anne that I thought I would finish on the podium.' Had Panis slept the sleep of the innocent or the deluded? Possibly both, it appeared.

When he looked out of the window and watched the falling rain drench the Mediterranean landscape his mood brightened, in stark contrast to the dull and grey weather. 'I saw the rain and I was more convinced than ever that I could be on the podium,' said Panis. 'I thought the weather was my ally and there was a chance to seize, really.' Anne was sceptical, as befits someone who understood the reality of her husband's position. 'You know where you are starting,' she reminded him, kindly. 'And in Monaco everyone knows you can't overtake.' Twenty years later, Panis smiled at the memory of what, in so many ways, had been a surreal conversation. 'Anne took me for a crazy man!'

When Panis arrived at the pits, the mood within the Ligier garage was buzzing. The engineers and mechanics' late-night work had reaped a rich dividend. The Mugen-Honda engine in the rear of his car was now making the kind of full-throated roar that was music to Panis's ears. In the traditional morning warm-up – which was dry – Panis recorded the fastest time. Faster than Schumacher, faster than Hill, and faster than the Benettons of Alesi and Berger. 'I was so happy for all the mechanics and engineers, as I felt so confident with this car,' said Panis. Rivals scornfully dismissed his performance as an illusion created by running with a light fuel load; they had been testing the balance of their cars with full or almost full tanks. 'Some people said we were fastest because we did not have the same fuel – but I didn't care,' said Panis. He felt relaxed, untroubled and excited by the challenge of the afternoon ahead.

Then it started to rain again. It rained so hard, drowning the streets, that the Porsche Supercup race, part of the support programme for the Grand Prix, had to be stopped. It also meant another headache for the organisers. Under F1 rules, if there is rain after a totally dry warm-up a further fifteen minutes' practice has to be scheduled to enable teams to trial their cars and make adjustments for a wet-weather race. Charlie Whiting, the FIA Technical Delegate, who was charged for the first time to start the Monaco Grand Prix, was less than enamoured with that regulation. 'A second warm-up was a complete pain the arse,' said Whiting. 'My argument is this: you don't stop the race if it starts dry and becomes wet so that the drivers can have a wet practice session, do you? You just get on with it.' Sunday morning warm-up disappeared altogether from 2003, but there was an obligation from the regulations to allow the drivers an acclimatisation practice that was held between 1.15 and 1.30 p.m. on this miserable afternoon in motor-racing paradise.

Some drivers explored the limit of the track with a greater appetite than others. None more so than Häkkinen. He was lapping close to two seconds a lap faster than anyone else when he crashed with violent repercussions – for his McLaren – at Tabac. Dave Redding, who was the number-one mechanic on Häkkinen's car, was dispatched by team manager Dave Ryan to assess the damage. Redding was picking his way through the scaffolding of the grandstand in order to get to the wreckage when Ryan came on his radio link.

'Dave wanted to know if we could use the car for the race or not,' said Redding. 'He was specific: "You need to be 100 per cent certain that we can't use the car." I told him, "I am . . . I can see the fuel cell." There was silence. Then Dave asked, "Did you say the fuel cell?" I confirmed that's what I said. Which meant the car, figuratively, was broken in two. That was an easy one to decide!'

Redding and other McLaren mechanics then had to hastily reconfigure the spare McLaren car, set up for Coulthard, for the use of Häkkinen in the race. 'Drivers have different front suspension set-ups, so to get the T-car ready for the race was a bit of a scene,' admitted Redding. 'It was full-on . . . and working outside in the rain. It was filthy, but all part of the unique fun of Monaco.'

Panis had been far more conservative during this wet-weather session. 'I didn't do a lot of laps,' he said. He used the time he was on the track as a useful reconnaissance, but he was not prepared to put his car under unnecessary exposure to such conditions ahead of the Grand Prix. 'I liked racing in the wet, so I thought, "Maybe it is raining for me because the weather gods want to help me because of the troubles I had on Saturday,"' said Panis. 'I knew, from all our tests, that the engine would be good in the wet. I was just so confident.' Nevertheless, Panis was still fourteenth on the grid, still a huge distance away from Schumacher's Ferrari on pole, on a circuit where opportunities to overtake are at a premium. At least, he thought, the rain was his friend. For rain meant that nothing, but nothing, was guaranteed. Rain created uncertainty, and for a racing driver looking to negotiate a passage from fourteenth position on the grid at Monaco, with its claustrophobic streets, and steel-clad perimeter, this was manna from heaven.

Intelligently, Coulthard had been much more circumspect during the warm-up than his team-mate, Häkkinen. 'It was so slippery,' he reported. 'I never went 100 per cent on the throttle once – not on the start–finish straight, not through the tunnel. I just couldn't get 100 per cent power, as the car was undriveable if you did. We were all in a bit of a flat-spin with the conditions. In those days, they did not grind off the white lines on the streets as they do now. If you touched a white line, it was like driving on ice. Mika's crash showed how difficult it was.'

Coulthard had a peculiar problem of his own to overcome. 'I was in a panic with my helmet,' he said. 'My visor was misting badly, which was possibly because I was hyperventilating!' His humour disguised an issue of genuine concern. It is virtually impossible to see anything driving in the spray of a car ahead, so imagine what it must be like when what little vision you have is obscured by a fogged visor.

Brundle once described driving a Formula One car in the rain to me in graphic detail: 'Blind people will tell you that other senses are developed and I can understand that. Momentarily, your hearing, your peripheral vision, is heightened driving in the rain; in fact, your whole sense of alertness is heightened. You are mostly listening for the guy in front, listening for him to lift off the throttle. It's hard. It's worse than driving your road car in thick fog, when roundabouts and corners come up and surprise you even when you know the road really intimately. I've known occasions in a racing car when you can't see your own steering wheel, let alone your dashboard – never mind the guy in front. Then you get the weird thing when everyone starts slowing down, because you know roughly where the next corner is. Then the spray reduces, and you see there is still 200 metres to the braking point and you all get back on the throttle. That's when you really earn your money.'

At Monaco, the lack of grip on a circuit contaminated by everyday traffic added to the complexity of racing in the wet. For Coulthard, the solution to his particular dilemma was found by asking a favour of Schumacher. 'We were both Marlboro drivers,' explained Coulthard. 'And I knew that Bell – a manufacturer of crash helmets – had a double-visor system, so I asked Michael if I could borrow one of his Bell helmets. He readily agreed. We just covered over the decals of his personal sponsors. He allowed me to keep the helmet. Michael and I were always hot and cold in terms of our relationship. Yet there was an underlying respect – I certainly respected him.'

Only one driver fell totally foul of the weather in this warm-up. While Pedro Lamy, Pedro Diniz and Giancarlo Fisichella all had gut-wrenching excursions, only Andrea Montermini excluded himself from the race. He totalled his Forti-Ford after he came out of the tunnel, and the team did not have a spare car. With his exclusion, twenty-one cars would start the 1996 Monaco Grand Prix. No one then could have accurately predicted just how many – or how few – would take the chequered flag.

Only Verstappen, who was twelfth on the grid, opted to risk starting on slick tyres; everyone else chose to run on the wet-weather compound. Like a man gambling the last of his chips on the blackjack table in the Casino de Monte-Carlo,

Verstappen felt he had nothing to lose. It was twist or bust. Calculations were much more complex for most drivers and teams. If the track remained wet for much of the race, or at best only partially dry, drivers would be unlikely to complete the scheduled seventy-eight laps and therefore would race for two hours, the maximum time allowed for a Grand Prix. On a wet track, top speed in each gear was estimated to be around 20mph slower than in the dry. This posed an extra dimension for teams to ponder: was it worth running on full fuel, slowing a car early in the race, to eliminate the need for a refuelling stop? Panis and Ligier thought it was. Of course, they kept this information to themselves.

As the cars weaved their way around the circuit on the formation lap, Schumacher controlled the pace of the cars behind him, as he was entitled to do. It was apparent that all the drivers were seeking to find grip on the wet streets, now more treacherous than usual. And it was just as apparent, during the journey back to their grid positions, that grip was in short supply.

This was the first year the FIA had brought their own set of standard lights to start the Monaco Grand Prix, a far cry from the long-ago days when it began with a man at the front of the grid waving a green flag before darting to the edge of the circuit for safety. 'What would have happened if he had tripped trying to get out of the way? It's unthinkable,' Whiting said, smiling. 'For this Monaco Grand Prix, it was the first time we had the system where five lights came on one by one and then go out in unison, as they still do today. We placed the lights on the far side of the circuit, opposite Race Control and the pits, so that the drivers round the bend towards the back of the grid could see them. I have spoken to a couple of drivers in the past who said that they could not see them.' Helpfully, Whiting had an answer for them. 'I told them, "Go when the others go." ' Whiting's droll sense of humour has served him well down the years, although some years later another set of these 'repeat' lights were installed between the sixth and seventh rows of the grid to make them more easily visible to the cars positioned at the rear of the field.

At Monaco, experience tells us that the rush to funnel through Sainte-Dévote makes it a habitual black spot. It is a rare opportunity to gain a place or two; it is also an accident waiting to happen. The sense of anticipation before the start of any Grand Prix is immense. Yet it somehow seems to be greater at Monaco. The apartment blocks towering alongside the circuit, their balconies crammed with people, make the start grid seem like a stage at a theatre. The noise of the engines at full throttle is amplified, as the sound reverberates from the buildings without relief. The appreciation of the teams, of the spectators, of the hundreds of millions of armchair fans, that there is so little room for so many cars to reside in harmony at such high speed on these streets underscores for the audience the realisation of the dangers ahead for the greatest drivers of their generation.

Then there is history to contend with. Murray Walker articulated the stakes in play as well as anyone when he told BBC viewers: 'You get no more points for winning at Monaco, but you get more publicity and prestige than for all the other races put together. Because Monaco is a unique challenge. Because Monaco is pressure all the way. Because one false move gets you into trouble.' And he might have added: *Because winning Monaco is a life-changing experience.*

So we watched in silent vigil as the five lights beside the track were turned on . . . one by one. Then waited – as the drivers waited, their engines screaming close to the rev limit – for the moment Whiting turned them off. It is fair to speculate that few would have been watching how Panis drove off the line on the outside of the seventh row, on the far horizon of the grid, apart from the Ligier crew and his wife. Yet before this afternoon was over, the 29-year-old Frenchman was going to be central to the story of a remarkable Grand Prix, a Grand Prix unlikely to be replicated.

Naturally, at the start of the race most eyes were focused on the front row. When Whiting turned off the red lights, Schumacher clawed his Ferrari from the line. Alongside him, Hill had a palpably cleaner start. His Williams was moving smoothly while Schumacher's Ferrari fought to gain momentum, real momentum. In a flash of time too minuscule to measure, Schumacher would have seen Hill in his left-hand mirror, getting closer, then in the next moment Hill drove past and Schumacher would have been overwhelmed by a sense of impotence. There was nothing the German maestro, winner of the previous two Monaco Grand Prix races, winner of the previous two world championships, could do other than to acquiesce and follow the British driver obediently through Sainte-Dévote. Instantly Schumacher's race strategy had been compromised. Instantly Hill's chances of winning the race had improved incalculably.

To lead at Monaco is to have command of your own destiny. Hill was clear of mind and clear of purpose as he told me: 'I wasn't thinking, "I have to get Michael." I was thinking, "I have to get to Sainte-Dévote first." Once I was past there, I knew I was gone.' I have left the profanities in what follows from Hill, not to embarrass him in any way, because Hill is as articulate and as thoughtful as any sportsman I have encountered in four decades of reporting from arenas around the world, but because they illuminate the intensity of the emotions he felt racing a motor car on these streets. 'Monaco is fucking intimidating. It is like getting in a ring with a bloke who is going to hit you; then any moment he is going to hit you harder. Can I blow my own trumpet a bit? I was fucking good in the wet – really good. When I was young I rode motor-bikes in fields, doing trials and stuff. That was all about understanding traction – getting tyres to grip in the mud and slime. It's where I learned clutch control, throttle control. It's something I have a good feel for.'

Verstappen was the first casualty, the turn of the cards pitching him out of the race at Sainte-Dévote. Fisichella did not get much further, as his Minardi and that of his team-mate Lamy pitched into one another, to the infuriation of Gian-carlo Minardi. However, what happened next was totally unexpected. After running through the Loews hairpin behind Hill, Schumacher lost control of the rear end of his Ferrari as he turned right to make the short dart to Portier, the gateway to the tunnel. In desperation, Schumacher piled on opposite lock, but he could not prevent his Ferrari from smacking the barrier with his left front wheel. The wheel collapsed, along with Schumacher's afternoon. He managed to get his Ferrari down an escape road before a marshal came to check if he was hurt. Only his vanity was pained, as he unfastened his steer-ing wheel and climbed disconsolately out of his car. The cause of the accident: driver error. Had Schumacher been pushing too hard because he had surrendered the lead to Hill at Sainte-Dévote? It is a reasonable question, yet one fact was indisputable: even the finest drivers were vulnerable in such atrocious conditions.

When Panis passed Schumacher's stricken car, he was reminded that an element of caution was advisable. 'I was cruising in the wet,' said Panis. 'I felt the cars ahead had slowed too much, that they weren't pushing. When I saw the Ferrari, I said to myself, "Careful, Olivier. If you are too confi-dent you will risk a crash." When I saw Michael, I thought, "This is an example of what can happen."' Like Verstappen,

223

Fisichella, Lamy and Schumacher, Barrichello also failed to survive the first lap, having planted his Jordan backwards into a barrier before Rascasse. It was a remarkable casualty rate, by any standards.

Some historical context is perhaps helpful here. At Monaco thirty years earlier, in the first race for the new three-litre engine cars, just four of the sixteen drivers who started the race were classified as having finished it. It was won by Stewart in a BRM. Behind him came Bandini (Ferrari), then Graham Hill and Bob Bondurant, who were also driving BRM cars. Some of the stars who failed to complete the race included Jim Clark, Jack Brabham, John Surtees, Jochen Rindt, Denny Hulme and Bruce McLaren, but these drivers all fell victim to mechanical gremlins, not accidents. Some sessions of this Grand Prix were filmed for the movie *Grand Prix*. Fourteen years later, in 1980, the drama at Monaco centred on a collision in the midfield between Derek Daly's Tyrrell and an Alfa Romeo driven by Bruno Giacomelli on the race into Sainte-Dévote. It was an accident with frightening-looking consequences, as Daly's car became airborne before landing between that of his team-mate, Jean-Pierre Jarier, and Prost. Mercifully, no one was hurt, but all four drivers retired on the spot. Later in the Grand Prix, René Arnoux, Didier Pironi and Elio de Angelis also crashed, and just eight cars were still running at the end.

But events in 1996 took the race to a new dimension. At the end of the first lap the order read: Hill, Alesi, Berger, Irvine, Frentzen, Coulthard, Villeneuve, Salo, Herbert, Häkkinen, Brundle, Panis, Katayama, Badoer, Rosset and Diniz. Hill's second passage through Portier allowed him to get a glimpse of an abandoned Ferrari – and he knew that the threat from Schumacher had been removed. 'I admit it made me feel a lot better in my car,' said Hill. 'All that stuff about Michael being invincible, you kind of go, well, he is just human like the rest of us. But if anyone was going to be a threat in the race, it would have been him, so that lifted a bit of pressure. There is the absolute heaven of leading the Monaco Grand Prix. Apart from anything else, how many people can say they have done that? The Williams was the best car that year, no doubt about that. So I had the luxury of that. But I also knew that leading the race was one thing, but getting to the end in front was another.' Hill set the fastest lap of the race on the third lap: 1:49.608. The slowness of that time reflected how difficult it was to get traction, but, for all that, Hill was placing mist-enshrouded daylight between him and everyone else. His lead was already over ten seconds.

Katayama was the next to crash, on lap 2. By now, Irvine was responsible for a line of traffic forming behind him, and Frentzen's frustration at being unable to pass was testing his patience to the limit. It was precisely as Lauda had claimed when he told me: 'If you know what you are doing here, there can be a car behind you that is five seconds faster and he can never pass you as long as you accelerate properly past the swimming pool, as long as you come out of the tunnel at top speed and stay in the middle of the road.'

Rosset was all alone when his race ended in the same igno-minious fashion as Barrichello's: by sliding backwards into the Armco at the left-hand corner before Rascasse. Pedro Diniz was ejected from this mayhem when his transmission failed in the second Ligier. The cranes stationed to pluck stricken cars out of harm's way were doing sterling business. With five laps gone, only thirteen cars remained. Hill's progress was smooth and unhindered. He was driving two seconds a lap faster than the Benettons of Alesi and Berger, as though he were on rails. Irvine continued to occupy fourth place, but at times Frentzen was so close to the rear of his Ferrari that he might conceivably have been on the end of a tow rope. At this stage, Brundle had Panis for close company; they were squabbling for twelfth position.

At last! Panis became the first driver to actually complete an overtaking manoeuvre as he expertly passed Brundle on the exit of Rascasse on the seventh lap. 'You used to come out of Rascasse and your inside rear wheel would always spin,' said Brundle. 'I have this clear memory of Panis coming past me. Whatever they had done on that Ligier, Panis came out of Rascasse and got alongside me with some tremendous traction and he was through.' Panis was clear-headed, and demanding more of himself with each passing lap. 'I am in traffic and not thinking about Hill, he has disappeared,' said the Frenchman, reliving the moment in Paris in 2016. He was unable to receive information over his radio as the reception, not good at the best of times at Monaco, was almost non-existent. He was dependent on reading his pit board, hanging over a wall on the start–finish straight, to establish the distance between him and the car in front. In actual fact, such was the closeness of the racing that he could almost tell for himself. 'I thought I had to overtake the maximum number of cars in the wet because this was when I was more competitive,' explained Panis. His next target was nearly under the nose cone of his Ligier: Häkkinen.

Hill was ever more in a race of his own: his lead over Alesi after eight laps stretched to over fifteen seconds. But there was another element for the drivers to factor in now: the circuit was slowly, slowly drying out. Soon the teams would have to choose the optimum moment to switch from rain tyres to slicks, but for the present Irvine's proficiency at keeping Frentzen behind him, and subsequently a line of other drivers in check, was commanding the narrative. Frentzen was exploring ways to pass the Ulsterman, at Loews, or on the approach to Tabac, or through the swimming-pool section, without fazing the Ferrari driver for a second. Irvine's Ferrari must have looked the width of a coach to Frentzen as he weaved one way in his Sauber, then another, trying to draw a mistake from Irvine without success.

On lap 11, Berger drove into the pits, surrendering third place to Irvine. Seconds ticked away and Berger sat in his car, shaking his head. He waited for instructions to leave, then seemed to stall the engine. It did not matter, for the Austrian knew – and the Benetton engineers knew – that the car was not going any further. 'It was a gearbox problem,' said Berger. 'Everything was under control, it was a shame.' He was the tenth retirement. At the rear of the race, Panis was now in tenth position, with Brundle eleventh and Badoer a long way back in twelfth and last place. Hill soon lapped Badoer. And his lead over third-placed Irvine was fifty-two seconds and counting.

Little wonder Frentzen felt he had stalked Irvine for long enough. Regrettably, his move to attempt to pass the Ferrari driver proved to be an injudicious one – as perhaps it was always going to be. On the eighteenth lap, Frentzen, slipping and sliding under acceleration, struck the front wing of his Sauber against the Ferrari before braking for Sainte-Dévote. Frentzen's car was damaged, and this allowed Coulthard to steal fourth place as he overtook the lame Sauber and powered uphill towards Casino Square. Frentzen's next stop would be a visit to the pits. Behind them, Panis had skilfully and successfully passed Häkkinen's McLaren to claim eighth place. He had the distinction of being the only driver to have overtaken a rival during the race, not once, but twice. After twenty laps the order was: Hill, Alesi, Irvine, Coulthard, Villeneuve, Salo, Herbert, Panis, Häkkinen, Brundle.

Panis was now thinking of how best to profit further. 'I felt the rain tyres were going away,' he said. 'I started to think of taking a gamble. I called the team and asked them to tell me when the first driver pits for slicks, then to tell me the lap time he does.' With his huge lead, it was Hill who swivelled right into the pits at the end of the twenty-eighth lap.

'People who haven't experienced this may not understand, but once you have wet-weather tyres on a dry track you cannot put the power down,' said Hill. 'I think it was the team's call, but I thought it was precisely the right moment. Put it this way, if the team had said "come in" and I didn't think it was right, I would have said something. Only three years before we had broken the record for the number of pit stops for tyre changes at Donington and were blown away by Senna and McLaren.' Each time Hill and Prost stopped during that European Grand Prix, they had to return with ridiculous monotony as the tyre swap had proved to be the wrong one. This time Hill knew from the moment that he drove up the hill towards Massenet and Casino Square, behind the new race leader Alesi, who was still on wet-weather tyres, that Williams had played a master stroke with his support. Williams refuelled Hill's car, too. He was scheduled to run now to the end of the race.

Once Panis had the news of Hill's pit stop, he called his engineer. 'I am coming into the box,' he said. Panis pulled up at his pit just as Irvine left the Ferrari box to rejoin the race on slick tyres. The Frenchman ripped a tear-off visor from his helmet and threw it across the pit lane as his mechanics changed his tyres. He pulled away without a hitch. Panis did not plan to stop again. Ahead, Hill picked off Alesi, who was lapping at close to ten seconds slower than the Williams driver as they headed at full throttle uphill towards Casino Square.

After the round of pit stops had been completed, Panis had catapulted forward to fourth place. 'Our stop was fantastic timing and a fantastic stop,' he said. No wonder he was ecstatic. Through his due diligence to the conditions, and the smart work of the Ligier pit crew, Panis had overtaken Coulthard, Villeneuve, Salo and Herbert. The order of those in position to score world championship points – just six in those days – looked like this after thirty laps: Hill, Alesi, Irvine, Panis, Coulthard and Herbert.

Coulthard was the least content. He felt he had been unreasonably let down by McLaren. 'It was a fuck-up of fuck-ups,' said Coulthard. 'As the track was drying, with Mika behind me on the road, I wanted to come in. Ron wasn't sure it was the right time to come in, or something, so they gave priority to Mika to pit. So Mika pitted and I had to do another lap on the wet-weather tyres. By the time I went round and came in to put slicks on, Olivier came from behind me to be in front. That was it – I never could get back to him. My recollection is that we gave that win away because the team pitted Mika first, in spite of me being ahead of him on the track. It was a missed opportunity. One of the things I have never understood about Formula One is that there is one pit box for two cars. In America you have a pit box for each car. In our sport they go on about saving the planet with all the new technology, but there are some fundamentals that would make the racing better. One is to let each driver have his own pit crew, and pit box, then you would get some really good inter-team battles. But the powers that be just go, "No, we don't do that in Formula One." '

Brundle was another man who would argue that this race of intrigue and high drama, of suspense and calamity, had been ruined unnecessarily. Only he had to accept culpability. He had barely returned to the circuit on slicks, filled with confidence that he could place himself in the mix at the front of the race, when he drove too hard into the left-hand entrance into Casino Square. He lost control of the Jordan and it pirouetted backwards into the Armco on the opposite side of the track, passing the Hotel de Paris in the wrong direction before finally parking on a zebra crossing facing the Casino. 'We made a brilliant call to pit for slicks, just perfect,' lamented Brundle. 'I just pushed too hard once I got up to speed. There was a wet patch in the shadow of the Hotel de Paris. I got a swapper – where the back of the car trades places with the front – and just touched the barrier and dropped the engine. The car was virtually undamaged. It was my fault – I was angry at myself.'

Brundle stayed where he had crashed, watching much of the remainder of the race as an irritated spectator. 'I have a memory of standing in front of the grandstand at Casino Square,' he said. 'It was one of those races where it looked like anyone could win. But to be honest, being a selfish racing driver, I would have been thinking at all times, "What an idiot."' Brundle, who never raced at Monaco again, instead migrating at the end of the season to a new and hugely successful career in broadcasting, added: 'I looked at where Ollie was and thought, "That's where I could have been." It is to take nothing away from him, though. Ollie had a great car and he drove it very well.'

Panis's immediate concern was precisely the one that had proved Frentzen's downfall. How do you get past Irvine? Only the racing line was dry enough to trust, and Irvine knew that while he kept to the line Panis could do little other than stick as close as he could to the Ferrari's gearbox. Irvine did not need to stop again either. Another fact: after one hour of racing, Hill had completed thirty-four laps, which meant that this Monaco Grand Prix would run for two hours rather than the scheduled seventy-eight laps. And Panis had established himself as the fastest driver, with a lap of just over one minute, twenty-eight seconds.

In the BBC broadcast truck, near the harbour entrance, Formula One editor Mark Wilkin was monitoring the race with the sense that Hill's drive was going to command a spot on the *Nine O'Clock News*. 'At that stage, I was planning how to close the show and thinking about what we were going to get from Damon,' he said. 'All that stuff is going through your mind. We were also trying to calculate how many laps the race would go. You think back now and see how little information we had in 1996. Today for Channel 4 we have a driver tracker to see where all the cars are in real time. We can see where the cars are going to come out after a pit stop. That is crucially important to read the race, to understand the strategies. I am in the ear of the commentators, telling them what I can see. Journalist Tony Dodgins is in the commentary box, keeping a lap chart and looking at what he can see. Karun Chandhok, a former driver, is in the pits and we are all talking to each other to make sense of the unfolding race. In '96, what we saw was on the screen and the viewers got what we got. With Damon that far ahead, there was never a point where Panis looked likely to win.'

Panis was dealing with his own calculations as the drama intensified, a member of the supporting cast being beckoned to claim centre stage. With the knowledge that he had such raw speed at his disposal, Panis recognised that he could not dither too long behind Irvine. On lap 36, the Frenchman drove as close as he dared to Irvine, placing himself in position for an audacious move as he darted from the slipstream of the Ferrari on the approach to Loews hairpin. Irvine moved a fraction to his right, making room to swing across the road to his left to take the apex at Loews but, in that instant, Panis kept on the throttle and drove his Ligier down the inside of the Ferrari. With some inevitability, Panis's car struck the Ferrari and pushed Irvine towards the barrier on the outside of the hairpin. Panis held his breath and planted his foot down again . . . and, to his relief, his Ligier responded and drove around the hairpin and away. He was in third place, in the race of his life.

Panis told me how he had realised that this was the one place on the track where there was a glimmer of hope of over-taking Irvine, and if it was no more than a glimmer it was a move he had to try to execute. 'On slicks I was really fast and when I got up to Eddie I asked myself, where can I overtake him?' he explained. 'I followed for some laps and saw that at Loews all the time he takes a wide line to turn in. I knew it was fucking risky, but, anyway, I had to take the risk otherwise I don't overtake him. Next time I saw Eddie do the same – whoosh, I am down his inside. But when I braked, I turn and locked the wheel. I touch Irvine with my front wing – and he goes out. In my head, I think the nose of my car is destroyed. I think that I fucked my race.' Irvine's car only brushed the Armco, but his engine stalled and he needed to bump-start it to get under way. He had to divert straight away to the pits for a new nose cone. Panis's move was brash, committed and one which, in the overly strict world of modern-day Formula One, might have attracted the attention of the stewards. Had it done so, Grand Prix racing would have been robbed of an epic storyline.

Panis knows that on this afternoon fortune smiled kindly on him. He mimed how he drove away, steering to his left, then to his right, to ascertain if his Ligier had been damaged in the low-speed collision. 'I carried on and spoke with my engineer on the radio,' he recalled. The transmission between him and the pits was dreadful, though. 'It took me two laps for him to understand what I wanted. I tell the team:,'LOOK . . . AND SEE . . . IF MY NOSE . . . IS BROKEN.' His race engin-eer, Paolo Catone, tried to identify any anomaly in Panis's

Ligier as he drove past the pits at full throttle, rattling through the gears. 'I could tell the steering was straight,' said Panis, but had anything else been weakened on his car? 'Eventually, they told me from the pit wall everything looked perfect. I was told I was the quickest on the track. It was a fight, they said, between Hill, Alesi and me for the fastest lap.' Even so, Panis was still some fifty seconds behind Hill.

'Then I came out of the tunnel and saw big smoke,' said Panis. 'It was from Damon's car. I was told by the team that I was second behind Alesi. I thought, "Fuck, this is not possible."' Hill thought much the same – for entirely different reasons. On the forty-first lap, with the race at his mercy, the Renault V10 engine in Hill's Williams belched a plume of smoke midway through the tunnel. Hill directed his car down the escape road to the right of the chicane and came to a halt. He climbed from the car and beat both hands against his helmet. His meteoric start to get the better of Schumacher, his flawless drive to open a huge lead over everyone else, his wish to add to the lustrous record his father had established at Monaco, had all gone up in smoke along with his engine.

Hill had received an indication that his race was in danger of ending prematurely. 'I had a warning light come on about a lap before,' he explained. 'The engine lost power in the tunnel because, basically, the oil had fallen out of the bottom of the car.' Ironically, with its lack of full-throttle straights, Monaco is not renowned as a circuit that is hard on engines. But Hill accepted then, as he does today, that fate is not an enemy you can outrun. 'I'm not saying the race was a cruise, but I had a massive lead over Alesi, in an inferior car, and the circuit was dry,' he said. Also, there was less than half the field still running, so there were fewer cars to lap. There was not going to be that much pressure put on me.

'I was just sad to be deprived of what I had loved doing. I

had lost the chance to win the Monaco Grand Prix, but then the whole year my mindset was on winning the world championship. I had already factored in not winning races due to mechanical failure. Sad that it had to be Monaco; it would have been fantastic to have won Monaco, of course. But then I won the British Grand Prix and my dad never won that. Maybe that evened it out.' And Hill did finish the 1996 season as deserved world champion.

With Hill out, Alesi inherited the lead of the Grand Prix. Panis was thirty-two seconds back down the road, followed by Coulthard, Herbert, Villeneuve and Salo. Only ten drivers remained on the circuit; the others were Häkkinen, Frentzen, Irvine and Badoer. On lap 45, Panis set a new fastest lap: 1 minute, 25.995 seconds. Alesi responded with a faster lap – 1 minute, 25.418 seconds – and nosed his lead over his fellow Frenchman to thirty seconds. Alesi was faster still again – this time with a lap of 1 minute, 25.366 seconds. Shortly afterwards, the Benetton driver was summoned for a second visit to the pits for fuel and fresh tyres. This stop enabled Panis to close the gap to Alesi to a fraction over eleven seconds.

Alesi, a Frenchman of Italian origin, had panache as well as natural speed at the wheel, which gave him a broad appeal to motor-racing fans. Yet the statistical evidence was not in his favour. Alesi was leading at Monaco with just one win to his name after more than seven years in Formula One. This proved not to be the day when he doubled that statistic. Without warning, Alesi returned to the pits. Clearly, the Benetton team were not sure what was wrong. Mechanics were belatedly given instructions to change tyres, but his stop looked more like a knee-jerk reaction than a planned stop for fresh rubber. With the front of Alesi's car off the ground in the pits, Panis went rushing through into the lead.

We had just witnessed the man who started fourteenth on

the grid driving to the front of the Monaco Grand Prix, an act in defiance of four decades of history on these streets. This was the furthest from the minds of the Ligier team, however. Instead an issue had presented itself – one deemed important enough to make an alarmed radio call to Panis. 'Be careful on your fuel,' he was told.

When Alesi rejoined the race he was behind the train of Coulthard, Herbert, Villeneuve, Salo and Häkkinen, but this proved to be of no consequence. His car had a flawed suspension and he came back to park his Benetton and add his name to the list of men with a hard-luck story to sell. Panis was determined not to join that club. He had been informed that he might not have enough fuel to reach the chequered flag if the race was to go the full distance of seventy-eight laps. However, if the race was stopped after two hours, there was a better chance that his fuel would last.

Either way, this was not ideal for a man leading a Grand Prix for the first time in his career, on the streets of Monaco, with a global television audience of hundreds of millions, for a team that had last won in Formula One fifteen years ago, with his wife in the pits carrying the secret that Panis had told her that morning that this was possible.

Panis had waited his entire life to lead a Grand Prix. What he promised himself within the solitude of his car, dealing with this new information, was that he would control his own destiny. Even so, there was suddenly a sense of optimism within the McLaren team. They knew Panis had not refuelled during his pit stop to change to slicks. The race, surely, would come back to Coulthard. 'I could tell the Ligier boys were getting really agitated,' said McLaren designer Neil Oatley. 'We were just convinced Panis wasn't going to make it, that he would have to come in, and we expected David to cruise to victory.'

Only Panis thought otherwise. 'Coulthard did a good job and got closer to me,' said Panis. 'I saw him in my mirrors everywhere. But I was changing gear earlier to save fuel, and when he came too close, I pushed a bit harder.' Then Panis heard his engineer, Paolo Catone, an Italian, talking in urgent tones to him on the radio. Catone spoke to Panis in French. 'Olivier,' he said, 'I think we need to pit. We don't have the fuel to go to the end. Save fuel . . . save fuel.'

Panis recalled his reaction. 'I upshift at very low revs. I didn't pass sixth gear after the tunnel. I tried to do my best and I saw, from my mirrors, David get back close to me.' This was a drama wrapped in a potential crisis. The clock was edging closer to the two-hour mark and it had long since been deduced Panis would not have to drive seventy-eight laps. Yet now even seventy-six laps seemed beyond the extent of his remaining fuel, according to the calculations being made on the pit wall.

'With two laps to go, Paolo is telling me that I have to come into the pits,' said Panis. 'I didn't answer. He said it in French, in Italian and English. I still didn't answer.'

Briatore had now arrived in the Ligier pit from the Benetton garage. He was riding the team hard to persuade Panis to make a fuel stop because, commercially, it was of great importance to win some points rather than have the Ligier parked on the side of the road, out of fuel. Catone came on the radio once more: 'Olivier you need to stop!'

Panis had another plan. 'I said to Paolo, "Look, we can be heroes or we can end up looking ridiculous. If I stop before the end with no fuel . . . bad luck. If I get to win . . . well, we win! I don't stop."' And he did not. 'I saw David on my gearbox, so I pushed again for two or three corners to give him the message that he could not pass.'

Beautifully, poetically and thrillingly, Panis was rescued

from this second-by-second tortuous journey by the only saviour possible: the sight of the chequered flag being waved at him after seventy-five laps, totalling almost 260 kilometres, or 155 miles. 'This is not possible, this is my dream all my life,' Panis thought, as he drove past the flag to the adulation of a crowd rising to applaud the man who, metaphorically at least, had just broken the bank at Monte Carlo.

Behind Panis there was yet a final moment of chaos as Irvine hit the barrier, at almost the same place Schumacher had done two hours earlier, and Salo drove his Sauber into the back of his Ferrari and was then hit himself by Häkkinen's McLaren. Frentzen had been lapped, so he drove into the pits without getting to the flag.

All of which meant Coulthard was second and Herbert was third and last. This was the fewest number of cars to have finished a Grand Prix anywhere in the world. *It still is.*

On his lap of honour, Panis grabbed a giant tricolour thrust into his hand and waved it at the cheering fans like a conductor waving a baton at an orchestra. Once he had braked to a halt on the grid, Panis freed himself from the cockpit of his Ligier and was engulfed by those waiting to shower him with praise for the remarkable job he had done. In the midst of the pandemonium of joy and disbelief, some mechanics tried to restart the car. 'But it wouldn't start,' recalled Panis. 'There was no fuel left.'

On the podium, Prince Rainier handed him the trophy he had driven through rain and traffic, through a trough of raging uncertainty, to win. 'It all was so confusing. I was in this place, I knew I had won, but it was hard to realise everything that happened,' said Panis. One of those waiting to greet him as the champagne flowed at Ligier was Jacques Laffite, a Frenchman who won all his six Grand Prix victories with the team, and a man for whom no one in Formula One has a bad

237

word to say, either about his thirteen years as a driver in the sport or as a broadcaster. Panis knew that his friend could comprehend better than most what he had just accomplished. 'I am very close with Jacques,' said Panis.

Guy Ligier called Panis straight after the race to convey how emotional he had been watching a car bearing his name win the most iconic motor race in the world. 'Guy was crying on the telephone,' said Panis. 'He thanked me I don't know how many times. He was saying I couldn't know what it meant to him to have his name on a winning car at Monaco, or know how much money he had put into the team to feel this moment one day. I loved Guy, he gave a chance to a lot of French drivers like me.'

No one begrudged Panis this moment of fame. 'The Ligier was a good car, but not a Williams beater, a McLaren beater or for that matter a Ferrari beater,' said Herbert. 'It was an extraordinary race and there was elation in our pit, at Sauber, as not many podium finishes came their way in those days. What you saw with Olivier was one of those rare occasions when the car seemed to come together, and he came together with the car. He produced a great performance and it was one of those victories no one ever thought would materialise. But this is Monaco.'

Brundle appreciated Panis's drive as the work of a professional scaling his Everest. 'Ollie was never a Prost or Senna, or anything like that, but he was a solid racing driver,' he said. 'He deserved that victory, no doubt about it. He kept his car on the road, stayed out of trouble and he drove it fast. He didn't make mistakes, but he won Monaco not just because he stayed out of trouble, but because he went forwards, too. Ollie was good round Monaco.'

That evening, Panis and Anne received an invitation to the traditional dinner hosted by Prince Rainier for the winner of the Grand Prix. While Anne had brought appropriate clothing to dine out in Monaco, her husband had not. 'I had just jeans and T-shirts,' he remembered. As it was Sunday the shops were mostly closed, but staff at the Beach Plaza hotel searched out a suit for Panis. At the dinner, Panis sat between Prince Rainier and Princess Stéphanie and at one point in the evening had to stand to take a round of rousing applause. 'It gives me goose pimples now to recall it,' said Panis, a man who added his name to the illustrious history of the Monaco Grand Prix as the driver who won on an afternoon just three cars crossed the finish line.

The next morning, as Panis went to check out of the hotel, he met Irvine in reception. It could have been a frosty exchange, but Irvine, smiling, shook the Frenchman's hand and said, 'Well done.' Panis did not know Irvine well, but he treasured the Ulsterman's comments. 'Eddie told me I had done a good job,' said Panis. 'He said that everyone had been complaining that it was not possible to overtake him in the race, but that I had managed it. His last words were, "Well done – fuck them!" Eddie was a tough guy, but a funny guy.'

When she reflected on what had happened on those streets of Monaco, Anne said, 'On race morning, he was very confident – too confident. It was very strange.' At what point did she think something special was going to happen? 'After!' Anne said, laughing. 'After the race a lot of things happened for us – it was unbelievable. It took a long time to realise that he won Monaco. Yes, a very long time.'

Panis is still stopped in the street in France and congratulated for winning the race. 'I thank those who say these nice things, but I do also remind them that it took place twenty years ago!' he said, smiling modestly. 'Wherever I am, it is what people want to speak about. I am very proud of this; it is part of my life. The track is not a racetrack, it is many streets and they have so much history to tell. It is true that after this victory people don't look at me in the paddock like they did before. I have a different level of respect. For my career, it gave me many more years to do my job.'

Panis and Anne have three children: Aurélien, a racing driver, and teenage daughters, Caroline and Laurène. Has he ever sat down with them to watch the day Monaco came under his spell? 'I have looked at some short clips of the race on Facebook with my kids,' he said. 'We laugh at me being so young.'

No Frenchman has won a Grand Prix since, and Ligier's name vanished from the grid when the team was bought by Alain Prost at the end of the 1996 season. In all, from 1994 to 2004, Panis started 158 times in Formula One, but this immensely talented and amiable Frenchman never reached the top step of the podium again. If it is a professional disappointment, it is not one he has carried as a burden. At the conclusion of our three-hour meeting in Paris, Panis happily admitted, 'If you told me I could win fifteen Grand Prix races or I could win Monaco, I would say I want Monaco.'

The trophy that he was allowed to keep – one went with his car, overalls and helmet to the Honda museum in Japan – is kept at the house of Anne's mother, who lives close to them in Grenoble. 'I see it every Sunday when we go to lunch or dinner there,' he said, smiling. 'It is one memory from the greatest day of my life. Monaco is a mystical Grand Prix, a trial of strength, of madness.'

Michael Schumacher, 2001

12

Schumacher: The Red Baron Rules

L ess than seven months later, Ross Brawn arrived for the first time at the factory of his new employers in Maranello, a town with a population of less than 18,000 in the region of Emilia-Romagna, in northern Italy. Some would argue it is better known as the spiritual capital of Formula One.

Brawn's departure from Benetton for Ferrari, if inevitable, had been clumsily managed by Flavio Briatore. A team under the technical guidance of Brawn, and driven by the mercurial force of Michael Schumacher, had won nineteen races in their championship-winning pomp in 1994 and 1995, yet failed to win a single race in the season Panis brilliantly upstaged the aristocrats of the sport at Monaco and Hill became world champion. 'It was a difficult year at Benetton,' said Brawn with classic understatement.

Yet like all those in the fast-moving world of Formula One, Brawn could empathise with the proclamation of British novelist L. P. Hartley in his book *The Go-Between*: 'The past is a foreign country: they do things differently there.' From the moment he walked through the door of the Ferrari factory to be met by Luca di Montezemolo, Brawn was struck by the grandeur and facilities of the only team to have competed in every season in Formula One history. 'I was given the royal tour by Luca,' he explained. Brawn's introduction included a visit to the office of Enzo Ferrari, a room that had been preserved as a shrine to the founder of the Scuderia Ferrari Grand Prix team, a man widely known as 'Il Commendatore', who died in 1988, aged ninety. 'The phone he used was still on the desk that was his,' said Brawn. 'On the walls there are shelves of handwritten race records. I was allowed to look at some and they are reports from engineers, technicians and team managers. Every season of his lifetime has a log with every race recorded.'

In time, Brawn and Schumacher would be empowered by the enormity of the resources at Ferrari. They would rise to conquer Formula One together once again; and they would enlarge their already substantive reputations for being able to deliver peak performance at the Grand Prix that assured maximum global attention: Monaco.

Yet Brawn understood the enormity of the challenge he had accepted – and he knew the responsibility of having to acquit himself with honours for the most demanding team in the sport would be onerous. But he was energised, not diminished, by the job ahead. 'Well, it was a dream to be joining Ferrari,' he said. 'The aura of Enzo was still strong. Everything lived up to what I hoped it would be.' But Brawn had joined not a team at the peak of its power, but one attempting to reverse its decline. One of the traditions in Maranello is that the parish priest of the church of San Biagio tolls the bells each time Ferrari registers a victory. Those bells had been rung in celebration just five times in the previous six years: a lamentable example of a team underperforming.

Brawn had been chosen to return the Scuderia to its former

glory, on the back of a stunning record of achievement, and at the helpful recommendation of Schumacher. Within two months Rory Byrne, who designed the championship-winning cars at Benetton, had also been hired by Ferrari. 'Ferrari has gone through these cycles of success and failure,' said Brawn. 'Yet when you arrive at Maranello and look at what they had there, you can't work out why they didn't win every world championship. There were wonderful facilities, two test tracks, a great budget and very good people. I didn't need to dramatically change the core group.'

At the point of his departure from Benetton, the only thing Schumacher had asked Ferrari to do was hire his race engineer, Giorgio Ascanelli. Brawn is adamant that it was not Schumacher's intention – at first, anyway – to be reunited with Byrne and himself. 'I honestly believe that Michael went to Ferrari almost wanting to show that he could have success without the infrastructure that he had before,' said Brawn. 'That's human nature, isn't it? Especially when you are young.'

Unlike John Barnard, Brawn's English predecessor at Ferrari who had been the creative influence as McLaren grew and bloomed under Dennis, Brawn opted to live in Italy. He chose a flat in Sassuolo, some seventeen kilometres south-west of Maranello. Often he was there alone as his wife, Jean – 'I courted her around various motor-racing circuits in the UK!' – stayed behind in England to ensure their youngest daughter, Amy, was not disrupted while she studied for her A levels. Later on, Jean was able to spend a greater amount of time with her husband in Italy.

The significance of the mission Brawn had embarked upon was made apparent to him from his earliest days in Italy. His memories offer a rare insight into what it is like to live and operate within the crucible of the most scrutinised team in motor sport. If his thoughts occasionally stray beyond the boundaries of Monaco, it is because Brawn is talking more candidly than he has been known to have done in the past. 'I particularly remember being abused by a floor sweeper at Bologna airport who was upset by how badly Ferrari were doing,' he said. 'He told me that I needed to get my shit together.' Brawn knew this to be the general tenor of the conversation as another engineer travelling with him interpreted the cleaner's indignation. 'It was pretty heady stuff at the beginning, in many ways,' he admitted. Any Italian with an interest in Formula One has an emotional investment in the fortunes of the team, it seems. For Italians, it is perfectly acceptable for neighbours or friends to support different football teams, whether Juventus or Inter, Napoli or Milan, but it would be considered perverse by the *tifosi* – the hard-core motor-racing fans – to cheer for anyone other than Scuderia Ferrari. The nationality of the drivers has always been largely incidental.

Brawn discovered a culture at Ferrari that reflected this deep public interest in the team. He recalled: 'Every member of management had an inch-thick pile of press cuttings on their desk each day. At the time, the policy at Ferrari was that you need to know what the press are saying about the team. That was alien to me. It wasn't a primary objective to placate the media. Inevitably, media opinion can sometimes steer things; and it was a country with very strong media opinions when it came to Ferrari. But having a pile of press cuttings on people's desks every morning meant that you didn't get any work out of anyone until 10 a.m. – after they had coffee and read the cuttings. If we had a decent race the cuttings pile might be two inches thick; if we had a bad race it would be three inches. I have never been blind to the media, but I wouldn't spend a couple of hours reading their thoughts. So I stopped them being distributed and had the cuttings put on the company intranet.'

Brawn had to wait until just his fifth race to experience the commotion that accompanies a Ferrari win. Of all places, it occurred at Monaco; the most famous team in the world had finally won the most glamorous motor race in the world for the first time in seventeen years. Bedlam reigned as Ferrari's vocal fans screamed their approval. Schumacher's third win on the streets of Monaco was his fourth victory for Ferrari, and timed to perfection to emphasise that the Scuderia was headed in an upward trajectory. 'This was the first time I really understood how important Ferrari was as a team,' explained Brawn. 'Monaco is very intimate. When you are walking back to the hotel at night, the fans are cheering you if you are in a Ferrari uniform. Walk from the pit lane to the paddock, and the fans on the hill, beneath the palace, blast their klaxons and chant your name. It is football-esque.'

We were talking in May 2016, in the conservatory of his thirteen-acre home in Oxfordshire, where a Ferrari 250 GTE – one of an enviable collection of cars owned by Brawn – was parked in the drive. In stature, Brawn is an imposing man, but there is a warmth and humour to his conversation that he was reluctant to express publicly during the years he was engaged in keeping one step ahead of his rivals. The narrative of his story is inevitably entwined with the rise to stardom of Schumacher, and his observations and judgements about the German's career must be first prefaced by Brawn's reaction to the shocking news that reached him one morning in late December 2013. 'I didn't give it too much credence originally,' he explained. 'I heard that Michael had an accident skiing and he was going to hospital for a check-up. I called Sabine Kehm, his manager, and said that I'd learned Michael had a shunt and that I would come and see him when I came back from a planned trip over New Year. Sabine replied, "If you want to see Michael, I think you should come now." The prognosis at that stage was that they could not be sure he was going to survive the fall.'

Brawn flew to France almost immediately. 'It was important to me to see Michael's wife, Corinna, and their family,' he said. Since then, he has maintained his close friendship with the family, but, most importantly, Brawn is respectful of their desire for privacy. 'It is just a terrible irony that a man with the kind of high-risk lifestyle that Michael had should have been struck down by what looks to have been, on the face of it, a trivial skiing accident.'

The Schumacher that Brawn willingly discusses is the one he stood shoulder-to-shoulder with during his record seven world titles, which harvested ninety-one Grand Prix victories from 307 races, where he annexed pole position sixty-eight times. In his Ferrari years, Schumacher was named variously by headline writers as 'Schumi', 'the Red Baron' or 'Regenmeister' (Rain Master). He was known to Brawn simply as Michael. 'For sure, Michael was the best driver I ever worked with,' he said. 'When I say that, it is a very narrow band in Formula One – they are all so good. Jenson Button is very, very good; Lewis Hamilton is fantastic; Nico Rosberg is fantastic. None of them are bad. But all the elements that matter in a major way, or a subtle way, Michael had them all covered.'

In Monaco in that spring of 1997, Schumacher gave a phenomenal exhibition of how to drive a Formula One car in the rain – in vivid contrast to the performance that had excluded him from the race twelve months earlier. 'When Michael came round at the end of the first lap, we thought there must have been an accident as there was no sign of anyone else,' chuckled Brawn. After five laps, his lead was twenty-two seconds. Schumacher was just never challenged – at least not by any of his rivals. But on lap 53, Schumacher missed his braking point at Saint-Dévote and detoured down the escape road. It cost him ten seconds, but not his lead. The atrocious conditions meant that the race had to be stopped after two hours, when Schumacher had completed just sixty-two of the scheduled seventy-eight laps.

'A strong recollection is the way that the *tifosi* celebrated,' said Brawn. 'Monaco is where you are fully exposed to the celebrations. Of course, when you do badly there is no hiding place, but when you are successful you really feel at one with the fans. If you are a Ferrari team member there is really nothing better. It was a massive moment for me – my first Ferrari victory in the best possible place. The victory is framed in my mind. It was very exceptional.'

Schumacher orchestrated the party after attending the black-tie dinner at the Sporting Club, the habitual honour given to the race winner by the royal family. The revelry then moved on to Jimmy'z nightclub. 'Michael was a very serious racing driver, but he always celebrated his success,' said Brawn. 'That was the fun thing of working with Michael. And Michael did get drunk! His poison was Bacardi and Coke. He was always very generous and he would invite his engineers and mechanics. We drove back late the next day. Normally we had our debrief meetings on Monday, but I think for Monaco we postponed them until Tuesday.' There was another party that night, too. Rubens Barrichello's second place for Stewart Ford – fifty-three seconds behind Schumacher – allowed Sir Jackie Stewart and his son Paul to devour the satisfaction of gaining a place on the second step of the podium in just the fifth race the team had competed in.

Panis lost third place to Schumacher's team-mate, Irvine, and the Frenchman accepted his disappointment without begrudging the Ulsterman's visit to the podium, as he was all too conscious of the fact that the outcome of their fierce duel a year earlier had been kind to him. Just one month later,

Panis experienced the cruel and capricious nature of Formula One when he was involved in a 150mph accident in the closing stages of the Canadian Grand Prix. His Prost Mugen-Honda suffered a rear suspension failure in the fourth-gear Turn Five. Panis was helpless as his car clipped one wall and then ricocheted across the circuit into the outside wall.

At home in France, his wife Anne looked at the pictures of the crash on her TV with a pounding heart. 'It was very difficult to watch,' she told me. 'I was stressed and very frightened.' Then Anne saw her husband motion from his car, and she sensed in that moment he would survive. 'Olivier made a little sign for me, a small wave, and I felt relief. When Olivier went to hospital, Alain Prost called to explain what happened.' Soon after the phone call ended she booked a flight to Montreal to be at the bedside of her husband as swiftly as humanly possible.

Prost had naturally hurried to the medical centre to see Panis as doctors prepared the Frenchman to be transferred to the Sacré-Coeur hospital in Montreal. Both his legs were broken. 'Alain took one look at me – and cried,' recalled Panis. 'When someone cries like this, I see this is the real man. It was tough for him, because he explained all the time that he was driving that this type of injury was his biggest fear.' Panis, who had been second to Jacques Villeneuve in the previous race in Spain, was third in the world championship when he was so violently put out of contention in a race won by Schumacher. He missed the next seven races. 'Even the accident is part of the job,' said Panis, all these years later. 'I knew straight away it would be a big crash. I was lucky that it did not finish my career, but I think in this season, before the accident, it was possible to finish in the top three of the championship; and that could have changed my life, too. All I could do was work to come back stronger.' Anne still thinks to this day that that crash proved a turning point in her husband's career. 'It was the worst accident Olivier had – and I think with this crash there was a change for him, a change for his career.'

The calamity to befall Schumacher at the end of that season was not physical, but devastating all the same; more so, as he was the author of his own humiliating downfall. At the final race, the European Grand Prix being staged at Jerez, in southern Spain, the German led the championship by one point from Villeneuve, who was seeking to deliver a fourth drivers' title in six years for Williams-Renault. Qualifying had never been more closely fought: Villeneuve, Schumacher, and Frentzen in the second Williams, all lapped the 4.428-kilometre circuit in the identical time of 1 minute, 21.072 seconds. Less than a second separated the top ten. As Villeneuve had recorded his time first, he was awarded pole, with Schumacher alongside him, and Frentzen in third place on the grid.

Schumacher led from the start, though. But when Villeneuve came to attack Schumacher on the forty-eighth lap, the German drove his Ferrari into the side of the Canadian's Williams. Schumacher was forced to retire, while Villeneuve continued. Prudently, late in the race Villeneuve conceded track position to both McLaren drivers rather than jeopardise his pursuit of the title by becoming embroiled in another collision. Häkkinen scored his first Formula One win, with Coulthard second, and Villeneuve finished third to close out the world championship. Those of us at Jerez felt no sympathy for Schumacher. He had discarded all semblance of sportsmanship.

While Brawn maintained his neutrality when Schumacher came into contact with Hill at the climax of the 1994 season, he took the view shared by all reasonable observers in the paddock on that afternoon in Spain. 'For me that was a blatant barge by Michael,' said Brawn. 'Yet Michael came back to the garage screaming blue murder and insisting Villeneuve had him off. He was yelling at me, "You have to get him kicked out of the race! The guy's outrageous – it is unbelievable what he did!"'

Brawn was calm and measured in his response. 'Michael,' he said, 'you have to take a look at the TV replay because that is not how we saw it.' Schumacher sidled away to do as he was advised. He came back with a revised opinion and said to Brawn, 'Yeah, that wasn't how I saw it in the car, but I can see now what you saw.' Unbelievably, the stewards at the Grand Prix concluded that the crash was a 'racing incident' and considered the incident closed. It was not, thankfully. Schumacher was condemned in newsprint in publications across Europe, including some of those in Italy and Germany. The furore ended just over a fortnight later when the FIA, prompted by its president, Max Mosley, took the unprecedented step of punishing Schumacher with disqualification from the 1997 world championship. However, he was allowed to retain for the record his five race victories, including the one secured on the rain-splattered streets of Monaco.

On that bright Oxfordshire afternoon in 2016, as the sun poured through the conservatory windows, Brawn remembered this controversy as a metaphor for Schumacher's career. 'I think in a way that was what made Michael so special – and what made him so vulnerable,' he said. 'He was so competitive, so obsessed with not letting anyone have an inch. That was his approach.'

Monaco 1998

It was perhaps a factor at Monaco in 1998 when Schumacher, having already crashed heavily in Casino Square on Thursday, tangled with Alexander Wurz's Benetton on lap 37 of the Grand Prix as he impatiently sought a route to properly chase the race leader, Häkkinen. Wurz declined to yield as they duelled downhill from Loews hairpin, but Schumacher edged the Austrian's car aside to gain track position momentarily. It was a place that came with a hefty price tag, for Schumacher damaged the rear suspension of his Ferrari and had to rejoin the race three laps down after pitting for repairs. Häkkinen, who started from pole, jubilantly provided McLaren with their first triumph at Monaco since Senna had had his record sixth win five years earlier. This was Häkkinen's fourth win of a season he dominated to become world champion, managed by Keke Rosberg, the last Finn to take the title sixteen years before.

Monaco 1999

Schumacher returned twelve months later to capture his fourth – and penultimate – win in the principality. It was particularly satisfying for the Red Baron as this was his sixteenth win for Ferrari, breaking the record held by Lauda. Irvine assured Ferrari a one–two finish, which contributed in the final analysis to the Scuderia winning the 1999 Constructors' Championship for the first time since Frenchmen Patrick Tambay and René Arnoux were driving for the team in 1983. Brawn recalled how the traditional dinner at the Monaco Sporting Club did not go entirely to plan. 'Eddie said that he couldn't come to the dinner as he didn't own a dinner suit,' said Brawn. 'Team manager Stefano Domenicali had anticipated this. Like all things, you don't want to tempt fate beforehand, but he told Eddie after the race that he had brought a black tie for him. Eddie mumbled "all right", but he definitely didn't want to go. We arrived at the Sporting Club and everyone was looking resplendent, then Eddie walked in wearing a leather jacket and jeans.'

Brawn was unamused. He asked Irvine, 'Why would you want to do that? You don't have to make a statement around here.'

'His excuse was that the suit didn't fit him very well,' Brawn continues. 'That was the slightly unfortunate side of Eddie. In all fairness, Eddie was very professional. He just took a pragmatic view to the way things were, and that Michael was faster than he was. But he could still do a pretty respectable job, so when opportunities presented themselves he most often took them. Eddie had an interesting balance in the way that he viewed life. He was actually good fun to be with, and I enjoyed my time with him. He was just that bit below Michael and he knew that he could never make it up. He came to terms with it. In fact, Eddie is probably the only driver who had written into his contract that he would get a bonus if the other driver at Ferrari won the world championship. He came to us and said, if he was helping Michael, surely, it made sense for him to get a bonus if Michael won the world championship. Logical, really!

'When Irvine left at the end of 1999 for Jaguar, he said, "I have been banging my head against a brick wall for ever, and that brick wall is called Michael Schumacher. It just needs to stop now. I managed to deal with it, but I can't deal with it any more." I respected him for that – and he went to Jaguar for a king's ransom, good on Eddie.'

That first Constructors' Championship under the management of Jean Todt and the technical prowess of Brawn and Byrne was to be the first of six in a row.

Monaco 2000

Their second Constructors' Championship claimed in 2000 had a dazzling centrepiece: the Drivers' Championship, won by

Schumacher, who became the first man to capture the coveted title for the Scuderia since Jody Scheckter in 1979. This title had been achieved at a monumental financial cost, according to Umberto Zapelloni, who reported in his authorised history, *Formula Ferrari*: 'After twenty-one years, 7,700 days and an investment of $3,500 million, Ferrari had won the drivers' title again – from Scheckter to Schumacher, from Enzo Ferrari to Luca di Montezemolo.'

Italians celebrated as if the country had won the World Cup. German Chancellor Gerhard Schroeder sent a congratulatory fax to Schumacher. No one was counting the cost now. 'Winning it with Michael was important,' said Brawn. 'He had been with the team for four years and been relentless in supporting everything that was going on. He was always giving his maximum. He had broken a leg in 1999 (at Silverstone), which everyone felt bad about as it was a car failure. Everything made the success in 2000 special. We had just missed out on the Drivers' Championship three times, with Michael in 1997 and '98, and with Eddie in '99, and I think that toughened the team up. Each time we had to go back and console everyone in the team and build them back up again.' Brawn has a vivid memory of returning to Bologna airport as champions, to be met by thousands of cheering, scarlet-clad fans – rather than an irate cleaner. 'Failure at Ferrari is like no other team,' said Brawn. 'And success at Ferrari is like no other team. It's felt in the extreme in both cases.

'At Monaco in that season Michael just disappeared and he was leading by a country mile, rather like he had done in 1997.' But this time there was to be a wake, not a party. 'We had an exhaust failure,' he explained. 'In those days the exhaust came out of the top of the bodywork, and we had an exhaust crack that started to blow hot gas on to the carbon-fibre rear suspension, which then failed on lap 56.' He told the story as though he was standing in the pit lane just minutes after Schumacher had retired. 'It was pretty soul-destroying,' said Brawn. 'Michael was a slam dunk to win.'

Brawn just wanted to escape, he said. 'I had some friends from the wine trade with me at the race. We'd become friends over the years and they had helped me build my wine cellar. They were staying at a small villa up in the hills and had asked me before the race to join them for supper, not supposing I could as they would have expected me to have been tied up afterwards. I rang one of them after Michael had gone out and asked, "Is that invite still open?" I had a quiet remorseful dinner with them.'

The race win was claimed by Coulthard, a huge milestone in his career. In one afternoon the pain and pleasure of Monaco was transparently on display to the world as Coulthard jubilantly embraced the celebratory mood within McLaren. Schumacher disappeared into the evening without a backward glance. Over the years, Brawn learned what to expect when a race failed to go to plan. 'If I have had a bad race I get a pain in my stomach, a pain in my chest, particularly if it is a race I feel we should have won or could have won,' he said. 'The physical pain afterwards is a horrible feeling. It takes two or three days to pass. Jean would never ring after a bad race. She knew I needed time to come round. Sometimes it might be late at night before I rang home. But Jean would always ring when we did well. On occasions I had calls from her on the pit wall!

'Then there is dealing with the despondency within the team after a bad race loss. You have to make sure they don't fall too far. Michael was good at this. He would come to terms with it and start to encourage the team again. It was our job to make sure that it didn't split the team. Ferrari became Michael's team. He knew all the mechanics' names, he knew the names of their wives, he knew their kids. It was natural to him to be involved like this. He was interested.'

Schumacher and Ferrari, with Todt, Brawn and Byrne, were an all-conquering alliance in Formula One for five years from 2000 to 2004. In that period, Schumacher's world-championship wins rose from two to seven. 'I think Michael raised the bar completely in the arena a driver operates in,' said Brawn. 'One measure of his professionalism was his fitness: no driver had been as fit as Michael. He did that himself – all his trainers worked for him and we never had to employ anyone. The Mercedes Academy had been a good school for him. He is an intelligent man. He had a naturally low heart rate. Michael had the genetics to be a great athlete. All the guys racing today are supremely fit – because of Michael. He was a superb team player. You will never hear of anyone who worked with Michael criticise him. He was so integrated within the team. He often organised a football match on Thursday night with the mechanics. They would all go out and have a beer afterwards; obviously, Michael would take it easy, but he just loved the camaraderie and teamwork.'

The example Schumacher set has percolated through each generation, all the way to Max Verstappen, a teenager widely predicted to be a world champion after making such a spectacular impact during the 2016 season with Red Bull. Verstappen, whose father, Jos, befriended Schumacher during his years in Formula One, recalled some shared childhood holidays with the German champion and his family when he told *Daily Mail* Formula One correspondent Jonathan McEvoy: 'Michael was a very friendly guy and he liked to hang out with the children. He was a very relaxed person around us. I would not say he was a hero of mine as such, but in the way he prepared himself he was way ahead of everyone else. He showed how you can take away the edge of your competition.

He was an example of how to go about sport. He is the perfect example to follow.'

Schumacher and Brawn redefined another aspect of Formula One: race strategy worked in total harmony from the pit wall to the car. 'I always used to say to the engineers at Monaco that they must let a driver have ten, twelve laps to get into the track,' explained Brawn. 'You are wasting your time tuning the car before then. This is the one track where a driver has to spend time to build up his confidence, build up his limits. If you put a driver out there without doing anything to the car, he will just go quicker and quicker as long as nothing else is deteriorating. Then, when you see that slight stabilisation, that's when you get him in and ask what can be done to make the car a little more forgiving. You have to wait until you have got to that plateau before you change anything. At Monaco the track changes tremendously over the weekend. It's the only track where you get ordinary traffic going round the circuit between the practice sessions on Thursday and Saturday. It means that it could be perfect on Thursday, then you go out on Saturday and have a completely different animal to deal with. It is important to think through how the track is going to evolve.'

In the earliest years of his career, Brawn was justly credited as being a master tactician before the new technology made planning a race, or altering strategy to deal with an unpredicted set of circumstances, an exact science. 'Later on the whole thing was being modelled in real time. The guys back at the factory, on computers, would pick the ultimate route to get where you wanted to go,' said Brawn. 'In the early days there could be some comparisons we did on a computer and you'd have printouts with that information with you on the pit wall and think those through as the race unfolded. I loved that part of the role; you were part of the race. If you have dealt with a crisis, or made a call that has worked out, you feel you shared in the race win. At Monaco there is the added complication that overtaking is very difficult. But there were opportunities to be exploited, such as when some cars were on old tyres and others on new. When you managed a successful strategy, you feel a sense of achievement.

'Michael understood that he did not have a helicopter view of what was going on in the race, or that the conditions could be about to change as he would not have seen the weather forecast update. Occasionally, he would give us another perspective; perhaps he had seen something or felt something, and there would be an exchange of information or views that would colour or influence your decision on the pit wall. But he could also appreciate that in his little cocoon, sat in the car, he could only see what was in front of him and what was behind. He couldn't see what lap times other drivers were doing, or know when they went out on fresh tyres. So he was in your hands to a fair degree. He knew you wouldn't get it right every time, but over time we built trust. He put his faith in you.'

Team radios were encrypted, but Brawn admitted: 'They weren't always great. Sometimes, you would have a little stunt to see who was listening. You would perhaps call a fake pit stop, and see if you got any reaction. Occasionally, we did!' But those who did eavesdrop on the Ferrari radio traffic found the most disarming aspect to be Schumacher's quintessential coolness, as Adam Parr, the former chief executive of the Williams team, confided in conversations during meetings for a recent collaboration with Brawn for a book entitled *Total Competition*. 'Adam said that once or twice they had got into our radio,' said Brawn. 'The most impressive thing for them was that Michael and I were having a conversation, as he drove, like the conversation we are having now. Adam said they could not believe the calmness in the voice of Michael on the track – no breathlessness, no hint that he was driving at ten-tenths. Michael was exceptional in that.

'Michael would understand what you were facing on the pit wall – he would understand that it is not a perfect science. Afterwards, he wouldn't be afraid, privately, to talk through the things that had not gone right. Which is why people within the team respected him – he never threw tantrums. He did get upset a few times, but not with the team. Mostly, he would be upset with other drivers.'

Schumacher never saw Formula One as a place to make friends on the track, just a place to make history, I suggested. 'Relationships within the team were very important to him,' said Brawn. 'But he had no interest in relationships outside the team. Outside the team you were the opposition. He always respected Häkkinen, I remember.' For two years in succession, 1998 and 1999, Häkkinen won the world championship for McLaren ahead of Schumacher; reason enough for the Finn to earn his respect. Häkkinen's pure speed was an extraordinary asset.

Monaco 2001

It is a testament to Coulthard's own pace that he took pole position for McLaren at Monaco that season, with his team-mate Häkkinen in third place on the grid. Between them was Schumacher. But before the lights went out on race day, so did the Mercedes engine in the rear of Coulthard's McLaren. 'The software switched the engine off when I selected first gear,' he explained. He had to start from the rear of the field. 'Regrettably, all the hard work was undone, the chance of winning gone in an instant.' To make matters worse for McLaren, Häkkinen detected his car pulling to the right and went into the pits to seek a remedy. Nothing could be done, and after trying to establish racing speed and failing he retired his car. Rubens Barrichello led in the second Ferrari for some laps after Schumacher had made his pit stop, but the Brazilian was complaining of his cramp in right foot. 'Ross became a physiotherapist,' he reported afterwards. 'At one time I could hardly feel my right foot and Ross was saying, "Drink water, drink water."'

Perhaps predictably – cramp or no cramp – Barrichello was powerless to prevent Schumacher from passing. The German drove unchallenged to his fifth win at Monaco, an accomplishment known only to two other men: Hill and Senna. Afterwards, Schumacher expressed his feelings without any real elation at joining such exalted company. 'Honestly, I don't feel that emotional because it had been a straightforward win,' he said. 'It wasn't anything exceptional. It's always nice to win in Monte Carlo, it is always special. It is easy to make mistakes here; it is a hard circuit and although it was an easy drive, it was still hard for those reasons.' What Schumacher could never have imagined as he left the circuit that evening was that he would never taste the champagne of victory in Monaco again.

Monaco 2002

Respect for Ferrari and for Schumacher was in short supply when they arrived in Monaco in May 2002. The team was at the centre of a huge controversy about how they had manipulated the result of the previous Grand Prix in Austria, to the benefit of Schumacher; and there were legions of fans who voiced their disapproval by booing the Scuderia when they returned to business in Monaco.

In Austria, Rubens Barrichello had taken both pole and control of the Grand Prix. It was only the sixth race of the season and Schumacher had won four of them, so was comfortably ahead in the championship. Nevertheless, a decision was taken by the Ferrari management to enforce team orders: Barrichello was repeatedly ordered to surrender victory to Schumacher. The angry Brazilian did so only after he exited the final corner of the Grand Prix, to show his contempt for the instruction, to show the world that the race had been stolen from him for no apparent reason other than Schumacher, the Red Baron, ruled. It was also felt across the world that Ferrari had shown contemptible disregard for the paying public and the millions of armchair fans. Schumacher's appearance on the podium was greeted by a hail of abuse. It mattered little that the German insisted Barrichello mount the top step. Or that he gave his team-mate the trophy awarded to the winner.

In Monaco, Brawn realised the extent of the dissent Ferrari had invited. 'If I reflect on it, it is a decision I wish I hadn't made – we hadn't made,' said Brawn, candidly. 'The reason I regret it is that the consequences were more severe than we should have anticipated. I think you get locked into your position on the pit wall and don't always reflect on the grave consequences of some of the things you are doing. But can we go back a step to explain the circumstances? Ferrari were still paranoid about winning the championships. Before the race, we had sat down with the drivers and played out some scenarios. We discussed everything with them at the same time so there was no subterfuge or any issues. Michael was way ahead in the championship and until he had it won we explained we wanted to give him the benefit of any one–two finishes that we could have. The final discussion took place on Sunday morning. We told them how we wanted the race to play out. Rubens agreed. Michael agreed.'

Barrichello's dominant start did not alarm Brawn. He said: 'At some point early in the race, we said to Rubens over the radio, "Remember our discussion, when there is an opportune moment, concede the position to Michael."' It was then the situation veered in the direction of becoming a crisis. According to Brawn, Barrichello argued, 'No, no! This is my race you can't take it away from me.' Brawn recalled how he continued to remind Barrichello of his pledge to comply with team orders. He told the Brazilian, 'If you change your mind now any trust between you and Michael is broken . . . any trust between you and the team is broken.' Todt was also on the radio to Barrichello, insisting he move over.

This was office politics at 180mph. Schumacher was demanding over the radio as he unsuccessfully pursued Barrichello, 'What the hell is going on?' Brawn produced a thin smile as he retold the story. 'Ideal, wasn't it?' he said. Ultimately, Barrichello radioed that he would yield position, but only when he was ready. And that was in sight of the flag. With the benefit of hindsight – that twenty-twenty optical panacea – Brawn told me: 'The fallout from that was far more serious, far more reaching, than the fallout would have been from Michael getting pissed off with Rubens. Michael had never been booed on the rostrum before and the distraction followed the team to Monaco and beyond. The whole consequence of what we did became much bigger than what we were trying to solve. We hadn't anticipated that.'

Tellingly, Brawn added: 'I don't have any excuses. But within Ferrari you can't believe the intensity of what's going on there. We had won a lot of races that year, but we were still paranoid that the championship might slip away from us. The pressure within Ferrari to win is as big as the pressure at any football club. I can try and justify the reasons why I did what I did – but I wish I hadn't. It looked very bad; and we should have anticipated how bad it would look. I suppose from that point we adopted a siege mentality, you know: the world is against us, let's stick together.' Subsequently, Ferrari were fined $1 million for breaking protocol on the podium and new rules were introduced to outlaw team orders. Two weeks later in Monaco, indignant fans let Ferrari know they had made a calamitous misjudgement. 'I don't think any of us were popular,' admitted Brawn.

Coulthard Strikes Again

Against this background, Coulthard approached the weekend with great optimism. He had won in Monaco two years earlier, but he is the first to acknowledge that his victory owed much to the fact Schumacher's race was ended by mechanical failure. 'In 2002, I just had an absolute belief that I could win,' explained Coulthard. 'The reason I feel so confident to talk about Monaco, to become cockier about Monaco, say, than Silverstone, where I also won twice, is because I did my homework. I used to get up and ride the circuit on my bike at sunrise on Wednesday morning. That is when all the barriers are up for the first time and as I rode around the circuit, inspecting how it might have changed from the previous year, there was no sign of anyone else on the track. For me, it was all about mental commitment. It is a bit like training on Christmas Day: you know that your rivals might be, but you also know they might not be. I tried to be the first car out on Thursday morning. I'd be down at the end of the pit lane, wanting to get the first lap on the circuit. I then felt: I have ownership of this race track . . . come and beat me if you can. Of course, that changes when others start going quicker than you! Yet the truth is you have to start building confidence at Monaco somehow. This was my way.'

Due to the traffic congestion in practice and qualifying, isn't trying to get a clear lap at Monaco as scientific as placing a bet on a roll of the roulette wheel in the hope your number might come up? I asked. 'Not necessarily,' said Coulthard. 'Obviously, with the team you try to work out a strategy. It comes down to management – and which team, and which driver, manages the circumstances best. I tried to be out on the circuit around quicker cars, because you know once they are there their laps they will be going quickly. I wanted to be around those with quality to give myself the best chance. Margins of error are so minute here.

'You are very aware of the silence of the crowd before you go out for qualifying. You had to be in your space. You had done the work to set up your car. You know the track evolves and continues to evolve during qualifying and you had to take that into account. It is important not to panic if the car is not quite right on the first run. I would feel more comfortable if I started the weekend with a bit of oversteer, which was not great for outright speed. But as the track evolves and the rubber in the rear tends to stabilise, you end up coming towards understeer. You need a great front end, come qualifying.'

His plan came to fruition, as he qualified on the front row alongside Juan Pablo Montoya, who had placed his Williams on pole. On race morning, the last thing Coulthard did before he walked out of his fourth-floor apartment was to place his kilt on his bed, so that it would be accessible for him to wear that evening to the dinner held in honour of the winner at the Sporting Club. 'I had a premonition I was going to win,' explained Coulthard. 'I knew I would out-start Montoya. If I could lead the race, I had the chance to win the race. I don't see myself as arrogant, but equally I think I earned my place in Formula One and I have a skill that enabled me in certain circumstances to be on a level with the best drivers.

'The reason I stayed for nine years at McLaren was not because I won lots of championships or races for them, but because Ron Dennis recognised my work ethic. He could have potentially employed faster guys, certainly younger guys, almost certainly cheaper guys. But I kept getting the gig because I had a work ethic. Mika was a much more natural, stronger qualifier. But there were times I could out-start him and times I could out-race him. I think wheel-to-wheel racing was my comfort zone. That was about respecting limits – and you had to know where that limit was.'

For a second time, Coulthard proved to be the driver most attuned to the challenge of mastering the streets of Monaco. He won the race from Schumacher by one minute and, like many before him, found the couple of steps from the track to the podium one of the most memorable walks in Formula One. 'It's wonderful that F1 has retained that heritage,' said Coulthard. 'You can spray the champagne with your mechanics on the race track.' That evening he wore his kilt to the drinks reception at the palace, then to dinner at the Sporting Club. 'I have been lucky enough to sit with Prince Rainier, then with Prince Albert after the second victory. As the winner, you are clapped into dinner – again, something so special. To get the chance to speak with Prince Rainier and know that he had sat there with drivers you had grown up watching and admiring was a privilege. He took an incredible interest – as does Prince Albert today.'

Monaco 2006

If this chapter of Formula One was dominated by the brilliance of Schumacher and Ferrari, it concluded with another controversy of the German's manufacture in his final season with the Scuderia in 2006 – at Monaco itself this time. As usual, Brawn had driven from Italy to the principality. 'The factory loaned me the most recent Ferrari,' he explained. 'It was a lovely drive, and usually Jean would fly to Italy so that we could travel together by road to Monaco.' Ferrari's long reign as champions was over, usurped in 2005 by Fernando Alonso driving for Renault. Alonso had maintained his winning habit into the new season and had been victorious in three races before the team assembled in the paddock beside the harbour. Schumacher held pole position as he neared the end of the final moments of qualifying, but the data indicated that Alonso's speed would enable the Spaniard to eclipse the German.

To the astonishment of those in the paddock and the media room, Schumacher drove in slow motion towards the barriers at the exit of Rascasse and came to a halt, his Ferrari blocking the road in the final corner. Alonso's hope of taking pole was ended, as he had to adhere to the yellow flags being waved by marshals. Even seasoned Schumacher watchers were astounded when he kept a straight face while pleading that he had lost control of his car. Few believed him. Rosberg, whose son Nico was in his first season of Formula One with Williams, felt such outrage that he told a knot of international reporters: 'He is a cheap cheat.'

Gratifyingly, the stewards met to adjudge this most improbable 'accident'. Hours passed as they evaluated the evidence. Then, approaching midnight, while parties on boats in the harbour were in full swing, and those of us waiting to file for the last edition of newspapers in London were pacing the paddock with growing anxiety, the stewards announced they had relegated Schumacher to the back of the grid.

Ten years after the scandal, I asked Brawn, 'Did you believe Michael had an accident?'

'No, he had an aberration,' replied Brawn. 'He couldn't explain it afterwards to us. All I said to the stewards was that if it had been a planned event I would have told Michael to put his car into the wall hard . . . because we could have fixed it overnight.' Neither Brawn nor Ferrari was implicated in the furore. It was Schumacher acting as a maverick; Schumacher protecting his turf and to hell with the consequences.

Brawn understood this, but his loyalty, and the years of success, drove him to speak in defence of Schumacher. 'It's like your kids do something wrong – you sort it out with your kids, but then defend them to the maximum,' he argued. 'I am not saying Michael was a kid, but he was part of the team and we had been through many things together. I was going to defend him whatever happened. It was just an aberration, a stupid one, because he had the fastest car there. He was blindingly quick in the race and finished seventh. It was a mad aberration that he had three or four times in his career. But it was all part of the magic of Michael Schumacher.'

All part of the legend of the man who caused the bells at the parish church in Maranello to be rung on seventy-two occasions in eleven years, in honour of Ferrari winning a Grand Prix.

Caterer's Tale

Lyndy Redding has been engaged in providing the catering needs for guests at Monaco for twenty-eight years. For the past two decades she was in partnership with McLaren, through a deal established with Ron Dennis in a company called Absolute Taste. She has supervised victory celebrations in the Monaco paddock for six McLaren drivers – Senna, Häkkinen, Coulthard, Räikkönen, Alonso and Hamilton. She has fed thousands of guests, and Lyndy is a friend to one and all because of her kindness and generosity of spirit. However, she does remember with particular fondness Coulthard's wins at Monaco. 'David was the most generous of all the drivers,' said Lyndy. 'I couldn't tell you how many times he took the team out. David is a gentleman – charming, respectful, a lovely, lovely man.'

Her rise has been as spectacular as some of the drivers she has come to know. Her inauguration was a nightmarish adventure as head chef on a boat caught in a massive storm in the Bay of Biscay en route to fulfil a charter contract for guests of Leyton House, who backed the March-Judd team at Monaco in 1988. 'Basically, all the fuel was in the hold and it ran loose in the storm,' she said. 'We had two nights sleeping on the bridge and there were conversations about having us airlifted to safety. Fortunately, the storm passed and we returned to Cardiff to clean up the damage. We arrived in Monaco on Thursday afternoon and went straight into this mad charter where the Japanese owners and mechanics thought it was a good idea to have a water fight on board. It was absolutely horrendous.'

Lyndy's second employment in Formula One proved a turning point as she learned the business alongside Sally Hart, from Wings, who catered for McLaren's sponsors, Marlboro. 'Three of us were cooking for the team and all the guests,' she said. 'It was wonderful food. I loved working for Sally, she taught me so much. When Ayrton arrived he wouldn't always speak as he could be somewhere else in his mind, but when he did he would always hold your face when he kissed you good morning. Ayrton was a beautiful man. Gerhard Berger was completely off his rocker and hilarious fun. I think there was a great chemistry between them.'

When the Marlboro contract with McLaren ended at the end of 1996, Dennis asked to speak with Lyndy. She had wanted to start her own business in event-catering in

London – but Dennis persuaded her to think of going into business with McLaren. 'Ron asked me to write a business plan,' she said. 'I had to hire an office for an hour as I never used a typewriter; I was a cook.' Dennis liked what he saw and together they formed a company called Absolute Taste. McLaren took a 55 per cent stake and Lyndy the remainder.

When she started out on 1 February 1997, she still didn't have an office. 'I got a Ford Escort Estate from McLaren and put a computer in the boot and drove back to my one-bedroom flat in Wandsworth,' laughed Lyndy. 'I was living and working there for two years. Two pallets of soft drinks would be permanently in my living room. Eventually, I acquired a secretary and by the end of the first year we had seven people on board.' With her staff, she catered races and tests.

The staff at Absolute Taste grew to approximately 300, with kitchens in London and Geneva providing in-flight catering for clientele operating private jets. The company's turnover increased to around £20 million. Monaco is still the most demanding race on the calendar. 'You feel the spike at Monaco time,' she said. 'Everyone is on 24-hour alert. Even if the circumstances of the team has changed a bit, we still did around sixty flights going to Monaco on the Friday of race weekend in 2016. For years we catered for guests in apartments and some boats for our sponsors. We hire kitchens – and have cooked in various different places. For a number of years we looked after the Lodge, the grandstand opposite the pits, so we had a big kitchen right on the harbour. We had our own tender to deliver to the boats. I suppose we have served as many as 2,000 people a day. Now we rent events kitchens in one of the hotels in Fontvieille and bring the food round by boat. We do a lot of parties in the evening, too.'

Lyndy is married to McLaren team manager Dave Redding; and the race after their son Josh was born, he was given the proud distinction of receiving the winning constructors' trophy on the podium after Hamilton triumphed at the 2010 Canadian Grand Prix. 'Dave was talking to me on the phone when Lewis poured a bottle of champagne over his head,' she said. 'Lewis signed a photograph for Josh.' These recent years have been harsh times for McLaren, a team without a win since 2012. Indeed, Dennis became a casualty of a boardroom revolt against him at the end of 2016, and at the start of 2017 One Event Management acquired Absolute Taste from Lyndy and McLaren. Lyndy remains the figurehead at the helm of the rebranded Absolute Taste. She explained: 'Being part of McLaren for twenty years has been amazing, and we will always have their DNA in the business. We look forward, together with One Event Management, to continue working with McLaren both in Formula One and at the team's headquarters at the McLaren Technology Centre in Woking.

'Most of the team don't know the euphoria of winning, but we all fervently believe that is going to change.' Lyndy goes to selective races these days, as the business demands her presence in London and, with her husband travelling for much of the year, Lyndy wants to be at home for Josh. There has been a shortage of success and some ruthless decisions taken at McLaren, but Lyndy is always first with a warm greeting whenever she is at the team's HQ in the paddock. 'I love our world,' she said.

Rivals, 2016

13

Family Business: The Rosbergs, the Hills and Hamilton

Ten days before the biggest motor race of his life in Abu Dhabi on 27 November 2016, Nico Rosberg looked like he had interrupted brunch on an ocean-going yacht to join me. He wore a casual-chic jacket, crew-neck sweater and shirt, in three complementary shades of blue, to offset his dazzling-white chinos. He was clean-shaven and immediately apologised for arriving five minutes after our scheduled rendezvous time, not beside the harbour close to his home in Monaco, but within the inner sanctum of the Mercedes-AMG Petronas F1 team's headquarters in Brackley, in Northamptonshire. Rosberg is a man possessed of great style outside as well as inside a race car.

Having spent three years driving alongside Schumacher, and getting the better of the seven-time world champion each season during the Second Coming of Michael after he came out of retirement in 2010, Rosberg was gearing up with

Mercedes' engineering staff for the final race of his fourth season partnering Lewis Hamilton. Schumacher and Hamilton were fast, hard, uncompromising and no strangers to playing mind games if they thought a need arose. Rosberg was in the same team as them, but they were hardly mates. So, eleven years of painstaking effort from Rosberg was being distilled into one afternoon's drive in the desert of Abu Dhabi. Win, and Rosberg would be elevated into the pantheon of Formula One world champions. Lose, and he would descend into despair.

I had first met Rosberg at his parents' snow-covered picturesque mountain lodge in Zell am See, in Austria, two months before he made his Formula One debut in March 2006 for Williams, the team his father, Keke, delivered the world championship for in 1982. It can be correctly assumed that there was no reason to believe that the conversation we shared in mid-November 2016 was taking place ahead of the last Grand Prix Nico would ever start.

That November, Rosberg's second place in the Abu Dhabi Grand Prix, behind Hamilton – whom he had first competed against when they were both teenagers in the European karting championship – confirmed the 31-year-old German as world champion. Before the Rosbergs, only Graham and Damon Hill had ever established Formula One as a family business on such an exalted scale; and the Rosbergs alone hold the unique distinction of being the only father and son to have won the Monaco Grand Prix – Keke once in 1983, and Nico three times in succession from 2013. The speculative storyline immediately after the sand had settled in Abu Dhabi looked a compelling one. Seasoned observers reflected on how Hamilton would, surely, spend the winter recess plotting to reclaim his crown in 2017. Only Rosberg was not listening. In his mind, he had written an alternative narrative.

After five days of parties and hangovers, of flying visits to Malaysia, Germany and the United Kingdom to offer his sincere gratitude to those who had assisted his climb to the summit of Formula One, we now know Rosberg stunned his paymasters at Mercedes, and the wider motor racing community, by announcing his retirement.

Rosberg said that prioritising his family – his wife, Vivian, and fifteen-month-old daughter, Alaïa – was the primary motivating force behind his decision to walk away from Formula One at the high point of his profession. It is significant, in trawling through my notes, to report that during our meeting in Brackley, where Rosberg spoke of his own childhood in Monaco, the champion-in-waiting revealed proudly: 'Today my wife is taking our daughter to enrol at my old school, the International School of Monaco. It is necessary to plan this far ahead with her schooling . . . and the fact she is there today is amazing to me!' Each May, classrooms at the ISM provide a window on to the world of Formula One, as the paddock for the Monaco Grand Prix is constructed on the waterfront of the harbour beneath the school. 'I remember how the Williams team worked right below me as I looked out of the window during maths class,' he said, laughing. 'That was spectacular. But I admit I never paid much attention to maths in those particular days.'

Instead, the cars below captured his imagination. As did the race weekend itself, which Rosberg witnessed on many occasions as a boy, from the grandstand provided by the family's wooden-hulled motor-sailer, *Vagabunda*, moored in a prime position in the harbour near the chicane after the tunnel. 'One year I was asleep on the roof of the boat and I got woken by Ayrton Senna coming out of the tunnel,' he said, smiling. 'The noise . . . it was insane. So loud.'

And then there were the stories his father told, and the films of old races at Monaco, and motor-sport articles to be devoured. 'I know a lot about the history of the Monaco Grand Prix,' said Nico. Of course, he grew up to feature heavily in that history. Also, he grew up to be world champion just as his father had been. For Hill, this meant the 'Son of Champs Club' had been doubled, as he pointed out to Rosberg when the just-crowned champion was feted during the 2016 Autosport Awards black-tie dinner in London at the beginning of December. 'I'm the president of the club, by the way; you're the vice president!' exclaimed Hill, a line he cheerfully attributed to his wife, Georgie.

Privately, a few days later, Hill told me: 'The idea that you have gone into the same profession as your dad, after he was very successful in the field, is not one necessarily to be advised. You always get that pressure created by what your dad achieved, I think. Even though you can deny it, the reality is that it is always there. Didn't Nico say after he won the championship that he was very proud of his achievement and that pride, he said, was related to the fact his dad was a champion? It is a way of measuring up in some ways, or saying thank you.

'I think I was slightly let off the hook, as my dad wasn't around. Nico has always had the shadow of his father in the background. The father influence is huge in this business. Jenson Button has said that when his father, John, died he didn't enjoy Formula One quite as much any more. Whether boys are pushed by their dads, or whether some dads didn't want their sons to race, which was the case with the fathers of James Hunt and Niki Lauda, there is an influence there, isn't there? I have thought much about this, and if my dad had lived I think I would have gone in a completely different direction. It's interesting to me that Nico got that something he wanted out of motor racing – then decided to stop. It was almost a box-ticking exercise, which, in some ways, it was for me. I know that driving a Formula One car represented some of the best years of my life. It's a privilege and a very enjoyable one, but the pressure is massive.

'It is about being put under the microscope in every sense, and that is not so much fun. It is all-absorbing. Even when you are away from it, you are not really away. It takes everything to succeed at that level. You can never really be disconnected; you can try, but you never really stop thinking about what you have to do. Since the championship ended, I can see there is a huge difference in Nico from the guy you see in front of the camera at the racetrack and the guy off-camera. In London at the Autosport Awards, and the BRDC Awards, where Nico was made an honorary member, he went round the room chatting to those he wanted. He was very relaxed, not playing the superstar, and he didn't seem uncomfortable in any way. He seemed to be in total charge of his life and free to go where he wanted and to do what he wanted to do. He has earned that right, 100 per cent.'

In essence, Rosberg and Hill are similar men. Both exacted every ounce of their skill, and devoted each waking hour, to finishing ahead of a formidable rival: in Hill's case, Schumacher; in Rosberg's case, Hamilton. 'I was older – thirty-three – when I began in Formula One than Nico was when he retired!' said Hill, smiling. His analysis of Rosberg, a man of proven tenacity, intellect and mental fortitude, is warm, but ringed with truth. Hamilton might – should – end his Formula One career residing in the company of the all-time great champions. Rosberg will be acclaimed as a champion who answered all the questions asked of him in one calendar year. For him, it rightly justified his lifelong quest to be recognised alongside his father, Keke.

'Nico's proved himself to be a top-drawer Formula One driver,' said Hill. 'He's just not from the very top drawer. That's the point, really. There are a handful of men, like Lewis, like Michael, like Senna, Prost, Stewart and Mansell, who are on a different level. Then there are those who are very good, who can beat them on given days, but to stay at that level, year in, year out, is of another order altogether. I have to be honest and say I looked at Schumacher and thought, "Why do you want to keep winning and winning?" I am staggered at his appetite for victory and titles. No one ever imagined one driver would win seven world titles. Prost thought four was good, and that he would leave Fangio up there on a peg with five. But for Schumacher six wasn't enough. *It was seven!* That's mind-blowing.'

If this is how Nico Rosberg's Formula One story ends, it seems appropriate to trace its beginning. To discover how a child with a racing heritage, growing up in the midst of the great wealth and security and educational opportunities enjoyed by residents of Monaco, found himself engaged in a lifelong rivalry with a kid from a council estate in Stevenage, Hertfordshire, called Lewis Hamilton.

*

Keke Rosberg received his big break from Frank Williams through circumstance rather than design. He was Formula One's original 'Flying Finn', a man who bucked the trend in Finland by deploying his enviable car control in a single-seat racing car, rather than in a rally car as other prodigiously competitive Finns – Hannu Mikkola, Markku Alén, Timo Mäkinen, Henri Toivonen, Juha Kankkunen, Pentti Airikkala and Ari Vatanen – had done in the seventies and early eighties. The words *swashbuckling* and *Rosberg* belonged in the same sentence.

Even in low-budget teams – Theodore, ATS, Wolf and Fittipaldi – the moustachioed Rosberg stood out. John Watson remembers first racing against him, driving for Brabham, when Rosberg made his debut in the South African Grand Prix for Theodore, in 1978. 'Keke drove a Formula One car like a

Scandinavian rally driver . . . with oversteer everywhere,' said Watson. 'That was his style, that's what he was outstanding at. He wasn't a conformist in driving style or personality. He was an individual, a character. Simply, he was Keke. In comparison to Nico, he was more flamboyant inside and outside of the car. Nico has been all his life in Monaco, he is an archetypal Euro child: multilingual, sophisticated, elegant, and educated to do pretty much what he likes if he sets his mind to it. Others in my time, or contemporary times, are more Lewis-type racers. Nico was a racer, but it wasn't the only thing in his life and now he is going to develop other elements of his life.'

Keke Rosberg's parents, a veterinarian and a chemist, had both competed in rallies, establishing a racing bloodline that passed through to a third generation. Keke had arrived in Formula One down a long and winding road from success in karting and junior formulas. In 1978, he drove in forty-one races on thirty-six weekends on five continents. This pattern of grinding graft and magisterial prowess at the wheel brought him to Formula One that same year. But it would be another four years before an opportunity to really compete presented itself, in a fortuitous manner.

At the end of 1981, the Australian and former world champion Alan Jones surprised Frank Williams by announcing his retirement. Rosberg was the one driver of competence, albeit without experience of running at the front of a Grand Prix, who could be recruited at such short notice from Fittipaldi, whose small budget disappeared at a speed their cars could never match. What he lacked in racing miles in a competitive Grand Prix car, Rosberg more than compensated for with his charisma and self-confidence. He would openly admit: 'I'm a cocky bastard.' Rosberg caused no offence with this attitude, because he made it no secret that he was there to succeed in the broadest definition of the term. Had your brief been to find a man who always drives to the edge of his resources, who blindly refuses to acknowledge defeat and who can make a racing car twitch and turn at his command, then you would have found it hard to ignore Rosberg. His invitation to travel to the south of France to test for Williams at the Paul Ricard Circuit at Le Castellet was manna from heaven, as he had been heading somewhere altogether different – towards obscurity. At thirty-three, life had suddenly taken on a new dimension.

Rosberg recalled the detail – or lack of it – of his life-changing test to Formula One journalist and author Maurice Hamilton for his book *Williams*: 'I had arrived the night before the test. Charlie Crichton-Stuart ([a bon viveur and Williams stalwart]) and I drank Beaujolais nouveau in the evening, and then at eight o'clock the next morning they put qualifying tyres on the car and, without warming it up, they said get in and see what you can do! Frank sometimes made strange decisions and this was one of them. I came from nowhere, did this test, and he signed me up more or less straight away.'

Irregular it might have been, but it was also most definitely inspired. In a season of remorseless misery, Rosberg's performances in his first fast and reliable F1 car lifted some of the gloom in 1982. For in this mournful year, tragedy followed tragedy. Gilles Villeneuve, one of the *tifosi's* most beloved Ferrari drivers of all time, died during practice at the Belgium Grand Prix at Zolder, while five weeks later Riccardo Paletti was killed in front of those of us seated in the media room when, in the young Italian's second Formula One start, he drove from the rear of the grid into the back of Didier Pironi's stalled Ferrari at the start of the Canadian Grand Prix in Montreal. Two months afterwards, as a heavy rainstorm broke over Hockenheim during practice for the German Grand Prix, Pironi damaged his legs so badly after crashing into the tail end of Prost's Renault that he never raced in Formula One again.

Watson won in Belgium, but that is not his abiding memory. What stayed with him as he left the paddock was the sight of Villeneuve's helicopter, parked and unattended. 'The reality and the tragedy of motor racing is that when someone dies someone else, a loved one or a friend, has to go to the driver's hotel room and collect his belongings,' said Watson. 'In Gilles's case, someone came to collect his helicopter after we had left. Gilles was a massive risk taker, because he had that supreme self-belief that he would always get away with it. He applied that to driving on the road, he applied it to flying a helicopter, sometimes on fumes, and he applied it as a racing driver. I don't subscribe to that school of philosophy, but maybe that's what made him an exciting racing driver and why many people still love him to this day.'

Two weeks after Villeneuve's fatal accident, Ferrari entered just one car for the Monaco Grand Prix as Formula One tried to come to terms with the heartfelt loss of the Canadian, who had driven and lived on terms of his own making. To compound the grief, Villeneuve's home had been in Monaco. One banner draped from a grandstand was laced with heavy poignancy: *Gilles sei sempre con noi*. Gilles, you are still among us.

Yet, as always, this is a show which stops only to doff its hat in the direction of its fallen heroes; then, it motors on. Remarkably, this was Rosberg's first-ever race at Monaco. He had failed to qualify three times in uncompetitive cars and missed the race altogether in 1979 as Wolf brought just one car for his team-mate, Hunt. Rosberg's debut on the streets of the principality coincided with an eventful, crazy and totally surreal motor race. Inevitably, the arrival of rain late in proceedings created the drama. Rosberg's own race ended on lap 65 of the 76-lap race when he broke the rear suspension of his Williams after he pinged a barrier. It was the prologue to a chain of events you simply could not make up.

The last three laps were manic. On lap 74, Prost surrendered the lead to Riccardo Patrese, driving for Brabham, when the Frenchman crashed his Renault heavily into the chicane. Patrese's chance of victory seemed to disappear as quickly as it had materialised, because shortly afterwards he spun at the Loews hairpin. Pironi passed the stationary Brabham, but his bolt for glory spluttered and stalled when his Ferrari ran out of fuel. Next in succession was Andrea de Cesaris, but his Alfa Romeo had guzzled all its remaining fuel before the Italian could reach Pironi's lifeless Ferrari. Irishman Derek Daly, driving for Williams alongside Rosberg, was the next man poised to inherit the race. However, his car was decidedly second-hand and was without its front and back wings due to earlier escapades. Yet that was not the cause of his demise. What actually accounted for Daly was the fact that his damaged gearbox seized up completely before he could begin the final lap.

In the BBC commentary booth, Hunt could not conceal his exasperation. 'Well, we've got this ridiculous situation where we're all sitting by the start–finish line waiting for a winner to come past and we don't seem to be getting one,' he said. Eventually, Hunt's vigil was rewarded. For Patrese's Brabham – apparently out of the race after the spin at Loews – came into view and crossed the line first. The Italian had received a nudge from marshals, who had deemed his car to be in a dangerous place. With this momentum, Patrese had managed to bump-start his car on the downhill sector from the hairpin and seized an improbable first-ever win in Formula One at the end of a plot beyond parody. Afterwards, no one seemed more surprised than Patrese that he had won. At the podium, he met de Cesaris, Pironi and Elio de Angelis.

'There was a big discussion over who was first, second or third,' said Patrese, telling the improbable story later.

'Somebody came to me and started to shout, "You won, you won!" Then, I finally realised . . .' As tradition demanded, Patrese was the honoured guest at the after-race party, an occasion that acquired greater significance than ever, as the Italian explained: 'That was the last time Princess Grace was there – she died in October of that year. I was quite young, and still a bit shy. She was really very kind and tried to make me comfortable in that situation.'

Patrese was one of eleven men to win in 1982, a season featuring sixteen races. Before the championship showdown on a circuit constructed in the car park of Caesars Palace in Las Vegas – which some thought was a low-rent stunt, designed to attract high-rollers to the Nevada Desert – Prost, Lauda, Pironi, Watson and Arnoux had all won twice. Nelson Piquet, Patrick Tambay, de Angelis and Rosberg had each won once. Yet as a consequence of his consistent points-scoring, Rosberg had to finish just fifth to be acclaimed world champion for a team who had hired him only weeks before the season began.

As the championship approached its climax, I had coffee with him near his luxurious home in Cookham Dean, Berkshire, complete with a sauna off the master bedroom. 'I was always rubbished at the start of my Formula One career because my driving was very hard,' said Rosberg. In truth, it was the only calling card Rosberg could present. 'Every driver says, "Give me a good car and I'll show you what I can do,"' admitted the affable Finn. 'But I suppose I said it louder than most.' He was multilingual from his nomadic existence during his years striving to reach the pinnacle of motor sport, yet perhaps his most valuable asset was that he was born street-smart. 'I enjoy making money,' said Rosberg. His property portfolio at the time included homes in England, Monaco, Ibiza and America. He flew his own twin-engined plane, liked a drink at an appropriate moment, and smoked – cigars or cigarettes. Before the championship showdown in Las Vegas, Rosberg travelled early to acclimatise to the time difference in California, where he spent some days increasing his flying hours at the controls of a light aircraft as a means of relaxation.

Watson was the man with the best chance of beating Rosberg to the championship. 'I had to win to be world champion,' said Watson, now seventy. 'To my mind the calculations were very much in favour of Keke, as they were for Nico in Abu Dhabi. Lewis could only do what he could do, which was to win the race. He tried to back Nico into the Ferrari of Sebastian Vettel and the Red Bull of Daniel Ricciardo. I don't condone what Lewis did – but I don't blame him for doing it. That was the only option he had to win the world championship. He was prepared to ignore the commands from the pit wall and deal with the consequences afterwards. The world championship was above company politics at that moment. He was driving for himself. When they told Lewis to speed up, he would have known that meant he could not win the world championship, and if he knew that, the bosses at Mercedes knew that, so in Lewis's mind that meant they wanted Nico to win. You can see how the paranoia built in his head.

'In Las Vegas, I came from the midfield to pass Keke, but, for reasons no one could have predicted, Michele Alboreto and his Tyrrell were quicker than everyone. I got to within ten or twelve seconds of Alboreto, but he was able to respond to whatever I had left in the tank.' Alboreto became the eleventh winner of the year, Watson finished second and Rosberg was anointed world champion by a margin of five points. Watson has never felt aggrieved that Rosberg became champion on account of a solitary victory. 'Keke won the world title on consistency, primarily,' he said. 'At all points of the season, he was competitive. I don't begrudge him that. It was an opportunity I had, or Niki might have had, and others had as well, but we all left the door open for Keke. On the racetrack, I found him very fair and very clean, and I can't say that about every competitor either that season or throughout my F1 career. Keke is an honourable man, one of the good guys. He has always been quick-witted, someone clever, funny and ready with a response to any comment.'

Rosberg told Maurice Hamilton years later how Frank Williams and Patrick Head had reacted to his title success without the fanfare or fuss that greets a champion today. 'It was business-like, no bullshit,' recalled Rosberg. 'When I won the championship, that was it for the day. "OK, that's done. Next?" So I didn't stay around, and went off to San Francisco with Mansour Ojjeh [a sponsor of the team and friend].' It was some party, by all accounts.

The following spring, Rosberg won the 1983 Monaco Grand Prix, the second win of his career. Reportedly, he had been feeling under the weather during the weekend, but this did not hinder him from putting his Williams-Ford in fifth position on the grid, making him the highest-placed driver without a turbo-powered engine at his disposal. It had been raining and the track was sufficiently wet to persuade the drivers around him to begin the race on wet tyres. Rosberg gambled by starting on slicks, as did his team-mate, Jacques Laffite. From the outset, Rosberg's throttle control gained an impressive amount of grip from the smoothness of his Cosworth engine, and he darted through the traffic ahead to arrive at Sainte-Dévote in second place. By the end of the first lap, he had passed Prost to assume the lead of the Grand Prix. Soon an abundance of rivals had to react to the drying conditions by pitting for slick tyres. Rosberg had the race in his hands – and he won with a masterful performance that was the hallmark of a world champion. 'It made sense to throw the dice as Keke and Williams did that afternoon,' said Watson, who watched the race with Lauda at the

Austrian's home in Ibiza. They had flown there for a burst of warm-weather training after they had failed to qualify for the race to the huge embarrassment of McLaren and their principal sponsors, Marlboro. 'In the end, Keke won comfortably.'

Rosberg never triumphed again in 1983. With the new Williams-Honda turbo car an unaccommodating package, he won just once in '84, his old friend Mansour Ojjeh having switched allegiance and provided the funds to develop the TAG Porsche turbo engine that enabled Lauda and Prost to dominate the season for McLaren. In the following summer, Rosberg illustrated his insatiable thirst for pure outright speed. During qualifying for the 1985 British Grand Prix, he brought the crowd at Silverstone to their feet. He travelled the 2.93 mile-long circuit in his Williams-Honda turbo-charged car, fitted with the super-sticky qualifying tyres of the era, in 1 minute, 5.967 seconds, at a preposterous average speed of 160.007mph. No Formula One car had ever lapped a track averaging over 160mph. It was a thunderous, ground-breaking sixty-five seconds' drive of staggering bravado. But Rosberg was not satisfied with that lap. Suspecting that his provisional pole position would come under counter-attack from men like Senna, Mansell or Piquet, Rosberg opted to make a second run. He wanted to improve his time in case one of his rivals eclipsed his record. As if; yet the Flying Finn went out again and promptly, very promptly, rewrote the history he had just created. His second lap, when he seemingly coerced his car to defy gravity, as he sped from one corner to the next in the blink of an eye, was timed at 1 minute, 5.591 seconds. His average speed was 160.938mph. He had stretched the boundaries of his mind as well as explored the limits of his racing car. Once out of the car, Rosberg lit up a cigarette. 'I got carried away, and that shouldn't be the case if you want to survive,' admitted Rosberg. 'But it only happened that one time . . .'

His only child, Nico, had been born less than a month earlier in Wiesbaden, Germany, the country of his wife's birth. Nico's childhood, though, would be spent in Monaco, and he was less than eighteen months old when his father retired from Formula One in 1986, having spent the final season of his career with McLaren. In all, he won five times in F1; it was a record that did not properly reflect his natural talent, or the dexterity of his racing mind, or the level of commitment he brought to a profession that was his passion as well as a means of securing the future prosperity of his wife and their young son. Later in life Rosberg managed Mika Häkkinen, accompanying his fellow Finn on his journey from the foothills of the sport to the summit represented by his world titles in 1998 and 1999. The last driver he managed was his son, Nico; but Rosberg Sr had stepped into the shadows some years before Rosberg Jr walked into Abu Dhabi as a contender and floated out as world champion.

*

Other racing drivers have migrated to this tax haven beside the Mediterranean, but, for Nico, Monaco has been his home for ever. 'It all seems very normal for me to grow up there,' he said, in Brackley. 'I started school for two years just above the paddock. Back in the day, they were still pushing the cars up to the pits.' As an infant, he was hooked on the magic and mystery of these noisy beasts unleashed on the narrow streets that his mother sedately drove down on the school run. 'The first time I drove a racing car at Monaco, in a GP2 race in 2005, I remember screaming going through the tunnel and thinking, "This is just insane!" The sheer speed of driving this racetrack, in the place I have known all my life, where mum drove me, or I went by bus, was unimaginable. Driving a Formula One car made it a different world.'

From an early age, he was consumed to learn as much as he could about Formula One. 'I loved watching old races, and I watched a lot from Monaco, even going back to the fifties,' said Rosberg. Did you see Panis win? I asked. 'Sure, I was at the circuit. I was eleven years old. That was an awesome result.' Was his dad a good raconteur? 'He told me stories from his time and from Mika's time when he managed him. Always crazy stories. One I remember is from the period when the drivers tested in Rio de Janeiro – they all loved that! He said that there was one day in Rio when he stopped his rental car at traffic lights and Alain Prost and Ron Dennis were in a car behind. They got out and started jumping on the roof of his car until it just got smaller and smaller . . .' Is it as crazy today? I ventured, suspecting I already knew the answer. 'Nothing on that scale,' he replied. The age of Instagram and Twitter – and the realisation that almost anyone you encounter has a phone camera – are formidable reasons to deter young, exceptionally well-paid men from behaving madly. As Brundle said, the sport has gone from the analogue to the digital age with good and less good consequences.

Rosberg's school days were ordered and unexceptional. He was an attentive and successful student. 'When I finished junior school, I transferred to a school in Nice. It took one hour to get there by bus in the morning and one hour to come home. It was fun – we messed about on the bus.' Rosberg and his friends spent time in the evening or at weekends playing with a ball on the promenade close to where they lived. 'We played soccer a lot, but sometimes it might be roller hockey,' he said. But unlike his friends, Rosberg was already making meaningful strides in another sport: karting. At six, he had been driving karts with his dad and other Grand Prix drivers, such as Gerhard Berger and Thierry Boutsen, in the garden of the family's summer home in Ibiza. At nine, the sport became more serious as he learned race craft; at twelve, he was testing engines; at fourteen, he had a truck from Bridgestone at his disposal at a circuit to test tyres; and before he was too much older, he hounded Schumacher in a round of the karting world championship on a wet track at Kerpen, the small town in Germany where the legendary champion grew up and competed as an honoured guest. 'I was stuck to Michael's bumper,' laughed Rosberg.

In 2000, he became team-mates for the first time with Lewis Hamilton when they shared the same dreams, and often the same camper van, as they travelled the continent to contest the European Karting Championship for a team known as MBM: Mercedes-Benz McLaren. The background of the two teenagers could not have been starker in contrast. Hamilton's father, Anthony, and his wife, Carmen, divorced when Hamilton was a toddler. At first he lived with his mother, but, aged ten, he moved in with Anthony and his wife, Linda, and their three-year-old son, Nicolas. He remained close to his mother, though. Anthony had worked three jobs simultaneously in the earliest days of his son's karting career, but Lewis's prodigious talent came to the attention of McLaren before he was twelve. From that point, the family had the financial muscle of the McLaren team behind them. Yet Anthony opted to manage his son's career path.

Were there occasions when Lewis ever shared a ride on a private plane that your father organised to take you racing? 'I'm sure at some point it happened,' said Rosberg. 'Sometimes, I went by private plane. It doesn't sound very good to say this, but yes, I did. It made a difference to my schooling. It was difficult to combine school in Monaco and racing all over Europe, and this saved time.' He added, with great emphasis: 'I didn't always travel by private plane, only when it made a difference to my education.'

Rosberg and Hamilton spent two years as team-mates in

karting, but the first day was either a comedy of errors or a glimpse into the future. 'I went out super-motivated and the track was dry, but for one puddle left from the humidity,' recalled Rosberg, during an interview when Hamilton had signed for Mercedes for the 2013 season. 'It was in the middle of a corner and I took it massively fast and went flying into the tyre barriers and destroyed my kart. As I was stepping out of my kart, I saw my dear friend Lewis arriving. He was even more motivated than me. He hit the same puddle and went flying off the track, smashing into my kart. I still had one foot inside it at the time. His kart broke, too. Of course, it was the most embarrassing moment ever. All the bosses had come to see us and there we were, both hanging in the tyres together with smashed karts – on lap 1.' It hurt neither of them, of course. The margins between them were always incredibly small. Fast racing and teenage pranks prevailed. Greatness beckoned both of them.

*

Between 2008 and 2016 Hamilton and Rosberg would win the Monaco Grand Prix five times; each man also became a world champion. Each of them attracted minute scrutiny: Rosberg because he had the advantage, and the burden, of being the son of a world champion; Hamilton because the colour of his skin, his childhood spent on a council estate, and his adoption by McLaren, made for an intoxicating backstory. In 2007, when Dennis felt Hamilton was ready to be introduced to Formula One – in a McLaren alongside double world champion Fernando Alonso – he wondered if Hamilton would be judged and assessed differently from other young drivers. 'There are people who want Lewis to be the Tiger Woods of motor racing, but no one in our organisation sees him that way,' said Dennis.

Rosberg had declined a place to study for a degree in aeronautical engineering at Imperial College, London, to concentrate on driving. 'It was Ron, through Dad's connection with him, who offered the possibility. He had a good connection with Imperial College, as a lot of engineers came to McLaren from the university,' he said. Rosberg had all the qualifications required and spoke five languages: German, French, English, Spanish and Italian. 'All of my friends were going to university – but I went motor racing. It was a little strange at the time that my life would take a completely different tangent. Strange and a bit worrying.'

But it was a decision he has never regretted. Rosberg beat Hamilton into Formula One by twelve months, having been hired by Williams for the 2006 season. It was while he trained at altitude, at the family winter retreat in Austria, ahead of his first race in Bahrain, that the Rosbergs shared some insight into the story behind the story. 'I thought I couldn't get much more mileage out of motor racing – now I find myself managing Nico,' said Keke. 'I was consciously looking for eighteen months for someone to manage him, but I don't think there's anyone better than me for now – so I'm stuck.' It was not always easy for either of them. 'It can be impossible,' said Keke, smiling. 'I still love motor racing, but as Bernie Ecclestone says, only a dictatorship works in sport. Unfortunately, this project with Nico runs as a democracy – and it's crap!' At twenty, Nico exuded the self-assurance of an educated young man, proud of his heritage but keen to be the author of his own history. Even so, he demonstrated a neat line in self-deprecation as he described how he had been received at Williams, a team where his father was much admired.

'I have an understanding of the car now,' said Nico. 'And at least the guys no longer mistake me for someone on work experience!' Tales from his father's years at Williams were leaked to him, and he relayed one anecdote with particular relish: 'In mid-race Dad's car caught fire in Brazil and he came into the pits. Patrick checked the car and told him to get back in. Dad said to him, "I can't – I've burned my moustache." Patrick yelled, "Who cares about your bloody moustache? Get back in."'

In that first season with Williams, Nico won four points, just three fewer than his team-mate, Mark Webber. His first Grand Prix at Monaco hardly passed to plan. 'Our car was good, but I had traffic in qualifying and ended twelfth on the grid, so that was that,' he said. 'In the race, the throttle stuck open and I crashed at the final corner on the circuit. Mark had been running third until his car broke down, so, all in all, I was disappointed.'

In contrast, the next season Hamilton entered Formula One and took the sport by storm. Instantly, he proved a match for Alonso, the two-time world champion who had switched to McLaren from Renault in return for an estimated £45-million, three-year contract. With that deal came an unspoken understanding that he would be the alpha male in the team. But Hamilton had not crept into the paddock in Melbourne for the first race of the 2007 season under the radar. The headline on a piece I filed for the *Mail on Sunday* a week before the season commenced read: 'Forget Button, this man is Britain's next champion of the world.' Within the feature, a cast list from British Formula One's aristocracy had all urged us to expect exceptional performances from Hamilton. 'Lewis will win a Grand Prix in his first year and there is no question that he is a future world champion,' forecast David Coulthard. 'I'll even predict he will be standing on the podium in Melbourne.' Nigel Mansell argued: 'I have no qualms predicting Lewis will be world champion in the next three to five years – it could be earlier. Lewis has been groomed and sponsored by Ron Dennis, probably to the cost of millions. McLaren are long overdue to be successful on a regular basis and with Alonso in the other car they are ready to win again.' Derek Warwick, these days the president of the BRDC, stared into his crystal ball and predicted the direction of

Hamilton's career with uncanny accuracy: 'Lewis is probably going to be the greatest British driver ever,' he said.

Hamilton did make the podium in Melbourne – finishing third – and by season end he had won four races, the same total as Alonso. The British driver was only denied the world title by Kimi Räikkönen in the last race of the year, in Brazil. But the season within McLaren had been an acrimonious one and concluded with Alonso's departure. Two quick drivers rarely cohabit within the same Formula One team without tantrums and tiaras being thrown, and Hamilton showed himself unnervingly accomplished at looking after his own interests in this macho world where there is nowhere to hide or dress your wounds without attracting derision. One year later, Hamilton arrived at the Brazilian Grand Prix with the world championship at his mercy. Hill, who had been the last British driver to be crowned champion twelve years earlier, told me in the countdown to Hamilton's duel with Felipe Massa in São Paolo: 'Lewis can become a global star. He could be elevated to that small category of sportsmen – Muhammad Ali, Pele, Tiger Woods and David Beckham – who are known around the world beyond the sport that made them famous.'

At that point, Hamilton had won nine of the thirty-four Grand Prix races he had driven, and started from pole position in more than a third of them. He dutifully completed his mission in Brazil – not without drama, naturally – yet that was swiftly forgotten as Hamilton rewarded McLaren's faith in him by providing them with their first world champion since Häkkinen. His five victories included wins on the streets of Monaco and at the home of British Motor Sport, Silverstone. At twenty-three, he was the youngest champion in Formula One history; and Hamilton's success reverberated around the world to reach an audience beyond the normal constituency of motor sport. He had revealed himself in the process as a man driven by cold-eyed ambition, and won over those who wondered if life had been too easily arranged for him. Berger, a veteran of 210 Grand Prix races, told me: 'I saw how Lewis had been spoiled, never had to fight for a drive, how everything was organised for him, and I wondered how he could have a killer instinct in a Formula One car. Well, like everyone, Lewis has made a fantastic impression on me. Ron can sometimes be a pain, but he deserves credit for what he has done with Lewis.'

Hamilton revelled in his maiden victory at Monaco in 2008. His childhood idol had been Senna, and Senna was the maestro of Monaco. The streets were wet, the conditions treacherous, and Hamilton touched the barriers on the outside of Tabac at lap 6, which necessitated an unscheduled visit to the pits for a new set of tyres. He was refuelled for a longer second stint and re-emerged in fifth place. Hamilton was leading when the safety car had to be deployed on lap 62 after Rosberg crashed at the swimming pool, scattering debris. Hamilton's car control, precise and light, was beautiful to behold. He talked beforehand of being aware of the spirit of Senna at Monaco more than anywhere else, and there was a gentleness and aggression about his driving that day that evoked memories of the brilliant Brazilian. In spite of suffering a slow puncture on the final lap, Hamilton claimed the victory he most craved when he took the flag as the race was stopped after two hours, two laps shy of the full seventy-eight. 'This has got to be the highlight of my career and I am sure it will be the highlight for the rest of my life,' said Hamilton as the euphoria engulfed him. 'I remember on the last few laps I was just thinking that Ayrton Senna won here a lot of times and to win here would be amazing. From the last corner onwards, I was screaming my head off basically . . .'

The following spring the victor's laurels at Monaco were taken by another British driver – Jenson Button. He ended the year as world champion for Brawn GP, the team Ross Brawn created as a salvage operation after Honda withdrew from Formula One in the winter of 2008 when the global recession bit deep. Button had suspected his career as a Formula One driver was destined for the scrapheap until Brawn bought the team for a nominal £1 and with Nick Fry contrived to make them unlikely champions. Button agreed to a reduction of his salary from £8 million a year to £3 million. 'Credit to Jenson, he understood the situation and wasn't at all difficult,' said Brawn, who joined the Honda operation in December 2007 after taking a year-long sabbatical from Formula One after leaving Ferrari when Schumacher did at the end of 2006. The only mistake Button made in Monaco was that he drove his car at the end of the race into *parc fermé* with everyone else instead of parking his car in front of the royal box, as tradition implored. Button rectified matters by sprinting down the pit straight to keep his appointment with Prince Albert II. 'This is the race everyone wants to win, isn't it?' beamed Button. 'The closing laps were the most enjoyable of my life.' It is an enduring theme, and one echoing down the ages from around these streets.

At the end of that triumphant season, Brawn sold a significant shareholding of the team to Mercedes, and the German car-manufacturing giant changed the name over the door at Brackley and on the entry sheet for the Formula One 2010 world championship to Mercedes GP. Ross recalled with understandable pride: 'Brawn GP existed for one year and won both championships, a 100 per cent record that I doubt anyone will repeat. It was just such a great adventure. Honda had put in a huge effort before they stepped out, leaving a car behind. I picked it up, and with a great team, we finished the job off.'

A new adventure awaited with Mercedes, who had become an official entrant in Grand Prix racing for the first time since 1955, with a German driver for good measure: Rosberg. 'I had discussions with McLaren as well,' said Rosberg. 'But I loved the Mercedes project as described to me by Ross, and Norbert Haug from Mercedes.' Yet all did not proceed quite to plan. Button caught Brawn by surprise by tendering his notice to join Hamilton at McLaren.

'We were caught off-balance,' admitted Brawn. His solution? To call Schumacher. 'We were having a beer at the end of the 2009 season and I knew he missed racing,' said Brawn. 'So, with Jenson gone I rang him to see if he was still missing Formula One. This led to a serious conversation and everything happened fairly quickly afterwards.' At McLaren, Hamilton also made a decision taken from the heart before the start of the 2010 season: he told his father he no longer wanted him to manage his affairs. The boy had become a man.

For Rosberg, the news that Schumacher was his new team-mate caused him to draw a sharp intake of breath. 'It was like God arriving . . . and I was not such a successful driver at the time,' remembered Rosberg. 'All the attention went to him – even internally.' Schumacher undoubtedly claimed centre stage at the first race of the 2010 championship in Bahrain. His media schedule began with a planned press conference at a local Mercedes dealership. Rosberg appeared on time – from memory Schumacher was almost an hour late. 'It became the story of my days,' said Rosberg, smiling. 'Waiting for Michael.' Rosberg barely fielded a question, while Schumacher offered monosyllabic or sarcastic responses to questions from the large international press corps covering his comeback after three years' retirement. At the circuit, Schumacher swept in and immediately commandeered the side of the Mercedes garage where Rosberg's mechanics had already established themselves. 'Michael loved the psychological stuff – he played it very well,' said Rosberg. 'You tell yourself that you shouldn't get messed around in the head, but it is not so easy sometimes.' In retrospect, it was a learning curve that would stand him in good stead for the duels that would come down the road with Hamilton. 'I love to challenge myself to grow from difficult moments and always managed to do that well,' he said. For an estimated £21 million-a-year salary, Schumacher left no one in doubt as to who was in charge. What was it like in an engineers' debrief ? 'Waiting for Michael . . .' Rosberg said, smiling again. He said their relationship was 'neutral'. Another word to describe it might be cold. They shared technical data, but had little else in common – hardly surprising, perhaps, given the sixteen-year age gap.

However, where it mattered most it was Rosberg who proved to be the dominant Mercedes driver on the track. When Schumacher retired for a second and final time, at the end of 2012, Rosberg had provided the team with their sole victory: in China, in 2012. Brawn admitted: 'It was frustrating that it wasn't as good as it should have been with Michael – and I think there were many reasons for that. We didn't have the funds to develop the 2010 car, and it took a while to sort ourselves out until Mercedes started to make a greater investment for 2012.'

In the spring of that year, Schumacher memorably rolled back the calendar to win pole at Monaco, aged forty-three. He could not start from there, though. He had arrived knowing that he had to take a five-place grid penalty for causing an avoidable collision with Bruno Senna at the previous race in Spain. 'Still, that was a pretty impressive lap,' said Rosberg, who qualified third after being hindered by a technical flaw. The next afternoon Webber won his second Monaco Grand Prix for Red Bull – and reprised his victory leap into the swimming pool on the team's three-storey Energy Station moored in the harbour – but Rosberg's second-place finish felt almost as rewarding, he insisted. 'It was really difficult towards the end, as it started raining and we all bunched up,' said Rosberg.

'It was so cool to be on the podium in Monaco – it felt in many ways like a win.' He partied the night away with around fifteen friends from his school days 'We finished in the Meridien Hotel, having burgers and fries at 7 a.m.,' said Rosberg. 'People were drinking from the flower pot on the table, mistaking it for the water jug. Others were falling asleep . . . it was out of control!' Also, a tradition had been established.

At the end of the year, Brawn had a decision to take. 'We knew Michael's career would come to an end – and we knew Lewis was on the scene,' he said. Hamilton had tired of Dennis's management style and he wanted to be freed from the constraints of a corporate lifestyle, which no longer felt right to him. 'I tried to work things in a fair way to both Michael and Lewis,' said Brawn. 'Michael had been undecided about his future, then I saw Lewis and it was clear he wanted to come to us. I explained this to Michael and he told me, truthfully, that he felt it was time for him to stop anyway.' If it was impossible to deny Sebastian Vettel a fourth consecutive championship for Red Bull in 2013, over the course of that season Mercedes put down a marker that the natural order of Formula One was shifting. Hamilton's signing was inspirational.

Yet it was Rosberg who posted the first message of intent when he won at Monaco that year. 'I dominated the whole weekend,' he said. 'We had to deal with tyre degradation and I had to slow down the pace massively at the beginning. Behind me there was a traffic jam. I had to make certain the tyres lasted – and at Monaco you can control the track to make sure no one gets past.' Brawn joined him on the podium, just as he had joined Rosberg Sr when he won thirty years earlier. Nico's mother came to the Mercedes garage to join the celebrations, but his father waited to see his son when the commotion had quietened down. How did Nico feel about his win? 'Well, it is the most glamorous Grand Prix, it has so much history and it gets the most attention,' he said. 'It's the most challenging track. It's *Monaco*. And for me, it is my home and it is where I grew up. Wow! It will always be the most special win.' The unique nature of the race is something all those who have won have attempted to describe. Nico told it like this: 'The whole weekend is very tiring as it is just so extreme to any other race. You can never relax. Look at Jack Brabham crashing out at the last corner when he was winning in 1970 – that is incredible. You can see what power the mind has. He probably did relax as he thought, "OK, I have done it." Senna's crash in 1988 is another reminder how this track bites. You need the highest level of concentration because everything has to be so concise. To understand what it is like, think how it would feel to drive on a country road in the rain at night, as fast as you can, for two hours. Then you start to get an idea of the level of concentration required. Some circuits are more physically tough, like Singapore. But Monaco is the toughest to achieve a win, yes. There is so much going on around Monaco, wherever you go. There is no peace and quiet. No easy route from one place to another. It's good to sleep at home in your own bed, but it doesn't help that much.' But the place reserved for the winning driver at the dining table with Prince Albert II on Sunday night is cherished because of what it represents: tradition and history. Later that evening, Rosberg met with his usual crowd of friends to go out on the town – after all, he had his own tradition to honour now. And a monumental hangover to deal with the next day.

At the beginning of 2014, Brawn had departed from Mercedes as he felt Toto Wolff and Lauda were diluting his role with the recruitment of Paddy Lowe from McLaren. By then, the team's momentum, and structure, propelled by the desire of two ambitious drivers, was such that Mercedes could wrestle control from Red Bull. As though shielded by a static ridge of high pressure, the sun has continued to shine on the Mercedes HQ in Brackley until the time of writing. Hamilton followed up his 2014 championship with his third title in 2015. Yet by this point, the mood between Hamilton and Rosberg had noticeably darkened. Hamilton's performances were illuminated by flashes of brilliance as he defeated and occasionally mocked Rosberg. Life was complex and their relationship turned hostile. All pretence of friendship had been shredded.

Of course, Rosberg claimed notable victories of his own. In those two seasons, although Hamilton won the world championships, Rosberg won eleven races. Two of them were obtained at Monaco, giving him a hat-trick of wins on those perilous streets. Only three legends of the business had done the same: Graham Hill, Jackie Stewart and Alain Prost. Rosberg's second win was coloured with controversy, a fact he willingly addressed. At the end of qualifying in 2014, Rosberg missed his braking point and failed to negotiate the right-handed Mirabeau, driving instead down the escape road ahead of him. Then he reversed out and marshals were obliged to wave yellow flags, slowing Hamilton, who was trying to claim pole from his team-mate. 'I understand that the circumstances were such that some thought I had done it on purpose,' admitted Rosberg. 'It's tough, not nice, when people have that judgement of you.' He was called in front of the race stewards after qualifying. 'That was not great,' he said. 'I just braked too late. Fortunately, it was easy to clarify from the data available to the stewards and the team.' Rosberg won the race the next day from Hamilton. 'I was under pressure from Lewis the whole way, he was pushing like mad. Yet for me, it was a perfect race; but the win wasn't as intense or as special as the first one.'

His third win in the principality, in 2015, will draw a smile from Rosberg in perpetuity; and it will haunt Hamilton. The reigning world champion had the race at his command when the stewards introduced the safety car due to Max Verstappen's accident with Romain Grosjean on lap 64 of the 78-lap race. On a big spectator screen, Hamilton had seen mechanics out in the pits – and as he navigated Rascasse he was directed to divert into the pit-lane entrance, which was just ahead on his right. The gap from second-placed Rosberg was twenty-one seconds. Had the management team on the pit wall – 'we used to call it the prat perch,' said Brawn – miscalculated the maths? In a word: yes. It was insufficient time to get Hamilton in and out of the pits for tyres before his team-mate passed the exit of the pit lane after Sainte-Dévote. 'When I went up the hill, I saw Lewis in my mirrors,' said Rosberg. 'I couldn't understand what the hell he was doing there. I thought to myself: "Holy moly, I am actually leading this thing."'

Vettel was also fractionally ahead of Hamilton, who hit the transmit button on his radio to express his anguish. 'What happened, guys?' he asked. 'I've lost this race, haven't I?'

Rosberg had too much street craft to be caught. 'For sure, I got lucky,' he said, smiling. 'I still thought Lewis would win, because he had fresh, soft tyres. We were on completely knackered, hard tyres. But there is nowhere to pass unless you make a mistake, and Sebastian did a good job in keeping him behind him.' Later Rosberg asked the Mercedes management if they would have asked him to concede first place to Hamilton if the British driver had overtaken Vettel. 'I was told they wouldn't have done that,' said Rosberg. 'It was explained that the other driver isn't penalised for things that go wrong on the other side of the garage. The team and Lewis made the mistake, because he thought I had boxed, or I would do so after him. It's always awesome to win, particularly if you think at the time that this one has got away from you.'

In 2016 the situation was reversed. Hamilton triumphed at Monaco, and Rosberg won the world championship that had been the reason behind his desire to be a Formula One driver since his teenage karting years. Rosberg out-qualified the British driver to put himself on the front row alongside Daniel Ricciardo's Red Bull, with Hamilton in third place on the grid. Ricciardo was ecstatic to win his first pole in Monaco, of all places. But of all places, a change of weather throws teams and drivers off-balance in Monaco like nowhere else. On race morning it rained hard. On the hillside beneath the Rock on which the royal palace reigns supreme, hordes of people sheltered under umbrellas of all colours. The weather could not dampen the humour, though. One makeshift camp of tents with the best view of Rascasse and the pit entrance had been named 'Tribune VIP'.

For some of us it was impossible not to recall how the atrocious weather had befriended Olivier Panis twenty years earlier. For certain, Hamilton arrived in the Mercedes garage sensing that the weather gods had offered him the break he needed. Like Senna and Schumacher, Hamilton was a man who could exploit such conditions in a racing car more profitably than most. The race started behind the safety car with its neon blinking lights and the drivers stayed in a procession, flashing in and out of vision through the flying spray, for seven laps. Impatient voices could be heard over the radios and the crowd stirred, wishing for the real action to begin. When it did, it was not long before it became apparent that Rosberg was holding up Hamilton's attempt to reach Ricciardo. 'I just had issues with the car and I was struggling in the wet,' he explained. 'I was asked over the radio to let Lewis past – which I did immediately.'

Ricciardo's race hopes vanished in a less likely manner: his tyres were not ready when he pitted, and Hamilton gained the lead during Red Bull's lengthy pit stop. The British driver was nerveless at the wheel. Peerless, too. He changed from full wet tread tyres, nursing them for a long stint on a drying track, to slicks. 'I don't remember anyone doing that here before,' said Coulthard, during his commentary for Channel 4. 'Pure genius.' Hamilton had not won at Monaco for eight years; more worryingly, he had not won anywhere for seven months, during which Rosberg had dominated.

'Honestly, I am kind of lost for words,' said Hamilton after a memorable drive. 'I prayed for a day like this and it came true.' He added, significantly, 'Nico was a gentleman.'

When I asked Rosberg how he had received that comment, he said unexpectedly, 'He didn't say that to me. I don't read the media, so, no, I didn't hear him say that. Strange. But then again, what I did is part of the game; it is expected. It was made clear at the beginning that such instances are part of our battle for the world championship. As a driver you can't afford to go against something like that. It would be damaging to my reputation at Mercedes; and that's not the way I want to go. You need the support from the team to have success. In the end, we are driving for the team. And we got the win, which I could not provide. It sucked for my championship right then; for the team, it makes sense.' Hamilton's forty-fourth win in Formula One corresponded with the number on his car; his favourite number and Senna's total of forty-one wins receded further in his rear-view mirrors.

After Monaco, it was a dogfight between Rosberg and Hamilton in identical 200mph cars. On that morning I spent with him in Brackley, Rosberg had been charm personified and had revealed, in closing, an indication of his mindset before the duel in the desert. 'It's been my best season, for sure,' said Rosberg. 'I am happy that I have been able to improve again and upped my game and battled Lewis in the way I have. He is the guy to beat out there. He is one of the best of all time – statistically as well. I am proud of racing him all the way to the end. Let's see how it goes. Of course, I have a good chance.' In the end, Hamilton's flurry of victories over the final four races of 2016 narrowly failed to enable him to hunt down his team-mate, who kept finishing second to keep him at bay, as required by the maths. With nine wins and seven podiums, Rosberg crossed the line five points ahead of Hamilton in Abu Dhabi. His career had its defining moment and his team embraced him.

Keke Rosberg only travelled to the circuit from neighbouring Dubai – where he had been shying clear of the media spotlight with his wife, Sina – after his son had started to celebrate with his wife, Vivian. Keke willingly lifted a six-year media blackout, self-imposed as he had not wanted to detract from his son's work, to draw an analogy between Hamilton and Nico. 'There is one guy in Los Angeles, here, there and everywhere, and then you have one guy concentrating on only one thing. Nutrition, time differences, training, emptying the brain at the right time and concentrating only on performance, performance, performance. So, it's a different approach. Both seem to work.'

For Nico, the next day dawned with a heavy diary of team commitments alongside Wolff. Then, five days into his reign, Rosberg announced his retirement. It was received as a bolt of lightning from a clear blue sky. Both Wolff and Lauda swiftly established that Rosberg would not change his mind. As he toured the awards' ceremonies in the following days, Rosberg quietly insisted his race in Formula One had been run. He knew what it had taken, he knew how deep he had quarried within himself, working with a sports psychologist, to side-step the traps and defeat Hamilton; and he saw no point in returning to have to do it all over again.

Yet one question drew a big smile from Rosberg. 'Will you miss winning Monaco?' asked Sky's Ted Kravitz.

'Hell, yes!' said Rosberg.

Epilogue

Friday, 27 May 2016: Noon

Charlie Whiting was talking about his daily routine during the Monaco Grand Prix as he sat at his desk in the new space-age control tower at the end of the pit lane. 'When I walk around the circuit shortly after 5.30 a.m., there are often bottles and cans on the track and people wandering about aimlessly because they are too drunk to know where they are going,' he said.

Whiting lives in Monaco. In spite of a life spent in constant motion, travelling from one Grand Prix circuit to the next in his multiple roles as the FIA Formula One Race Director, Safety Delegate, Permanent Starter and head of the F1 Technical Department, he is at home often enough to watch the track being built as the local population uncomplainingly adjusts to the disturbance. 'The circuit grows over weeks of high activity, but life goes on,' said Whiting. 'It is the same during the Grand Prix. The roads are open at the end of each day for the principality to get back some version of normality. Early each morning of the Grand Prix, from Thursday to

305

Sunday, I walk the track. As well as debris, and people still trying to get home from parties, there might be an odd car parked on the circuit. The local police, very efficient and strict, know what they have to do to get it cleaned up.'

Whiting's office has a window overlooking the pit lane and starting grid, a better view than the one afforded by his old location, out of sight of the cars. On his desk there is a computer and a television. Across the corridor is a room with forty TV screens covering every inch of the track. 'It is what we call our Race Watch System, which automatically detects incidents. The system will then find video film of all incidents for us; normally, we get that within twenty seconds of an incident taking place. We judge each of them on merit – once we have scrutinised the video tape there can be quite a lot of false positives.'

Behind his office is the stewards' room, and if an incident is deemed worthy of their attention then it is electronically dispatched to them. 'They have a guy with them who shows them what we have just seen,' explained Whiting. Former drivers are appointed as stewards on a one-race basis, and Whiting outlined what is expected of them. 'I tell them that they are not here to be a driver adviser, but as someone called upon to know the rules, and to be a part of every decision that is made, and not just those involved in driving standards.' Whiting said that he is rarely present in the stewards' meetings, but the reaction and response by the stewards to any incident is flashed across his desk.

He remembered clearly the day a decade earlier when Schumacher crashed in slow motion at the end of qualifying to ruin Alonso's attempt to steal pole from him. 'That was one of the daftest things, a pathetic attempt at crashing,' said Whiting. 'I can remember Mark Webber telling me – in his candid way – how he had asked Schumacher what had happened: "Michael, what the fuck did you do there?" According to Webber, Michael replied, "Mark, sometimes you start to go down a road and you can't turn back." ' Whiting deduced from that conversation that the seven-time world champion was without a coherent defence. 'So, Schumacher had it in his mind to do what he did, but he did it in a half-baked way that was just awful,' he said. Schumacher's relegation from the front to the back of the grid won the approval of all in the paddock bar those wearing uniforms embossed with a prancing horse.

At Monaco, each step that has been taken over the years to increase the security for the drivers and public is an important step forward, no matter how small it appears from the outside. 'Safety has been improved little by little,' said Whiting. 'It took quite a lot on the part of the Automobile Club de Monaco to get the principality to accept taking down two trees; the trees were highly thought of. But taking them down provided another forty metres of run-off in a precarious place. Yet, if you look at the way a modern street circuit is built, we are always playing catch-up here. Apart from anything else, the topography in Monaco doesn't lend itself to great change. They have a certain way of doing things here; as I say, they are willing to take steps little by little. Having garages in the pits, as we do now, was the stuff of dreams thirty years ago. There used to be a normal guard rail in the tunnel, but now there is a permanent 1.5-metre-high wall.'

The tunnel is a unique feature. It is also a profound source of concern. 'You can see from the on-board camera of a car how long it takes for a driver's iris to adjust to the change of light,' explained Whiting. 'It is very tricky; the drivers are travelling at 290kph coming out of there – that's pretty damn quick on a circuit like this. It's bumpy. It's a corner. It's quite hairy trying to brake, especially if you are trying to out-brake someone to overtake. It's quite a feat: proper racing.'

His days involve a continuous round of meetings. One is

with the drivers. 'It is no longer called a drivers' briefing – I prefer to call it a meeting,' said Whiting. 'I don't take a school-teacher approach to them, being more inclined to respect the fact that they are the best drivers in the world – unless proved otherwise. It's more of a discussion for the drivers to raise any ongoing issues from the last race. For example, in the meeting yesterday there was a discussion with the tyre manufacturer to reassure drivers that tyre malfunctions were not an issue.'

On race morning, Whiting expects team managers to seek him out. 'Teams always want to ask last-minute questions to get everything clear in their minds for the race,' he said. 'Especially so, if the weather is changeable like it is this year. They want certainty. In previous times, going back twenty years, you would have a race stopped and the race director would be surrounded by team managers asking what was going on. I used to think that was laughable, as it is all written in the rules. These days they are all very professional, but they still just like that comfort of being assured that their understanding of the regulations is right.'

This was Whiting's thirty-ninth Monaco Grand Prix. In 1978, he was in the small band of mechanics that looked after the Brabham team owned by Bernie Ecclestone. 'There were less than fifteen of us,' said Whiting. 'Our truckie used to drive the three cars down to Monaco on his own. He would unload the truck, then look after the spares and tyres. Afterwards, he would load it all up again and drive home. No questions asked.' For this, the seventy-fourth Monaco Grand Prix, in 2016, the McLaren team had deployed forty-eight drivers to transfer the team's cars, kit and three-storey paddock HQ, known as the Brand Centre, from the previous race, and subsequent test, in Barcelona. At Whiting's first race the staff list looked like this: two mechanics per car, a tyre man, a truckie, designer Gordon Murray, and team management comprising Dave

North and Herbie Blash – the latter an immensely popular figure who retired as FIA Deputy Race Director following the final race last season, in Abu Dhabi, after a lifetime in Formula One.

'Bernie had a motorhome, but we never got to see it,' said Whiting, smiling. 'We used to stay in the Hotel Diana. Herbie was recalling the other day that it cost then the princely sum of £5 a night.' Whiting was chief mechanic on Nelson Piquet's car when the Brazilian was world champion with Brabham in 1981 and 1983. Did the team stay at a more salubrious hotel in Monaco in those giddy times? 'No, we just had slightly better rooms in the Diana.'

At sixty-four, Whiting still views Formula One with the same sense of wonderment a child reserves for Christmas. 'I do, I do,' he said. 'It's just a shame I am called to work sometimes! To see the teams striving for perfection all the time is quite awesome.' At Monaco, nothing is permanent, though; and like the perimeter fencing and barriers, the new control tower would start to be taken down as soon as the Formula One circus left town to head for the next show somewhere else in the world. Whiting would be there, of course.

When I reflect on the journey that this book has taken me on, there is a line of truth connecting the past to the future in Formula One. For all its imperfections, for all its flaws, F1 has an unremitting capacity to make the pulse quicken. It does this most dramatically of all at Monaco. Of course, there is a legitimacy to the argument that race day can sometimes be reduced to a procession of cars, running one behind the other, for lap after lap, as though coupled together like carriages on a TGV train. But that criticism is to miss the point. The point is having the privilege of watching men like Lewis Hamilton winning the Monaco Grand Prix. Hamilton had to overcome the sheer madness of driving a Mercedes Formula One car powered by an engine capable of 950 horsepower, at 15,000 revs, on streets barely wider than a country lane in Cornwall, flanked not with hedgerow but with unforgiving Armco barriers, while being harassed by drivers from behind and threatened by the presence of slower-moving traffic ahead created by cars almost a lap down. This cannot be conceived as boring, can it?

The point is to appreciate that in Monaco, more than anywhere else in the world, Hamilton has raced almost the very same route as those who attained their legendary status on this circuit in the decades before him: men called Graham Hill, Jackie Stewart, Ayrton Senna, Michael Schumacher and Alain Prost.

The scenery is unchanging, too. The Casino de Monte-Carlo, the Hotel de Paris, the harbour, the tunnel, they are all still the most identifiable landmarks on a racing circuit anywhere around the globe. You may recall what Murray Walker memorably declared twenty years earlier: 'You get no more points for winning at Monaco, but you get more publicity and prestige than for all the other races put together.' Keke Rosberg specified what determined, in his eyes, a successful career for a Formula One driver in these terms: 'You have to win your first race, your first Monaco Grand Prix, and your first world championship.' It is as clear a barometer to greatness today as it was when the Finn raced over thirty years ago.

I reported from my first Grand Prix in Monaco in 1981 – and I had been to more than twenty-five others when I returned this year. One of my earliest dispatches centred on the red-blooded rivalry between Brazilian Nelson Piquet, driving for Brabham, and Australian Alan Jones, who was Frank Williams's first star. Jones had grown tired, shall we say, of Piquet's lack of etiquette on the track and wished him to know that if he repeated it he would have no compunction about shoving him into the harbour. From memory, I think he meant car and all. Those were the days! Drivers were not shielded by PR personnel or surrounded by an entourage then. Reporters like me could approach them in the garage, or the paddock, and they would answer questions or just chew the fat. Trust was forged. The sport received more than its share of column inches.

In time, corporate stakeholders demanded a more controlled media environment; and TV broadcast corporations seized on the marketable aspect of Formula One and if the drivers have become blander as a consequence it is not a concern to them. Armchair fans get a great spectacle – the camera work at Monaco is nothing less than sensational. However, the drivers are barely distinguishable behind the same, short soundbites. This has to change.

Gilles Villeneuve won that first race I saw with charismatic flourish at the wheel of his Ferrari Turbo, and the *tifosi* celebrated with wild abandon. He was another larger-than-life character. Tragically, Villeneuve never returned, as he was killed two weeks before the 1982 Monaco Grand Prix. Senna was his natural successor as a man who could bring a crowd to its feet at Monaco. But, as we discovered, Senna's speed was reinforced by an utterly ruthless mind. His first drive in the rain at Monaco, in 1984, was a masterclass. The awful weather may have forced a premature end to the race before he could launch a final assault on Prost's McLaren, but we had seen enough to understand these streets would become in thrall to his brilliance.

Up close, there was something magical in the manner Senna made a car weave and dance to his command, apparently millimetres from doom. As he put the power down, heading uphill towards Casino Square from Sainte-Dévote, the rear of his car would flick from side to side, as though waving farewell, sparks bouncing against the tarmac. He had no trouble overtaking, I can tell you. Rivals caught sight of his yellow helmet in their mirrors and made themselves as small as

possible on the circuit. Yes, in this mood he was that dominant; but, having said, it must be acknowledged that there was
a smoothness to Prost's driving round this circuit that Senna
could not match. Their decade of dominance at Monaco was
at times beautiful, at times alarming. At no time was it dull.

But while Senna won at Monaco a record six times – and his
duel with Mansell in 1992 will be never forgotten – the circuit
exacted a price from him for his excellence by humiliating him,
too. It is still hard all these years later to comprehend properly
how we witnessed him drive on an empty road into a barrier
approaching the tunnel. While Prost took his place on the
podium, Senna was locked inside his apartment a few minutes'
walk from the scene of his nonsensical accident, crying with
shame. If Schumacher was also guilty of pushing himself
beyond the limit, his supremacy at Monaco was also compelling on the eye.

Those who raced against the great champions never lacked
passion, of course. Twenty years after he last competed in
Formula One, Martin Brundle still feels a certain emptiness for
not having won a grand prix in spite all that he achieved,
which included second place at Monaco. In 158 Formula One
races – the same number as Panis – he scored 98 points; which
was 22 more than the Frenchman accumulated. But my parting question on that morning we spent together in his London
apartment clearly struck a nerve. Surely it hasn't hurt you too
much not winning an F1 race, I asked. Brundle responded, as
only a racer can I suppose: 'Psychologically, it is really painful.
It's the races that got away, isn't it? It does frustrate me, of
course it does. I was good enough to win grand prix races; but,
for whatever reason, I didn't make it. It doesn't eat me up, far
from it; but it does annoy me. The fact is I know a lot more
now than when I was living with blinkers on trying to be a
racing driver.' In retirement, Brundle managed David Coulthard

for years and the two men remain good friends travelling the world together for rival broadcast corporations. Coulthard has no regrets; nor does he share Brundle's still insatiable desire to drive a fast car whenever he can. 'Martin would race at Le Mans tomorrow if someone gave him the opportunity,' smiles Coulthard. 'But with the greatest respect to my friend – and I have this conversation with him – you have to know when to give it up. Martin and I were good racing drivers – if that doesn't sound arrogant – but we were not exceptional. That's not being disrespectful to Martin, or me; it's just that some people capture the imagination in a way others don't. I had better opportunities than Martin, but in the end results talk.' It is this dichotomy of thought, and analysis, which makes men who drove a Formula One car, at circuits as diverse as Monaco and Monza, men of endless fascination.

Nico Rosberg's three wins at Monaco were the fulfilment of an exceptional talent, even if the last was gifted to him by a schoolboy error from the Mercedes management to the detriment of his team-mate, Hamilton. As for the future, if Mercedes retain a competitive edge it is logical to suggest that Hamilton's exuberance, speed and tenacity will keep him in contention to build on the two wins he has already achieved in Monaco. Two other younger men who have already announced themselves as fast and nerveless are Daniel Ricciardo and Max Verstappen from Red Bull. Both will be desperate to install themselves on the honours board. Indeed, changes to the governance of Formula One occurred dramatically in January 2017 when Liberty Media, the American media organisation, was given approval by the FIA to complete a £6.4 billion takeover of the sport with the acquisition of 100 per cent of Formula One's shares from the consortium led by private equity firm, CVC. Bernie Ecclestone's near forty year reign was over. At 86, perhaps Ecclestone was the only man in Formula One who did not realise that time had caught up with him. His autocratic authority – less kindly critics called him a dictator and Ecclestone took that to be a compliment not an insult – had become an obsolete style of management. His role at the helm has passed to American Chase Carey, aged 62. Carey immediately appointed Ross Brawn to be managing director of motorsports within the new management structure.

Brawn will provide much needed experience. He will also be a voice of reason within the teams as Formula One looks to adapt and modernise; and to distribute its wealth more transparently – and evenly – to prevent, hopefully, more teams going out of business as Manor did before the ink was dry on the sale to Liberty Media. When we met at his Oxfordshire home in May 2016, Brawn acknowledged the problems confronting Formula One without playing the blame game. 'Formula One is in a difficult place at the moment,' he told me. 'I think some of the changes that have been made over the past few years have had consequences, intended or not.' He insisted as a parting shot: 'Never say never – but I have no plans to go back. I am not actively looking and no one has come to me with anything appealing enough to change my life again.' Then Carey called; and Brawn was sold on a role to which he is eminently suited. Former ESPN executive Sean Bratches was appointed as managing director of commercial operations.

Doubtlessly, Ecclestone will have been amused that it has required three men to take over a job he did alone for almost four decades, making himself a multi-billionaire and some team owners, and a platoon of drivers, multi-millionaires in the process. Ecclestone had been a visionary unlike any other man in sports administration. He did deals on a handshake, and he is amusing, and mischievous, but his word was law. With such an unorthodox manner, Ecclestone brought

Formula One out of the wilderness to become a sport that commands a TV audience counted in hundreds of millions. Yet, of late, that audience has been in decline, and races have vanished from Formula One's heartland in countries like Germany and France. However, if Ecclestone took Formula One to soulless tracks in Malaysia, Korea, Turkey, China and Russia, apparently in exchange for a government's ransom payment. He is also to be commended for keeping the flame burning as brightly as ever over this improbable race track on the streets of a tax haven beside the Mediterranean. It is a museum of motor-racing treasure.

As recently as the end of last year, Ecclestone said, 'If you ask a driver what race he would like to win more than any other, the immediate answer would be Monaco.' That question would have delivered the same answer for more than half a century; and Formula One under new management is certain to preserve its rich heritage at Monaco. Times may change but the challenge of Monaco is timeless.

Friday, 27 May 2016: 6.30 p.m.

Music greeted me the moment I had left the paddock and joined the track at Rascasse. Already a sizeable crowd had assembled on this popular strip of bars and restaurants. This part of the circuit had become a dance floor as music from the stereo systems of different establishments competed with each other. Loud music. Chalked blackboards promised beer and a slice of pizza for ten euros. A van selling Badass Burgers offered alternative nourishment. Across the track, those on board the yachts in the harbour were drinking cocktails more sedately in the soft sunlight of a glorious evening. At the swimming-pool section, a fleet of recovery vehicles was parked for the night alongside the circuit as though it was a designated truck stop. The scene was just warming up, but I was headed for another part of town.

Two decades had passed since Olivier Panis last set eyes on the Ligier JS43 Mugen-Honda that he had driven to the least-expected victory in the history of the Monaco Grand Prix. But there it was on the rest day of the 2016 Monaco Grand Prix: showroom-clean and parked in the atrium of the Casino de Monte-Carlo. Champagne flowed, and Panis posed for photographs with the car bearing number nine. His wife, Anne, and his son Aurélien, along with friends, absorbed the ambience of the reunion organised on the twentieth anniversary of his unforgettable triumph by Hirotoshi Honda, the son of Soichiro Honda, who founded the Honda Motor Company.

'After I won the race, the Japanese took the car, still covered in shit, straight to the Honda museum in Japan,' Panis told me. 'I have so many good times with this car; it is special.' Guy Ligier had died ten months earlier, but it was with affection, not sadness, that Panis recalled the life of the charismatic man who championed the cause of French racing drivers. 'Two weeks after I won at Monaco I had dinner with Guy at Magny-Cours,' he said. Ligier may no longer have been calling the shots at the team racing under his name, but he was still a major shareholder in it. 'I don't know how many times Guy said thank you to me! You know, his funeral last year was a sad time, but if you told me that you could live like him and die at eighty-five years old, I'd sign up now. He was drinking and smoking like a chimney . . . I loved this guy. He was the guy who gave a chance to a lot of French drivers. I was one of them.'

The regional newspaper *Nice-Matin* published a two-page spread of the commemorative party that put Panis back on the international stage again. The coverage included an excerpt – translated here into English – from Ligier's reaction to the victory, taken from Henri Charpentier's book *Monaco: 60 Grands Prix de Légende*: 'That day I was dreaming with my eyes open in front of my television like a child at the foot of a Christmas tree. Olivier truly deserved his victory. He went after it with panache and control. There is never really any coincidence in Monaco: his will, his courage, his intelligence, his skill at the wheel allowed him to execute an admirable race and to believe in his chance until the end.'

But Panis was never given the possibility to provide a winning encore to his success at Monaco, in part through misfortune with his serious accident in Canada, in part through a missed opportunity that he did not discover until four years later. After three years of driving for Prost, Panis asked his management team of Didier Coton and Keke Rosberg to get him a contract as a test driver for the McLaren team in 2000. Mika Häkkinen had been world champion for the previous two seasons in a McLaren with his team, David Coulthard finishing third, then fourth in the title race, and Panis wanted to discover how quick he could be in a competitive car. 'I wanted to know where I am, where is my speed,' said the Frenchman. 'If I have this opportunity in a McLaren, maybe I show to everybody that I did not win Monaco by luck.'

A week or so after he had made the proposal to Coton, he received a call back from the man who manages him solely these days. 'Didier said that he had spoken with Keke and maybe it was not such a stupid idea,' recalled Panis. Yet when Ron Dennis was approached at McLaren, the notion was met by a blunt rejection. Panis explained: 'I was told that Ron said that he wouldn't give the winner of a Grand Prix a test-driver job out of respect for what I had done. But I said to Didier to tell Ron that I didn't care about respect. I wanted to do this. In the end the guy who pushed hard for me at McLaren was chief designer Adrian Newey, who thought it would be good for the team if they employed me.'

Dennis agreed to a meeting. 'Even then, he said that he felt sad to give me this post because I was a winner of a Grand Prix,' said Panis. 'I told him not to worry about that!' A deal was struck, and Panis stepped from the limelight into the shadows without fuss. 'In 2000 I drove 27,000 kilometres over sixty-three days of testing; I was all the time in the car,' he said. 'But I think it was one of my best years in Formula One to meet Ron, Adrian, Martin Whitmarsh and Mansour Ojjeh.' Then, one evening, Panis had dinner with Dennis and he found out how his life might have easily taken a different direction after the glory of Monaco but for the alleged subterfuge of one man: Prost. The four-time world champion had been attached to McLaren in 1996 as a consultant, and he had been on the pit wall as Coulthard finished second before Prost later completed his purchase of the Ligier team. Panis recalls the conversation that night with Dennis going like this:

'Ron suddenly said, "And your friend is OK?"'

'Which friend?' Panis asked.

'The small one.'

'What do you mean, the small one?'

'Alain, he's OK?'

'I suppose so. Why do you ask?'

'You don't know the history of 1996?'

'I don't know what you are talking about.'

'I will explain. I asked Alain to arrange for us to meet, but he did not do this. He said that you didn't speak much English, that you were a big character and not an easy man to manage.'

Panis was dumbfounded by the revelation – and he was angry. As soon as dinner had finished, he called Prost and relived the conversation he'd had with Dennis. At the end,

Panis had just one final question – asked in exasperation: 'What the fuck, Alain?' He remembers that Prost did not make any kind of denial, but told him instead: 'Olivier, I am sure you want to kill me right now. But at the time I bought the Ligier team I needed you to stay.'

Panis accepted Prost's objective was to do the best he could for the team and not to further his career. 'When Alain explained it like this I could not think of him as a bad guy,' said Panis. 'This is business, that's all. I like this guy very much and I pass good times with him. As a driver, for me Alain was one of the best in history. But being the best driver in history does not make you the best team principal. It is something you need to learn. I learn a lot from him – sometimes good decisions; sometimes bad ones. We may not always agree.'

In his year away from racing, Panis clearly proved with his work as a test driver that he was competitively fast. He returned to Formula One under a race contract with the BAR Honda team in 2001 and remained with them for two seasons before switching to Toyota in 2003. In his second season for Toyota, underperforming in spite of a mammoth budget, Panis sensed his time was up. 'I began to think of stopping in 2004, but I wanted to prepare myself,' he explained. 'I knew of sportsmen who became depressed after they stopped; so, for me, it was important the decision was mine. I spoke a lot with Didier and Keke. I told them that I was tired – not from driving, or from the risks, but *tired*. We did a lot of PR days. I give an example: in 2004, Toyota sent me to China for one day to present a car. So I said to Didier that I wanted to know if Toyota thought they had a car that could win the championship in 2005. If the answer is yes, I will prepare myself to win the championship. If the answer is no, I will stop at the end of this year.'

Of course, Toyota, who finished eighth in the Constructors' Championship in 2004, could make no such predictions

319

of success. And Panis made good on the promise he made himself. The Frenchman finished his F1 racing career in Japan on 10 October 2004, two laps behind the race winner, Michael Schumacher. He had driven in 158 Grands Prix, but it had been seven years since he had made the last of his five visits to the podium. 'Toyota asked me to stay with them as test driver for the next two years,' said Panis. 'I asked for time to decide. I had one month off – then I said to Didier I would do it if he gave me a contract that I am just doing the testing, no promotions. All these things I was finished with.'

Panis performed testing duties until the end of 2006. 'I was so happy when I stopped,' he admitted. 'I loved F1, I loved the people I worked with, but now it was time for my family. For one month this was fantastic. But one day I turned open my diary – and it was blank. What am I doing today, then? Drive the kids to school. Fantastic. Pick them up. Fantastic. Have dinner with my wife. Fantastic.'

The reality was that Panis was adrift; at thirty-nine, his worst fears were manifesting themselves. 'I felt depressed, to be honest. I was going down. I thought I was sick and I went to see my doctor for a thorough check-up. He told me that I was perfectly fit, but, psychologically, I was tired. Every day I was depressed. I didn't want to talk. I didn't answer the phone. Sometimes, I left home for a week to see a friend in Brittany, in the middle of fucking nowhere. I did some shooting. For six months it was hard, hard for me. I was the one who wanted to stop – and I was sure this would not happen to me. But it was happening.'

Then one day, from out of the blue, he received a call from . . . Prost. He asked if Panis wanted to race with him in the Andros Trophy, a championship for racing on ice. 'My wife said, "Go, I am sick and tired of you!"' He went with Prost, and Panis was still competing in the competition over the winter of 2016–17; indeed, he won the Elite Pro class at the round of the series in Alpe d'Huez nine days before Christmas. His son Aurélien was competing in the electric car category. 'I have told Aurélien that it is possible to be a professional racing driver outside of Formula One. I try to explain F1 is closed – that is the reality. He is intelligent and he knows, but the dream is bigger than the reality. When you are twenty years old and he knows what I did, against all possibilities, he thinks, "What is this old man talking about?"'

Panis has forged himself a new career, broadcasting on sports-car racing for Eurosport, and hosting a show each weekend of the season with his great friend Jacques Laffite, a six-time winner for Ligier, and one of those in the team garage when Panis prompted wild celebrations at Monaco. On that evening in the atrium at the Casino de Monte-Carlo, back with his car once more, Panis moved around the room with a quiet dignity, a little overwhelmed by the attention. 'It will always be part of my life, Monaco,' he said. 'I am proud of this.'

Privately, Panis had hoped this might have led to greater success. 'That was my desire every day,' he said. Yet he comprehends that to have had the privilege of racing on these streets, and to drive a Formula One car for a dozen years, was the realisation of a dream beyond his imagination. 'We are lucky in life to have done such a thing.'

And his name is woven for eternity into the fabric of the most fabled motor race in the world of Formula One.

As the party in honour of Panis in the Casino de Monte-Carlo wound down, the Frenchman confided: 'In five or six years' time my Ligier will be eligible for the Historic Grand Prix of Monaco. Mr Honda said to me we will come back and win Monaco again.' Panis smiled as he revealed his response. 'OK, no problem.'

Acknowledgements

Having left my privileged role as Chief Sports Reporter for the Mail on Sunday for 18 months, I had grown accustomed for the first time in my adult life to living without copy deadlines or editorial pressures. I tried to learn to play golf – a work still in progress as my new companions at the Drift Golf Club in East Horsley will testify – and I travelled extensively with my wife, Rachel, to faraway places in Australia and New Zealand, to the United States and to the Caribbean. More closely to home, we spent a greater amount of time within the vineyards of the south west of France where we have had a small house for many years. Idyllic would correctly summarise my appreciation of retirement. Then the idea for this book manifested itself.

Formula One had been integral to my professional agenda during the majority of my 39 years' career as a reporter for national newspaper titles. One of the six books I have previously written had been a recreation of the rivalry between Ayrton Senna and Alain Prost. The truth is, the sport, and the people within it, never ceased to fascinate me. If there was one race that presented the beauty and the glamour of

Formula One, that also encapsulated the thrill of motor racing, and its incumbent risks, it was the Monaco Grand Prix. If I did not miss writing to deadline I did miss writing – in telling stories from Monaco, if not its history in its entirety, I had found a labour of love!

So, I shook the cobwebs from my contacts book, and made some calls to men and women within Formula One with whom I'd not spoken with for an age. It was humbling, as well as gratifying, that they all agreed to share with me their time and their memories without condition or favour. I put this down to their own immense affection for the Monaco Grand Prix, and for a willingness to discuss their part within the history of the most famous motor race in the world.

In no particular order I wish to thank: David Coulthard, who courteously gave me a driver's eye view guide to the circuit and much more besides; Sir Jackie Stewart, Ross Brawn and Martin Brundle invited me to their homes to talk for hours with candour and insight about their experiences on these streets, good and bad; Niki Lauda, Damon Hill, Nico Rosberg, Johnny Herbert, Jonathan Palmer and John Watson told stories rich in drama and humour; and Olivier Panis devoted an afternoon in Paris to relive in minute detail, for the first-ever occasion in English, the day that he caused the greatest upset ever witnessed at Monaco.

I am also indebted to the invaluable contributions to these pages made by Charlie Whiting from the FIA; Michel Ferry and Richard Micoud from the Automobile Club de Monaco; Neil Oatley and Dave Redding from McLaren; John Hogan, once of Marlboro; Mark Wilkin, Formula One Editor with the BBC, and nowadays Channel 4; PR Tony Jardine; photographer Steven Tee; caterer Lyndy Redding; travel agent, Lynden Swainston; and Betise Assumpcao Head, personal press officer to Ayrton Senna. I am also appreciative of the assistance offered by Bradley Lord, from the Mercedes Formula One team, Matt Bishop, from McLaren, Didier Coton, a driver manager whose client list includes Panis, Matteo Bonciani, head of F1 communications for the FIA, and journalists Joe Saward, Agnes Carlier, Dino Allsop and Maurice Hamilton. I have also drawn from the contributions provided from an earlier time by Alain Prost, Gerhard Berger, Nigel Mansell and Jo Ramirez, formerly team manager for McLaren, and journalist Gerald Donaldson. Sincere thanks to one and all.

Fortunately, when my agent, Jonathan Harris, a tireless veteran of the literary world, accompanied me to discuss an outline for this story with non-fiction commissioning editor Ben Brusey at Century we found a man who instantly grasped the scope offered by Monaco as the star witness to a compendium of motor racing tales involving the biggest names in the annals of Formula One. Ben's inestimable support, along with the efforts of his assistant, Huw Armstrong, and all those at Century, has made delivering this book a source of pleasure. It's elegant appearance is their work. As for the photography, I have to thank LAT Images for opening their archive to allow us to publish a pictorial history of Monaco through the ages,

I am probably deluding myself when I suggest that writing a book, without the stress of a day job, has made it easier for Rachel to deal with this time around. But it is my story and I am sticking to it. Thanks as always, Rachel.

Finally, our daughters, Sian and Megan, may have professional careers in London, but, it is probable they have felt at times like they had moved to Monaco! Thanks for your endless enthusiasm at seeing me back at work.

Year	Name	Nationality	Car
1929	William Grover-Williams	Great Britain	Bugatti
1930	René Dreyfus	France	Bugatti
1931	Louis Chiron	Monaco	Bugatti
1932	Tazio Nuvolari	Italy	Alfa Romeo
1933	Achille Varzi	Italy	Bugatti
1934	Guy Moll	France	Alfa Romeo
1935	Luigi Fagioli	Italy	Mercedes-Benz
1936	Rudolf Caracciola	Germany	Mercedes-Benz
1937	Manfred von Brauchitsch	Germany	Mercedes-Benz
1938-1947	Not Held		
1948	Giuseppe Farina	Italy	Maserati
1949	Not Held		
1950	Juan Manuel Fangio	Argentina	Alfa Romeo
1951	Not Held		
1952	Vittorio Marzotto	Italy	Ferrari
1953-1954	Not Held		
1955	Maurice Trintignant	France	Ferrari
1956	Stirling Moss	Great Britain	Maserati
1957	Juan Manuel Fangio	Argentina	Maserati
1958	Maurice Trintignant	France	Cooper-Climax
1959	Jack Brabham	Australia	Cooper-Climax
1960	Stirling Moss	Great Britain	Lotus-Climax
1961	Stirling Moss	Great Britain	Lotus-Climax
1962	Bruce McLaren	New Zealand	Cooper-Climax
1963	Graham Hill	Great Britain	BRM
1964	Graham Hill	Great Britain	BRM
1965	Graham Hill	Great Britain	BRM
1966	Jackie Stewart	Great Britain	BRM
1967	Denny Hulme	New Zealand	Brabham-Repco
1968	Graham Hill	Great Britain	Lotus-Ford
1969	Graham Hill	Great Britain	Lotus-Ford
1970	Jochen Rindt	Austria	Lotus-Ford
1971	Jackie Stewart	Great Britain	Tyrrell-Ford
1972	Jean-Pierre Beltoise	France	BRM
1973	Jackie Stewart	Great Britain	Tyrrell-Ford
1974	Ronnie Peterson	Sweden	Lotus-Ford
1975	Niki Lauda	Austria	Ferrari
1976	Niki Lauda	Austria	Ferrari

Year	Name	Nationality	Car
1977	Jody Scheckter	South Africa	Wolf-Ford
1978	Patrick Depailler	France	Tyrrell-Ford
1979	Jody Scheckter	South Africa	Ferrari
1980	Carlos Reutemann	Argentina	Williams-Ford
1981	Gilles Villeneuve	Canada	Ferrari
1982	Riccardo Patrese	Italy	Brabham-Ford
1983	Keke Rosberg	Finland	Williams-Ford
1984	Alain Prost	France	McLaren-TAG
1985	Alain Prost	France	McLaren-TAG
1986	Alain Prost	France	McLaren-TAG
1987	Ayrton Senna	Brazil	Lotus-Honda
1988	Alain Prost	France	McLaren-Honda
1989	Ayrton Senna	Brazil	McLaren-Honda
1990	Ayrton Senna	Brazil	McLaren-Honda
1991	Ayrton Senna	Brazil	McLaren-Honda
1992	Ayrton Senna	Brazil	McLaren-Honda
1993	Ayrton Senna	Brazil	McLaren-Ford
1994	Michael Schumacher	Germany	Benetton-Ford
1995	Michael Schumacher	Germany	Benetton-Renault
1996	Olivier Panis	France	Ligier Mugen-Honda
1997	Michael Schumacher	Germany	Ferrari
1998	Mika Häkkinen	Finland	McLaren-Mercedes
1999	Michael Schumacher	Germany	Ferrari
2000	David Coulthard	Great Britain	McLaren-Mercedes
2001	Michael Schumacher	Germany	Ferrari
2002	David Coulthard	Great Britain	McLaren-Mercedes
2003	Juan Pablo Montoya	Colombia	Williams-BMW
2004	Jarno Trulli	Italy	Renault
2005	Kimi Räikkönen	Finland	McLaren-Mercedes
2006	Fernando Alonso	Spain	Renault
2007	Fernando Alonso	Spain	McLaren-Mercedes
2008	Lewis Hamilton	Great Britain	McLaren-Mercedes
2009	Jenson Button	Great Britain	Brawn-Mercedes
2010	Mark Webber	Australia	Red Bull-Renault
2011	Sebastian Vettel	Germany	Red Bull-Renault
2012	Mark Webber	Australia	Red Bull-Renault
2013	Nico Rosberg	Germany	Mercedes
2014	Nico Rosberg	Germany	Mercedes
2015	Nico Rosberg	Germany	Mercedes
2016	Lewis Hamilton	Great Britain	Mercedes

Index